New slaveries in contemporary British literature and visual arts

Manchester University Press

New slaveries in contemporary British literature and visual arts

The ghost and the camp

PIETRO DEANDREA

Manchester University Press

Copyright © Pietro Deandrea 2015

The right of Pietro Deandrea to be identified as the author of this work has been asserted by him in accordance with the Copyright, Designs and Patents Act 1988.

Published by Manchester University Press
Oxford Road, Manchester M13 9PL
www.manchesteruniversitypress.co.uk

British Library Cataloguing-in-Publication Data
A catalogue record for this book is available from the British Library

ISBN 978 0 7190 9643 3 hardback
ISBN 978 1 5261 5582 5 paperback

First published 2015

Paperback edition published 2021

The publisher has no responsibility for the persistence or accuracy of URLs for any external or third-party internet websites referred to in this book, and does not guarantee that any content on such websites is, or will remain, accurate or appropriate.

Typeset in Sabon by
Koinonia, Manchester

To my beloved father,
Francesco Deandrea (1933–2012),
and his silent teachings.
And to my enslaved neighbours:
may I never fail to see them.

Contents

List of plates	*page*	ix
Acknowledgements		xi
1 Introduction		1
2 Investigating migrant domestic workers		33
3 The ghost and the concentration camp in the twenty-first century		49
4 The British concentrationary archipelago in cinema, photography and drama		97
5 Dystopian narratives		140
6 Conclusion		177
References		209
Index		228

Plates

1 From Nick Broomfield's *Ghosts*: Ai Qin is made to hide in a box in the back of the smuggling truck (copyright Tartan Films) — page 100
2 From Nick Broomfield's *Ghosts*: Ai Qin at the window (copyright Tartan Films) — 101
3 From Nick Broomfield's *Ghosts*: The group of Chinese cockle-pickers on the roof of the van, surrounded by the rising tide (copyright Tartan Films) — 103
4 From Dana Popa's photographic exhibition *Not Natasha*: Maria behind a window (p. 9; copyright Dana Popa) — 111
5 From Dana Popa's photographic exhibition *Not Natasha*: Elena's face covered by her wig (p. 67; copyright Dana Popa) — 112
6 From Dana Popa's photographic exhibition *Not Natasha*: Poverty and absence back in Moldova (pp. 72–3; copyright Dana Popa) — 113
7 From Alfonso Cuarón's *Children of Men*: Migrants caged along railway platforms, while Theo is walking by (copyright Universal Studios) — 146
8 From Alfonso Cuarón's *Children of Men*: The pregnant Kee in a cowshed (copyright Universal Studios) — 147
9 From Alfonso Cuarón's *Children of Men*: Military violence at the entrance of Bexhill detention centre (copyright Universal Studios) — 148
10 From Philippe Lioret's *Welcome*: Migrants are denied entry into a Calais supermarket (copyright Nord-ouest Productions) — 179
11 From Sylvain George's *Qu'ils reposent en révolte*: A migrant with his head covered by a hood and sweater (copyright Noir Production) — 180
12 From Philippe Lioret's *Welcome*: Bilal's head in a plastic bag, in the back of the smuggling truck (copyright Nord-ouest Productions) — 181

13 From Philippe Lioret's *Welcome*: Simon forcing Bilal's head
   into a plastic bag (copyright Nord-ouest Productions)   181
14 From Sylvain George's *Qu'ils reposent en révolte*: Burnt
   fingertips, erasing one's identity (copyright Noir Production)   186

Acknowledgements

During the years that I have spent researching into British new slaveries, I have met many people (students, friends and colleagues) expressing their concern for this issue, and who have kindly shared their thoughts with me. I am deeply indebted to them, for their inspiring and encouraging words. Thanks to them, I have managed to publish a few essays on the topic (see References), which have been re-elaborated and expanded for the writing of this book.

My thanks, therefore, to the London staff of Anti-Slavery International, and to Melanie Abrahams, Esterino Adami, Moniza Alvi, Hazel Andrews, Adelaide Bannerman, Cristiana Bartolini, Shaul Bassi, Paolo Bertinetti, Ross Bradshaw, Bianca Bressy, Paola Brusasco, Elena Carraro, Francesco Cattani, Grazia Cerulli, Carmen Concilio, John Graham Davies, Ashley Dawson, Giulia D'Agostini, Barbara Del Mercato, Bianca Del Villano, Lidia De Michelis, Alison Down, Edin at the Royal Court bookshop, Laura Fantone, Moris Farhi, David Farrier, Chiara Giobergia, Francesca Giommi, Anna Gomes, Claudio Gorlier, Zaria Greenhill, Carlo Greppi, Indra Khanna, Stanley Langer, Hannah Lowe, Roberto Lupis, Alan Maddock, Tiziana Magone, Raoul Mancin, Giulia Marcassoli, Claudio Maringelli, Valentina Martini, Anna Nadotti, Stephanie Newell, Annalisa Oboe, Claudia Pasquero, Bettina Pfanmoeller, Griselda Pollock, Marco Ponti, Alan Rice, Les Roberts, Francesca Saggini, Efisio Serra, Max Silverman, Catherine Spooner, John Sutherland, Chika Unigwe, Camilla Valletti, Nicoletta Vallorani, Cristina Viti, Abigail Ward, Sara Wasson, Stephen Watts, Patrick Williams.

Special thanks to Christine Bacon, Sylvain George, Anna Jordan, Sonja Linden and Dana Popa for their generosity in letting me use their invaluable work; to Ruth Anne Henderson, for her punctual correction of my faulty English and her impassioned observations on my writing. And of course, to my much loved Cinzia Gallotti and our two children, Rebecca and Ettore, for being here with me.

1

Introduction

Appeals to the past are among the commonest of strategies in interpretations of the present. What animates such appeals is not only disagreement about what happened in the past and what the past was, but uncertainty about whether the past really is past, over and concluded, or whether it continues, albeit in different forms, perhaps.
Edward Said, *Culture and Imperialism* (1993: 1)

As the world map is being redrawn after 1989, postcolonial studies has done little to keep pace with the changing forms of imperialism as an actual set of strategies and developments.
Timothy Brennan, 'The image-function of the periphery' (2005: 107)

1.1 Crossing the 2007 bicentenary: Transatlantic memory and the slaves of globalisation

Can we hope that the *sans-papiers* and their supporters in this country (and in all other countries) will establish a Museum of Illegal Immigration, so that the memory of those detained and deported, of those who fought and resisted with success, will not be forgotten, will not be annihilated, will not be vaporized?
Steve Cohen, *Deportation Is Freedom!* (2006: 153)

The year 2007 marked the bicentenary of the abolition of the slave trade. The same year saw the publication of *Chords of Freedom*, J. R. Oldfield's investigation into the construction of the memory of transatlantic slavery. Examining a long history of monuments, commemorations and museums, Oldfield brings to the fore Britain's tendency to celebrate itself as a champion of civilisation which put an end to the abominable trade. The gradual dismantling of this view, according to Oldfield, is a quite recent phenomenon related to the rising importance of multiculturalism: 'since the 1980s the dominant discourse has been disrupted and, to some extent, replaced by overlapping narratives that, in turn, reflect broader cultural and political changes within British society' (Oldfield 2007: 2).

Amongst other things, Oldfield studies how monuments in Bristol and Lancaster began to turn public attention towards the African victims of the trade (78–81), and how some slavery museums have involved Black communities in their activities with the aim of including multicultural perspectives in the conception of their own exhibitions (121). When dealing with the monument *Captured Africans* by Kevin Dalton-Johnson (erected in October 2005 in front of the Custom House in Lancaster), the book dwells on the mixed reactions it received:

> Not everyone has welcomed the appearance of *Captured Africans*, some preferring to *throw a veil over* Lancaster's slave past as if it were best *forgotten*. Nevertheless, such responses and the *anxieties which lie behind* them should not blind us to the significance of what has been happening in Lancaster. In a city that remains predominantly white, STAMP [the Slave Trade Arts Memorial Project] has been instrumental in shaping a new agenda that has less to do with the moral triumph of British anti-slavery than with the voices of the *forgotten*, the slaves themselves. (80–1; italics mine)

If Oldfield's language alludes to a disquieting resurfacing of the repressed, when reflecting on the same monument Alan Rice (involved in the STAMP project) has recourse to images that are explicitly spectral; he quotes James E. Young, who writes that memorials of the Holocaust are meant not to reassure or console but to '*haunt* visitors with the unpleasant, *uncanny* sensation of calling into consciousness that which has been previously – even happily – repressed' (Rice 2007: 331; italics mine).[1] Commemorations of the slave trade can certainly be related to Gothic elements from an obscured past, and transatlantic slavery often presents itself as a ghost haunting contemporary Britain. The coming of the 2007 bicentenary seemed to shape the image of Britain's present as enveloped in a spectral aura.[2]

Even though these cultural critics deal mainly with how transatlantic slavery is remembered and commemorated as a thing of the past, they sometimes end by pointing to what is happening in Britain today. Inevitably, their studies of memory hint at the relationship between remembrance and present life, and this is true not only for the descendants of the African diaspora. Oldfield (2007: 63) narrates the late recovery of the figure of abolitionist Thomas Clarkson and the tablet embedded in the floor of Westminster

Abbey in 1996, not far from the statue of William Wilberforce (who had long dominated the arena of the memory of transatlantic slavery):

> every effort was made to ensure that the memorial campaign was inclusive rather than exclusive, and that it linked Clarkson to the ongoing struggle against slavery and oppression, particularly in the Third World. ... [the committee] included two representatives of Anti-Slavery International: ASI, for its part clearly regarded the committee's work as an important means of establishing foundations (not least, in terms of raising public consciousness about slavery) from which it might 'leap into the twenty-first century'.

The campaign for the Clarkson memorial, then, acted as a linkage between the memory of slavery and awareness of present and future slaveries – and it did so in the mid-1990s, the period immediately following the publication of the pioneer texts on new forms of slavery in Britain (see Chapter 2). Oldfield's passing references[3] point to a global context scarred by contemporary versions of slavery, without significant comments – as this is not within the scope of his volume – on the new forms of slavery scarring Britain today. Alan Rice's essay on Dalton-Johnson's *Captured Africans* moves closer to the issue, when he reports that the artist was clear about not limiting the significance of his work to the past:

> Well, it's just a fact that black people could be treated like that, and if it could happen then, it can happen again now. The reason why we need to have a memorial is so it isn't repeated – it operates on that level. ... [W]e live it every day, the way we are treated brings it all back, what our ancestors went through, even though it's not the same degree. (Rice 2007: 330–1)

Following Paul Ricoeur,[4] Alan Rice comes to the conclusion that memorials can 'speak to their future contexts as much as to the past they commemorate, to a future-oriented responsibility', and in order to demonstrate their potential significance he mentions the Morecambe Bay tragedy, an event of key significance for this book (see Chapter 4.1). Rice also reports what the artist Lubaina Himid said during the launch of the STAMP project – a warning about the ghosts of slavery who are still haunting Britain: 'If you are going to honour the dead who have been ignored, suppressed or denied when in peril in the past, you must do it because as a city you want to show that you would do differently now, that you would be able to defend those people now' (Rice 2007: 325).

Slavery *now* is precisely the subject of this volume, in which I take up the challenge of analysing the literature and the visual arts regarding new forms of slavery in Britain. The book assigns a central place to this phenomenon, which in texts such as Oldfield's and Rice's is present only in embryo and beneath the surface.

The study of present forms of slavery requires, first of all, some modifications in the definition of slavery itself, given that ownership of a slave is no longer legal. In 1982 the UN updated definitions of slavery to take into account its contemporary forms:

- slavery is any form of dealing with human beings leading to the forced exploitation of their labour.
- slavery is any institution or practice which, by restricting the freedom of the individual, is susceptible of causing severe hardships and serious deprivation of liberty. (Anderson 1993: 11)[5]

This association between forced labour and slavery is nowadays widely accepted. In their pioneer study, Bridget Anderson and Ben Rogaly (2005: 15) showed how, according to international legislation, 'forced labour and trafficking are closely linked'. In turn, the UN Convention against Transnational Organised Crime includes, amongst forms of trafficking, 'forced labour or services, slavery or practices similar to slavery'.[6] A highly debated aspect of this phenomenon is the purportedly voluntary assent of the enslaved – but in the definition of 'trafficking' included in the abovementioned UN Convention the consent of a victim 'shall be irrelevant' (Anderson and Rogaly 2005: 8).

Two years after Anderson and Rogaly's study, a report commissioned by the Joseph Rowntree Foundation explicitly employed 'slavery' as an appropriate definition for such phenomena: 'Human trafficking, for sexual or forced labour purposes, is the most numerically common form of modern slavery' (Craig et al. 2007: 25). The report identified three main features characterising 'contemporary slavery': 'severe economic exploitation ... absence of human rights' and the control over a person by 'the prospect or reality of violence' (1, 12). The report's authors concede that there are many gradations of forced labour, so that the question of where slavery begins constitutes 'a complicated debate' (17). Another complication concerns the documented/undocumented issue: it would be simplistic to affirm that all undocumented migrants are enslaved; what seems certain is that an undocumented status is likely to increase three factors of vulnerability to forced labour, i.e. dependence on recruiters, blackmailing and isolation.[7] However, the scenario is further complicated by the fact that documented forms of migration, too, can easily lead to slavery (Anderson and Rogaly 2005: 43–7). In Monica Ali's *In the Kitchen* (2010: 420), the Labour MP Fairweather describes this phenomenon thus:

> traffickers use regular migration routes and work visas, but then charge fees for arranging work which put the workers into debt before they've even arrived in the UK. Sometimes their documents are removed, they're kept in poor housing and charged a fortune, charged for transport through and from work, ... Threats, abuse, all sorts of things. ... [being] an illegal immigrant is neither here nor there.

The number of exploited and enslaved migrants living in contemporary Britain is very difficult to estimate; attempts to produce reliable figures have often been contested.[8] Both the existence of new slaves in today's Britain and the near impossibility of quantifying them remain highly controversial issues, not least because – before and after the 2007 bicentenary commemorations of the abolition of the slave trade – British institutions have often been part of the problem. The date 18 October 2010 was chosen as Britain's first ever Anti-Slavery Day, as part of a long and massive campaign against the lack of action by successive British governments: 'Britain's anti-slavery legislation is now weaker than the rest of Europe's, thanks to the coalition's decision to opt out of an EU directive on human trafficking' (Dugan 2010: n.p.).[9]

Within a European context where economic liberalism and institutional persecution of migrants have contributed to the growth of new forms of slavery, and where state policies on immigration control reproduce, rather than eradicate, illegality, which 'then becomes the *raison d'être* of the security apparatus' (Balibar 2004: 62), Britain is recognised as the country where these changes have produced the worst effects. This is accounted for by some 'systemic features in the UK labour market ... one of the most flexible labour markets in Europe', with its pressures for flexible pay arrangements and working hours, easier hiring and firing, short-term contracts and geographic mobility, conducive to heightened exploitation of those who are most vulnerable to these conditions – that is to say, migrant workers (Anderson and Rogaly 2005: 23).[10]

Alongside (and commensurate with) this economic system, Britain has also distinguished itself for its increasing criminalisation of migrants, leading, amongst other things, to punitive administrative detention, a practice which has constantly increased;[11] as far as the neglect of basic human rights in its detention centres is concerned, Britain has again played a leading role (Bosworth and Guild 2008: 703–12; Fekete 2009: 150).[12] This kind of policy has certainly increased migrants' vulnerability to potential exploitation (Fekete 2009: 23), but in some cases it has also created official forms of slavery: there have been asylum seekers turned 'into a pool of forced labour as a price for their being given a roof over their heads', where 'local authorities are specifically designated as an agency that can contract for' this (Cohen 2006: 136).[13] Unsurprisingly, the outsourcing of detention centres to multinationals[14] has exacerbated the conditions in which the detainees live: several complaints of maltreatment were addressed to G4S, which has contracts worth £4.6 billion with the British government (Casciani 2011: n.p.), while in Yarl's Wood removal centre, run by SERCO, migrants were made to work for 50p an hour (McVeigh 2011: n.p.). Another form of institutionally induced exploitation has to do with the asylum policies aiming at the destitution of both claimants and failed asylum seekers, constraining them to an 'enforced non-productivity'[15] that leaves them vulnerable to extreme poverty and consequently to exploitation (Farrier 2011: 86, 97–8); this accounts for the occasional inclusion of asylum seekers in the category of new slaves in the chapters that follow. One case worth mention here is the Turkish character of Senay in Stephen Frears's film *Dirty Pretty Things* (2002), since her sexual exploitation results from her pending application for asylum.[16]

Since the early 1990s, this outcome of globalisation has been variously studied and defined. Étienne Balibar (2004: x, 9, 43–4), for instance, underscores the existence of a virtual European apartheid. In this regard, Zygmunt Bauman's *Wasted Lives* (2004) is perhaps one of the most widely read attempts. He also articulates an extended analogy between these human beings (economic migrants and asylum seekers) and rubbish: he defines refugees as 'the human waste of the global frontier-land ... "the outsiders incarnate", the absolute outsiders' (Bauman 2004: 80). Although it is undeniable that today's slaves are cheaper and more disposable than in past forms of slavery (Bales 2005: 9), Bauman's analysis of the rejects of globalisation can be applied only partially to the object of this book. Bauman stresses how we consider refuse disposal sites and urban ghettos or asylum camps off-limits – in other words, how we tend to reject human and non-human waste by avoiding and distancing them. However, as the following chapters will show, one of the main features of British new slaveries consists in their being disseminated throughout the country, potentially everywhere and thus potentially contiguous to any 'respectable' citizen, who indeed is far from living, as Bauman writes, in a 'comfortable, soporific *insularity*' (Bauman 2004: 27; italics mine). De Genova (2002: 422) makes clear how the services provided by migrants lead to a state of inseparability among the undocumented, documented migrants and citizens, in a 'quite intimate proximity'.

In the following pages I argue for a more composite imagery, and more fitting critical paradigms, to understand British new slaveries and their specificities. Terminology-wise, I opted for using *'new slaveries'* and *'new slaves'* (rather than the more blandly chronological but equally widespread 'modern-day slavery' or 'contemporary slavery') in order to emphasise the changed features of this phenomenon. In doing so, I was encouraged by the titles of some signal publications, such as Kevin Bales's *Disposable People: New Slavery in the Global Economy* (1999)[17] and Christien Van den Anker's *The Political Economy of New Slavery* (2004); compared to them, my employment of the plural form is designed to underscore the diversity of the phenomenon.

One final note regarding terminology, which anticipates my reflections on naming in Chapter 2.2 and 3.1. The widely employed label 'illegals' is here avoided because of the disparaging connotations that it carries, and the hierarchical exclusion that it implies (Gunning 2011: 142); as Georges Bensoussan writes (2002: 65), words can lower our moral vigilance. The definition 'undocumented' is preferred: in comparing the language of British immigration controls to Big Brother's self-justifying propaganda, Steve Cohen (2006: 28) avers that *undocumented* 'helps politically to stand Newspeak on its head. It describes rather than derides, and unites rather than divides.'[18] This choice is meant to pay homage to those migrants who occupied the church of Saint Ambroise in Paris in 1996 (Balibar 2004: 48–9), whose protest against French restrictive laws included their rejection of the term 'clandestine' for the less disparaging 'sans papier'.[19]

1.2 New slaveries in literature and the visual arts

> what visions of a postcolonial world can we as humanists offer that will interrogate, perhaps even interrupt, the forms of globalization now dictated by politicians, military strategists, captains of finance and industry, fundamentalist preachers and theologians, terrorists of the body and the spirit, in short, by the masters of our contemporary universe?
>
> Ania Loomba et al., *Postcolonial Studies and Beyond* (2005: 13)

> I write ... because there is some lie that I want to expose, some fact to which I want to draw attention, and my initial concern is to get a hearing. But I could not do the work of writing a book ... if it were not also an aesthetic experience.
>
> George Orwell, 'Why I write' (1968: 6)

This book deals with the literature and visual arts concerned with those human beings who have moved to Britain as part of the global migratory movements of the late twentieth and early twenty-first century; accordingly, it takes into consideration primary works produced, approximately, between the early 1990s and the end of the following decade.

The main driving force behind this volume is a conception of the role of artistic representations as pivotal for raising awareness of an issue that is largely hidden and unacknowledged, as demonstrated by the recurrence of spectral tropes related to it (see Chapter 1.3). It must be plainly stated, then, that one fundamental aspect here has to do with denouncing, with making public. Nevertheless, this is mostly *literary* criticism: in the spirit of Orwell's quotation above, the following pages attempt more than mere exposition.

If museums and monuments, as Oldfield writes (2007: 56), have the function of educating the living, literature and art may be seen as the most powerful means to make the living feel three-dimensionally. Composed in 1821, Percy Bysshe Shelley's *Defence of Poetry* captures the core of the question, the essentially ethical thrust of literature – which becomes inescapable when dealing with problems such as new slaveries. According to Shelley, the power of poetry resides in its awakening of the sympathetic imagination, 'a going out of our own nature, and *an identification of ourselves with* the beautiful which exists in thought, action, or person, not our own' (Shelley 1888: 11; italics mine).[20] Even though the term 'beautiful' certainly does not fit the subject of new slaveries, Shelley's definition is appropriate for the potential role of the arts in so delicate a field: the pressing question is to help readers/viewers become socially conscious and fully aware of the ordeal of human beings who live side by side with them, albeit often invisibly, and are enslaved in order to make the citizens' lives proceed smoothly, to have their food ready, to keep their surroundings clean.[21] This particular faculty of literature may also account for the way in which some non-fictional texts have recourse to narrative strategies, in order to better convey the lives of new slaves (as discussed in Chapter 3.1); the overall impression is that their experience is so shatteringly complex that the analytical language of investigation cannot, in itself, transmit it exhaustively. This unique role of literature is lauded by Caryl Phillips with regard to the future of Europe, in what seems to be a translation of Shelley's principles for the twenty-first century (together with a Coleridgean quote):

> All of us are faced with a stark choice: we can rail against European evolution, or we can help to smooth its process. And, if we choose the latter, the first thing we must remind ourselves of is the lesson that great fiction teaches us as we sink into character and plot and suspend our disbelief: for a moment, 'they' are 'us'. I believe passionately in the moral capacity of fiction to wrench us out of our ideological burrows and force us to engage with a world that is clumsily transforming itself, a world that is peopled with individuals we might otherwise never meet in our daily lives. As long as we have literature as a bulwark against intolerance, and as a force for change, then we have a chance. Europe needs writers to explicate this transition, for literature *is* plurality in action.... This truly is my hope for Europe, and I *know* that the writer has a crucial part to play in this. I believe this. And this only. (Phillips 2011a: 16–17)[22]

The categories of actors involved in the works here analysed, then, are basically two: the new slaves proper, and the so-called citizens whose lives capitalise (in differing degrees) on the new slaves' labour. As regards the former, I wish to refer to Yosefa Loshitzky's analysis of Stephen Frears's film *Dirty Pretty Things* (2002), where she rightly concentrates on the image of the human heart found in a toilet bowl by the protagonist:[23] 'This, the film implies, is what London and capitalism are doing: flushing human hearts in the toilet and treating the refugees like a form of waste' (2010: 71). I take this image as challenging the potential function of literature (and consequently of literary criticism): namely, to recompose, albeit imaginatively, what reality is constantly disrupting, to offer a humane vision where humanity is denied. Or, to put it in the terms of Giorgio Agamben's definition of the function of 'intellectuality' (2000: 11), it 'incessantly reunites life to its form or prevents it from being dissociated from its form', against 'state sovereignty, which can affirm itself only by separating in every context naked life from its form'.

With regard to the category of citizens, it is obvious that this conception of literature and art does not only impinge on new slaves themselves (as discussed in Chapter 6.2). Poetry 'makes familiar objects be as if they were not familiar', Shelley also wrote (1888: 11), and this could be applied to the case of new slaveries, where art has the potential to shake one's supposedly stable world by showing how it placidly rests on daily acts of inhumanity, and how easily it denies exploited migrants something that this book often touches upon, their 'right to complex personhood' (Gordon 2008: 4).

What this chapter has claimed so far is obviously indebted to a humanistic function of art that has been sidelined by much theory. The main thrust behind the following pages is very close to what Edward Said asserts in *Humanism and Democratic Criticism*: 'humanism is critique' (2004: 22) – a concept that he untiringly repeats in this manifesto of his intellectual engagement.[24] Certain passages of Said's book represent guiding templates behind my research on British new slaveries:

> situating critique at the very heart of humanism, critique as a form of democratic freedom and as a continuous practice of questioning and of accumulating knowledge that is open to, rather than in denial of, the constituent historical realities of the post-Cold War world, its early colonial formation, and the frighteningly global reach of the last remaining superpower of today.... Humanism, I strongly believe, must *excavate the silences*,[25] the world of memory, of itinerant, barely surviving groups, the places of exclusion and *invisibility*, the kind of testimony that doesn't make it onto the reports but which more and more is about whether ... marginalized peoples outside as well as inside the maw of the metropolitan center can survive the grinding down and flattening out and displacement that are such prominent features of globalization. (Said 2004: 47, 81–2; italics mine)

For scholars in postcolonial studies the dark side of humanism is a well-known axiom: as Fanon wrote (1967: 252), 'When I search for Man in the technique and style of Europe, I see only a succession of negations of Man, and an avalanche of murders.' The present book (and especially Chapter 5.2 on Ishiguro) shows awareness of systemic organisations that overwhelm the power of individuals, and attempts to make fruitful use of 'post-humanist' thinkers such as Derrida and Foucault. At the same time, shadowing Said's concept of humanism-as-critique, it does not exclude two aspects of artistic production that his *Humanism and Democratic Criticism* brings to the fore: the potential of human agency and the centrality of the reader (Said 2004: 10, 43, 76).[26] The role assumed here for literature obviously impinges upon my priorities for research; it points back to the key question posed by Loomba in the first epigraph above, and to the aesthetic component called for by Orwell in the second. If the procedure privileged here consists of textual analysis, what specific tropes, figurations and devices are employed to represent new slaveries in both artistic and analytical works? What kinds of renditions of the phenomenon prove more or less effective, and why? What particular theoretical paradigms are most qualified to interpret them?

1.3 Troping new slaveries: Ghosts of postcolonialism, Marx and deconstruction

> 'I am thy father's spirit; doomed for a certain time to walk the night … and … and for the day confined to fast in fires, till the foul crimes done in my days of nature's … nature are burnt and purged away … But …' He broke off and grinned at Michael Adonis, and then eyed the bottle. 'That's us, us, Michael, my boy. Just ghosts, doomed to walk the night. Shakespeare.
> Alex La Guma, *A Walk in the Night and Other Stories* (1986: 28, original ellipsis)

> Slavery is the greatest human rights challenge of my generation. … But in the first couple of weeks in any new country that I visited, my greatest challenge was finding a single slave.
> E. Benjamin Skinner, *A Crime So Monstrous: Face-to-face with Modern-day Slavery* (2008: xvii)

> 'How come I've never seen you people before?'
> 'Because we are the people you do not see. We're the ones who drive your cabs. We clean your rooms, and suck your cocks.'
> Stephen Frears, *Dirty Pretty Things* (2002)

The ghost is the first of the two tropes taken here as central for the study of new slaveries in Britain. As the following chapters show, the image of the ghost is highly appropriate for today's enslaved migrants, whose hidden condition (see Chapter 1.1) is the main reason why they are frequently described as phantoms: 'The "ghost population" in Britain: the almost invisibles' (Pai 2008: xix). Étienne Balibar (2004: 42) traces a clear connection between this invisibility and the colonial structures of Europe's globalisation:

> the prohibition of access to the public sphere and to rights of free expression and the possibilities for struggle they offer, and confinement in ghettos and in some cases in an 'underground', seek to prevent both the individualization and the socialization of foreigners ... exactly as it occurs in colonial situations, since that would threaten dominant positions and the possibilities of exploitation offered by the rule of non-right.

The role of the ghost image must necessarily be positioned in the wake of its (post)colonial antecedents, representing the latest point of a long historical and cultural imagining. First and foremost, as suggested at the beginning of Chapter 1.1 in relation to the 2007 bicentenary, the image of the spectral alterity haunting Western monolithic social and ideological constructions constantly surfaces in postcolonial studies, becoming even more intense when related to slavery and to the ways in which it has been repressed by Western modernity. Ian Baucom's *Specters of the Atlantic* (2005), for instance, offers a vision of our globalised contemporaneity as part of a long twentieth century that stretches back to the transatlantic slave trade, as an intensification of the rise of finance capital in the late eighteenth century with its equating human beings with abstract value, exemplified in the infamous *Zong* massacre. Baucom contends that this logic makes the 'dominant protocols' (Baucom 2005: 24) of our age, and therefore our present is 'more than rhetorically haunted by the spectre of the Zong's 1781 voyage' (18). By my reckoning, Baucom's vision of history (indebted to Benjamin and Arrighi) finds in British new slaveries a telling incarnation.[27]

Transatlantic slavery, however, represents only one of the declinations of the spectral in postcolonial studies.[28] In the first epigraph above, for instance, the reference to *Hamlet* is taken as exemplary for the spectralised lives populating the apartheid ghetto.[29] Another case in point is Sam Durrant's study of Coetzee, Harris and Morrison, *Postcolonial Narrative and the Work of Mourning*, centred on the definition of postcolonial literatures as 'haunted by the memory of colonialism', an oppressive presence leading characters to perform collective acts of mourning which 'exceed the proportions of the individual subject' (Durrant 2004: 3, 11). A similar concept – colonial atrocities in Australia and Canada reappearing as spectres – is present in Gerry Turcotte's *Peripheral Fear*

(2009). In Italian academia, Bianca Del Villano (2007) employs this trope with regard to the fractures of Western thought in the field of Anglophone literatures. Each of these volumes, according to its own subject, centres its reflections on the undermining work of spectral tropes, and they share a remarkable ethical thrust that, as I have said in Chapter 1.2, I consider fundamental. Sam Durrant, for instance, acknowledges his debt to Robert Young's definition of postcolonialism as 'grounded in an appeal to an ethical universal' that entails 'a certain simple respect for human suffering' and a 'fundamental revolt against it' (Durrant 2004: 3).[30]

Moreover, all these books, in varying degrees, pay homage to the influential *Specters of Marx* (1993) by Jacques Derrida. At the time when the end of the Soviet bloc and the birth of the so-called New World Order were prompting some philosophers and historians to insist upon the renewed urgency of Marxist categories, Derrida commendably aimed at translating this urgency into the symbolic realm. Even more interestingly for the present volume, Derrida did so through his reading of the trope of (Marx's) ghosts as irreducibly haunting neo-liberalism. *Specters of Marx* presents a sort of evil Decalogue, what Derrida terms the 'ten plagues' of the New World Order (Derrida 2006: 100–4). Significantly for the present book, Plague number two foresees the significance of exploited and persecuted migrants:

> The massive exclusion of homeless citizens from any participation in the democratic life of States, the expulsion and deportation of so many exiles, stateless persons, and immigrants from a so-called national territory already herald a new experience of frontier and identity – whether national or civil. (Derrida 2006: 101)

Elsewhere, Derrida also mentions xenophobia (2006: 100). His call for a 'New International' capable of operating a critique against the neo-liberal powers-that-be (105–7) imagines an uncoordinated, nationless, institutionless, citizenshipless organism belonging to anonymity (113), evoked by Marx's spectres. Because of these very characteristics envisaged by Derrida, this New International could embrace not only researchers into new slaveries but also new slaves themselves. Derrida's relevance for this book is compounded by the motivation supporting his focus on spectres, namely the need 'to learn to live with ghosts. ... To live otherwise, and better. No, not better, but more justly' (xviii). The publication of *Specters of Marx* was contemporaneous with the first works on British new slaveries, discussed in Chapter 2. In the years after 2000, the ghostly dimension of new slaves became increasingly evident, as shown by the Skinner's and Frears's quotations above.[31]

Driven by the urgency of the phenomenon of new slaveries, my research reaches beyond the boundaries of strictly literary studies, as also demonstrated in Chapter 1.4. As far as the trope of the ghost is concerned, the following pages often refer to the sociologist Avery Gordon's *Ghostly Matters* (1997) and the centrality of haunting in her topics of investigation, including slavery as one of the 'key problems of our time' (2008: xix). Introducing the republication of her book, Gordon (2008: xvi) defines haunting as

> when the people who are meant to be invisible show up without any sign of leaving, when disturbing feelings cannot be put away, when something else, something different from before, seems like it must be done. It is this socio-political-psychological state to which haunting referred.

1.4 Troping new slaveries: Holocaust studies and the concentration camp

> It can happen, and it can happen everywhere. I do not intend to nor can I say that it will happen; ... it is not very probable that all the factors that unleashed the Nazi madness will again occur simultaneously, but precursory signs loom before us. ... It only awaits its new buffoon (there is no dearth of candidates) to organise it, legalise it, declare it necessary and mandatory and so contaminate the world. Few countries can be considered immune to a future tide of violence generated by intolerance, lust for power, economic difficulties, religious or political fanaticism, and racialist attritions. It is therefore necessary to sharpen our senses, distrust the prophets, the enchanters, those who speak and write 'beautiful words' unsupported by intelligent reasons.
> Primo Levi, *The Drowned and the Saved* (1989: 167)

The ghost is not the only image guiding my investigation into the artistic representations of new slaveries. From Chapter 2.2, through Primo Levi's piercing reflections on the experience of the Nazi Holocaust, the concentration camp is seen as foreshadowing the imprisonment of new slaves in today's Britain. The interaction between the camp and the spectre image constitutes the backbone of this book – and, in Chapter 5.2 and 6.1, one of its signal arguments.

Although I am aware of the ethical risks involved in this kind of operation, I am firmly convinced, in light of Georges Bensoussan's reflections (2002: 37), that considering the Holocaust to be open to comparison does not necessarily entail a denial of its exceptionality. My intention is not to belittle the importance and uniqueness of the Holocaust. Far from it: I want to unveil its contiguities with British new slaveries in order to place it in a historical perspective capable of throwing light on what remains of it today.

Hence, the texts on the Holocaust employed here (among the composite field of Holocaust theory)[32] envision this tragedy not as an event circumscribable to a past but as something constantly lurking in our contemporaneity, albeit in modified shapes. Georges Bensoussan's *Auschwitz en heritage?* (1998) reflects on how Holocaust memory interrogates our present: it should be seen, he writes, as a *living* memory that educates us to question authority, group mentality and the powers-that-be. Holocaust commemorations are sterile, if they do not inspire a *political* examination of our civilization (Bensoussan 2002: 51).[33]

This perspective is shared in two earlier volumes that are equally important for this book; curiously, and perhaps not by chance, both of them were published in the years immediately preceding the horrors of the Yugoslavian war (and of the rise of new slaveries in Britain). The first is Zygmunt Bauman's *Modernity and the Holocaust* (1989), a book that sees the Holocaust as the palimpsest of our modernity, and offers a sociological analysis that should be inspirational in our times for both institutions and individuals. The second one is by an Auschwitz survivor, my fellow townsman Primo Levi: his last book *The Drowned and the Saved* (1986) is a chilling testament concerning many aspects of the Holocaust, but also prophetic in its reflections on what might still happen, as the quotation above shows. It must be clearly stated, however, that Levi did not trace this connection between the Holocaust and late twentieth-century Europe in his last book alone. In 1973 (and later in 1976) Levi edited *If This Is a Man*, his famous 1947 autobiographical narration of his deportation to Auschwitz, for secondary school students. The footnotes, preface and appendices added by Levi to these editions are pervaded by his feeling that new forms of fascism and intolerance (and concentration camps as their most extreme consequence) hang over contemporary society:[34] as he writes in his '1972 Preface to young people', it is precisely to communicate this that he agreed to re-edit his book (Levi 1986: 7; translation mine). And that edition still included Levi's original 1947 'Author's preface', where he had already claimed that, when a society is dominated by the belief that 'every stranger is an enemy', concentration camps are a predictable effect (Levi 1996: 15).

For the same reason, the following chapters are also indebted to studies by Hannah Arendt, Giorgio Agamben and Vinay Lal, who emphasise that the institution of concentration camps is not limited to the extermination of Jews operated by the Nazi regime but involves a longer history, a disquieting present and a foreseeable future in the relationship between the West and the rest of the world. Following on from Hannah Arendt's *The Origins of Totalitarianisms* (1951), Lal contextualises Second World War concentration camps in a wider frame, starting from the genocides committed in the name of European colonialism; he points his finger at economic neo-colonialism, at the invisible genocides committed today in the name of so-called 'development' all over the world. Inevitably, he asks questions concerning the present and the future:

> If Arendt could reach back to the Boer War and to British colonialism in India to describe the origins of that totalitarian form of terror known as the concentration camp, it is just as reasonable to ask what the concentration camp of the future might look like. Is the concentration camp only a thing of the past, or has it metamorphosed into different forms? ... Has the concentration camp, unmoored from its precise location, shorn of its physicality, freed from its chains, bounded no longer by barbed wires, come to occupy a different space? (Lal 2005: 230)[35]

Lal's questions resonate thunderingly within the scope of this book.[36] It is the purpose of this volume to confine itself to a more restricted geographical context – namely, Britain. Its objects of analysis are those who escape from the invisible genocides described by Lal. And, as a way of answering his crucial questions, this book argues that the scattered sites of imprisonment for new slaves represent a contemporary development of the institution of the concentration camp. This book shows that the camp has metamorphosed into not only normative but also illegal forms, retaining some of its previous features. My analysis focuses precisely on the ways in which it has changed, and my conclusion is that in today's Britain the concentration camp has been atomised, vaporised into a myriad of ever-changing, ever-shifting places. This new form of the camp embodies the dynamic features of transnational capitalist mobility, its most emblematic case being represented by Chinese sex slaves

Introduction 17

forced to shift around a network of brothel-flats on a weekly basis (Pai 2008: 172). The name that I give to this very fragmented and mobile system is 'concentrationary archipelago', in the wake of David Rousset's well-known 'concentrationary universe' (Rousset 1946) but also of Aleksandr Solzhenitsyn's 'gulag archipelago'. New slaveries in Britain form a system that, precisely like Solzhenitsyn's world, 'though scattered in an Archipelago geographically, was, in the psychological sense, fused into a continent – an almost invisible, almost imperceptible country' (Solzhenitsyn 1974: x).

In a 1967 talk, Michel Foucault described contemporary society as 'the epoch of space': 'We are at a moment, I believe, when our experience of the world is less that of a long life developing through time than that of a network that connects points and intersects with its own skein' (Foucault 1986: 22). Foucault's remark is to be posed against Gilroy's warning (2004a: 165) of the dangerous centrality of the migrancy problematic, since it becomes misleading 'when it alone supplies an explanation for the conflicts and opportunities of this transitional moment: fascination with the figure of the migrant must be made part of Europe's history rather than its contemporary geography'. I part company with both Foucault's and Gilroy's visions in arguing, however, that the British concentrationary archipelago rests on twin foundations: it is composed of the tangled network that this volume attempts to unravel, an ever-moving matrix that emerges as extremely unstable, composed of innumerable skeins constantly unravelling and re-forming,[37] while being part of a long history.

The insertion of paradigms pertaining to Holocaust studies, together with postcolonial ones, might be seen as a diluting of my theoretical frame. Steady maintenance of a single, orienting critical paradigm would probably have made this work apparently more solid – but, I feel, much less complete. As a postcolonial literary critic, the principal lesson I am drawing on here is Spivak's call for 'reconstellating' the text as a way to approach subaltern experience (Spivak 1988: 241). In opting for a larger perspective uniting postcolonial and Holocaust studies, I am much indebted to Michael Rothberg's *Multidirectional Memory: Remembering the Holocaust in the Age of Decolonization* (2009), where the author concentrates on an issue echoing this book's concern, 'one of the most agonizing problems in contemporary multicultural societies: how to think about the relationship between different social groups' histories of victimization' (Rothberg 2009: 2). In order to do so, he argues for the eschewal of any mutually exclusive approach: memories of slavery or colonialism and of the Holocaust are seen as 'subject to ongoing negotiation, cross-referencing and borrowing; ... the productive intercultural dynamic that I call multidirectional memory' (3).[38]

I argue that this *historical* approach is equally productive for an analysis of the imagery of artistic products dealing with *current* forms of slavery in Britain, even though they sometimes include peoples whose history was involved neither in British or European Imperialism nor in the Nazi extermination of Jews. I will return to the relationship between theoretical models and the national origin of new slaves in Chapter 6.2. Suffice it here to say that one of the aims of this book is to verify whether and how the study of British new slaveries can rest on what Rothberg (2009: 5) considers multidirectional memory to be, namely an 'intercultural dynamic [... with] the potential to create new forms of solidarity and new visions of justice'.

1.5 A theory in the making

> Any teaching that does not question our present is bound to turn into a sort of antifascist catechism for conformists.
> Georges Bensoussan, *Auschwitz en héritage?* (2002: 59, translation mine)

So far, my declaration of critical intent has involved areas as diverse as the studies on the memorialisation of transatlantic slavery, globalisation studies, postcolonialism, Derrida's deconstructive reading of Marx's contemporary relevance, and Holocaust studies. In order to construct working paradigms capable of fruitfully investigating a new, complex and elusive phenomenon, I deem all these perspectives crucial, each one through its particular contribution.

However, the very complexity and the material, contextual specificities of British new slaveries make several qualifications necessary with regard to all these critical perspectives. The concept of 'Traveling Theory' developed by Edward Said in his 1983 essay of that title is extremely useful here. Close to the spirit of Bensoussan's above epigraph, Said aptly observes that, when theoretical concepts are applied too passively to a context that is different from the one in which they originated, they tend to become dead critical instruments, ideological traps. To remain alive and significant, any theory must always be localised; this, according to Said (1991: 241–2), is what distinguishes general theory from a critical consciousness. Similarly, the construction of a theory for a cultural study of new slaveries in Britain necessarily eschews any passive embracing of established models. A constant tendency towards adjustment is what is needed here, as shown by my adoption with reservations of Bauman's *Wasted Lives* (Chapter 1.1) and by some specific examples illustrated in the following paragraphs.

When I visited the Liverpool International Slavery Museum,[39] I was inspired not only by my reading of Oldfield's *Chords of Freedom* (see Chapter 1.1) but also by the museum's temporary exhibition entitled *Trafficked*. Disappointingly, it proved to be only the nucleus of a future concern for new slaveries: little more than one corner of a room was dedicated to it, with three panels recounting the case histories of three enslaved individuals and a richly informative leaflet by the international association Stop the Traffick, presenting data on international trafficking of human beings and suggestions on how to become involved in the cause. After appreciating the permanent collection, I felt even more convinced of the need and the potentialities to engage with new slaveries. On the other hand, I found myself asking what curators *could* do, if they decided to enlarge the room dedicated to new slaveries. The following chapters bring to light the extreme fragmentation of the phenomenon, in most cases composed of isolated, imprisoned individuals. How could curators possibly be 'seeking their [minorities'] active participation in the planning and organisation of museum displays', and how could they 'go out into the community' when new slaveries imply a shattering of the very existence of communities of minorities? How should an 'outreach worker' (Oldfield 2007: 121–2), like the one appointed in Liverpool, work?[40]

Another powerful allusion for the concerns supporting this book is expressed by Sam Durrant; the authors that he analyses are presented as inviting us

> [t]o participate in a ceaseless labor of remembrance, a labor which radically redefines the borders of community by teaching us how to live in memory of both the dead and all those whose living presence continues to be disavowed by the present world order. (Durrant 2004: 1)

It is not exactly clear what Durrant means by living in memory of those living, not least because this is a point he does not elaborate on. Curiously enough, Rothberg and Derrida, too, take scant measure of the fallout of their paradigms on to the enslaved living. Rothberg's emphasis on how the apparently competitive histories of (de)colonisation and the Holocaust can become mutually inspiring for the development of *group* identities raises questions about its own viability for the study of contemporaneity. How far can a cultural study employ key tropes from both fields in a similar manner, when it is concerned with a most diverse universe of *isolated* individuals who are not simply reflecting on their past but living through the most appalling kinds of victimisation *now*? When Rothberg writes 'Meanwhile, labour migrants and their descendants in Europe often find themselves confronted with the ghosts of the past at the same time that they experience the prejudices of the present' (2009: 28), he clearly refers only to certain specific categories of labour migrants in Europe in the present time: the subjects of postwar migrations and their descendants, most of whom occupy the position of 'citizens', albeit discriminated against (whose difference from new slaves I will not neglect).

The need to develop Rothberg's theory along different lines, with regard to British new slaveries, becomes even more pressing apropos his reading of Caryl Phillips, one of the most influential authors for Black British and postcolonial studies. Rothberg takes Phillips as an emblematic case of 'multidirectional memory' from the realms of non-fiction and novelistic writing. He emphasises Phillips's 'intertextuality and fragmentation' in so far as they eschew easy analogy between Jewish and African diasporas, but rather convey 'similar structural problems within those histories and missed encounters between them' (Rothberg 2009: 137).[41] However, he is rather vague about how Phillips's *The European Tribe* (1987) offers glimpses of 'the genocidal past, *present, and perhaps future* of Europe ... [through Phillips's] prescient sense of latent violence' (Rothberg 2009: 153–4; italics mine). This, I think, is an aspect worth developing. In his 'Foreword' to the 1992 edition of *The European Tribe*, Phillips notices what violent forms his former intuitions of the tribal leanings of Europe had later assumed – first and foremost, ethnic cleansing in Yugoslavia (Phillips 1999: xi–xiii).[42] More interestingly for the present volume, the 1987 edition of the book included revealing observations on the increasing importance of foreign labour, especially in its chapter on Germany:

> German *Gastarbeiter* [guest-workers] have no civil rights and are liable to be deported if arrested. They have no vote and are ineligible for social security; *in other words they do not officially exist*. ...

Immigrants form 22 per cent of Frankfurt's population, but because they have no vote politicians are able to ignore them. (Phillips 1999: 84; italics mine)

The issue of *Gastarbeiter*, dating back to the 1960s, was a unique element in the discourse of migrants' rights which dominated Western Europe (Albrecht 2011: 178–9); only later was this discourse disrupted by the massive displacement following the fall of the Soviet bloc and, more markedly in the UK, by the criminalisation of migrants and by the threat of international terrorism (Howarth and Ibrahim 2012: 203–4). But what counts here is that not only did Phillips sense the marginalisation of non-citizen workers as one of the dark sides of Europe, but also he grasped one basic trope of their condition, i.e. their ghostliness. Rothberg's selection of Phillips's preoccupations seems even more partial in the face of some of the novelist's later works, where he shows an increasing interest in the predicament of contemporary migrants.[43] In his travelogue *The Atlantic Sound* (2000) he describes the Ghanaian Mansour, formerly a migrant in Britain who had been imprisoned and then expelled for overstaying his visa (2001a: 148–58). Mansour had been advised to 'go underground' by a solicitor, and in Phillips's novel *A Distant Shore* (2003) the same advice is given to Gabriel, a war refugee who contrives to reach England after experiencing atrocities and an almost fatal journey (Phillips 2004: 166).[44] Even though Phillips never deals with new forms of slavery in Britain (and this is why no chapter of this book focuses on him specifically), *A Distant Shore* deftly touches upon many related issues, as shown in the following chapters: spectrality, racism, the anxiety-laden balance between the impossibility of telling and the wish to tell one's story, a background of violence and sexual abuse. More generally, I consider Phillips's concern extremely significant for the topicality of British new slaveries, given the widely recognised importance of his *oeuvre*,[45] and this is why the present book is interspersed with his illuminating comments on contemporary Britain.

As far as Derrida is concerned, despite his explicit references to the persecution of migrants, he too seems to envisage the ethical function of the ghost as *not* including the *living* victims of the neoliberalism that he deplores:

> It is necessary to speak *of the* ghost, indeed *to the* ghost and *with* it, from the moment that no ethics, no politics … seems possible and thinkable and *just* that does not recognize in principle the respect

for those others who are no longer or for those others who are not yet *there*, presently living, whether they are already dead or not yet born. (2006: xviii)

Derrida, then, eludes any concrete unravelling of his theory within the material coordinates of the present, of the 'there' that he italicises. His employment of the ghost trope tends to be circumscribed within the realm of textuality, in a typically deconstructive attitude that risks sidelining the concrete referent of cultural productions. Despite its valuable suggestions for the present volume, my thinking on *Specters of Marx* has, I feel, affinities with Aijaz Ahmad (1994: 103–4) when he takes exception to Derrida's 'New International' and to its renunciation 'of social class, of ideology and its representations, of the idea of superstructure. [...] In Derrida's language of metaphoric indirection, the range of possibilities remain [*sic*] infinite.'

While relying on textual and aesthetic analysis (see Chapter 1.2), this book intends to avoid a critical approach *exclusively* limited to the field of textuality. I argue that new slaveries cannot be investigated, even in their cultural products, without the material referents valued by Ahmad – without attempting, in Avery Gordon's words (2008: 26), 'to make the fictional, the theoretical and the factual speak to one another'.[46]

1.6 Argument and outline of the book

Chapter 2 starts from the first half of the 1990s, with the first publications acknowledging the unexpected presence of new slaves in Britain.[47] Bridget Anderson's *Britain's Secret Slaves* (1993) is recognised as the pioneer text on the issue. Its investigation into the condition of many domestic workers – deprived of basic labour and human rights – unveiled the fact that British institutions pandered to wealthy foreign families who wished to settle in Britain, by not granting independent status and passports to their domestic workers. In Anderson's groundbreaking research the chapter identifies the first traces of the use of the ghost trope to describe the 'non-existence' of these migrants, the first sign of the ghosts of globalisation. Anderson is also seen as initiating a strategy that recurs in the present volume: the recovery of these spectral migrants' voices (in the first person, too) as a way to counter their effacement.

Chapter 2.2 is centred on the first fictional product on British new slaveries: Ruth Rendell's *Simisola* (1994), a bestselling crime story that acknowledges its inspirational debt to Anderson's volume.

Thanks to Inspector Wexford's inquiring mind, the social setting created by Rendell conveys (and questions) the complexity of a multi-ethnic Britain made up of stratified minorities, with globalisation's new slaves being its lowest rung. The unidentified corpse of a new slave places a spectral void at the centre of the novel, and Wexford's crime-solving will not be enough to fill this gap. This induces a rethinking of Rendell as belonging to a conservative strain of crime fiction. Moreover, it represents a chilling warning about today's Britain being potentially scattered with private homes effectively working as prisons: the brutal violence oppressing Simisola is construed through Primo Levi's observations on the Nazi concentrationary system.

After acknowledging a general attitude of neglect towards new slaveries in the second half of the 1990s,[48] Chapter 3 moves to the first decade of the twenty-first century, marked by a renewed interest in the subject that first surfaced with the publication of Benjamin Zephaniah's *Refugee Boy* and Kay Adshead's *The Bogus Woman* (both 2001), and with Pawel Pawlikowski's film *Last Resort* (2000). Without following a chronological order, the following parts of Chapter 3 focus on two investigative reports and four key novels on British new slaveries. Chapter 3.1 takes into consideration two volumes of research, Louisa Waugh's *Selling Olga* (2006) and Rahila Gupta's *Enslaved* (2007). Given their emphasis on the victims' voices, they are both seen as developments of Bridget Anderson's work, albeit not limited to domestic workers. I here examine new slaves in their continuities with, and breaks from, the postcolonial category of the subaltern: one important feature of Waugh's and Gupta's works is the manifold ways in which the recovery of these voices is problematic, not least because of their ghostly and secluded conditions of living; these, in turn, are exacerbated by institutional neglect, to put it euphemistically, in addressing the problem.

In Chapter 3.2 Chris Abani's raw, lyrical novel *Becoming Abigail* (2006) exemplifies new slaves' anguished need to escape the violent subjugation and imprisonment imposed on them; in this case, a Nigerian teenager-turned-prostitute enslaved in a 'respectable' London house. The pervasiveness of the ghost trope associated to the protagonist's life, and the literal animalisation that she is subjected to by her gaoler, point to the many true stories unearthed by Waugh and Gupta in Chapter 3.1. Abigail's bodily degradation, and her obsessive writing on her own body as if to affirm her denied identity, are construed through Giorgio Agamben's concept of 'bare life', and compared to testimonies of the Holocaust – together with the recurrent concern for the body in postcolonial studies.

Chapter 3.3 concentrates on Little Bee, the protagonist of Chris Cleave's novel *The Other Hand* (2008), another sexually persecuted Nigerian teenager who travels to England. Despite being scarred by an oil-related massacre and unspeakable atrocities, she is made to spend two years in a British detention centre, and then fortuitously set free to roam the country like a ghost. *The Other Hand* offers a glimpse of the continuities between the traumas that many asylum seekers come from and the enforcement of British immigration policies – a phenomenon that, appallingly, does not spare children. I construe the events around Little Bee's deportation by tracing some analogies between British immigration procedures and the bureaucratic machine behind the Holocaust, both incarnated in the figure of the 'desk killer' (originally associated by Hannah Arendt with Adolf Eichmann).

Chapter 3.4 and 3.5, both on genre fiction, elaborate on two essential facets of *The Other Hand*. In 3.4 Marina Lewycka's *Two Caravans* (2007) undertakes the difficult and controversial task of narrating such a tragic topic as new slaveries through humour – something that is partially present in Cleave's novel, too, thanks to Little Bee's ebullient imagination. The picaresque travels of Lewycka's characters expose the variety of places and sectors in today's Britain where new slaves are exploited, much wider than the private home and forming what I call the concentrationary archipelago of British new slaveries. *Two Caravans* also suggests similarities with the Nazi concentrationary system, thus proving that narrative humour and profound reflection are not necessarily incompatible. In Chapter 3.5, Ian Rankin's crime novel *Fleshmarket Close* (2004) is interpreted as exploring in depth the disquieting connections between illegal exploitation and institutional detention of new slaves, already suggested in Cleave's *The Other Hand*. Ten years after Rendell's *Simisola*, Rankin's sleuth John Rebus embodies a criticism of the powers-that-be that sounds even harsher than Inspector Wexford's. On the surface, Rankin's Edinburgh is much rougher than Wexford's respectable Kingsmarkham; in fact, the similarities between the two novels and their settings are many and suggestive.

Chapter 4 examines the analogies, differences and mutual influences between written publications on new slaveries and visual arts. The movie, photographs and plays examined here share a marked tendency to explore the complex relationship between the visual manifestations of new slaveries and the spatial locations that they occupy. Chapter 4.1 elaborates on Rankin's inclusion of the Gothic attractions of Edinburgh's city centre in the exploitative scenario of new slaveries: in Nick Broomfield's film *Ghosts* (2006), the co-ordinates of the Gothic genre are read as needing readjustment, under the pressures of the British concentrationary archipelago. Narrating the tragedy of the Chinese cockle-pickers who eventually drowned in Morecambe Bay in 2004, *Ghosts*'s filmic language conveys the many claustrophobic spaces where they are imprisoned and the spectral dimension of their daily lives. At the same time, its Gothic atmosphere is given a significant slant thanks to Broomfield's documentary-like aesthetics, aimed at inspiring an ethical awareness, rather than an unsettling obscurity, thereby countering the ghostliness of these migrants. In its apparent simplicity, *Ghosts* subtly gestures at issues related to the transatlantic slave trade and the Nazi Holocaust: the trope of the double, for instance, shows that slavery affects both victims and perpetrators – and here again, Primo Levi's works prove an unsurpassed critical inspiration. Chapter 4.2 continues the reflection on the specific contribution of visual arts to the narration of British new slaveries, and Dana Popa's photographic exhibition *Not Natasha* (2009) is briefly commented upon: her hidden, covered subjects are taken as emblematic of the secluded spectrality of the sexual slaves she photographed. Her exhibition is also significant in that a good number of her pictures depict the degraded emptiness of these migrants' home villages in Eastern Europe, once again proving that the focus on new slaveries in Britain cannot imply a neglect of the global roots of the issue.

Chapter 4.3 is centred on four plays where the main characteristics of British new slaveries highlighted thus far are elaborated through a creative rethinking of theatrical spaces. The claustrophobic truck where Clare Bayley's *The Container* (2007) is staged is seen as potentially triggering a passive self-identification in the audience, to the detriment of critical reflection and characterisation. On the other hand, Cora Bissett and Stef Smith's *Roadkill* (2011), Abi Morgan's *Fugee* (2008) and Lucy Kirkwood's *It Felt Empty When the Heart Went at First but It Is Alright Now* (2009) develop their stories through Brechtian, alienating effects (sometimes harking back to Augusto Boal's theatre of the oppressed) that are more profoundly suggestive; with the help of non-naturalistic devices, they are likely to inspire a detached attitude towards, amongst other things, the complicity of our media culture and British institutions exacerbating spectralisation and violence. In these plays, the temporal and spatial disruptions of the stage are also compared to the analogous disruption caused by the traumas (with their ensuing Post Traumatic Stress Disorder) that many migrants go through. A field of study already referred to in Chapter 3.1, trauma theory is here employed as an illuminating critical tool, not least because of the marked interest in the Holocaust that it shares with the present book.[49] The final parts of Chapter 4.3 are devoted to the crucial issue of agency and to the recovery of these new slaves' humanity in the four plays.

Chapter 5 further develops Chapter 4's concern for artistic form. Conceiving of the dimension of dystopia as appropriate for a critical approach to new slaveries, it deals with the ways in which art imagines new slaveries changing Britain without limiting itself to the present state of the nation. In addition, Chapter 5 again takes up the chronological pattern of this study's contents (by going back to the late 1980s and early 1990s) and its multi-generic focus (thanks to a comparative study of fiction and cinema). Dystopia, I contend, is much closer to reality than might be expected. In 1988 the magical-realist England of Salman Rushdie's *Satanic Verses* uncannily anticipated the processes of spectralisation and animalisation imposed on migrants by xenophobic authorities. Chapter 5.1 demonstrates how Alfonso Cuarón's film version (2006) of P. D. James's *The Children of Men* (1992) radically alters the novel in order to emphasise the urgency of migration issues. The centrality of the concentration camp for contemporary Britain is likewise present in Cuarón's movie, and it is here seen from the perspective of Agamben's theoretical works on the camp's contemporary transformations. Chapter 5.2 presents a bio-political reading of Kazuo Ishiguro's unforgettable alternative-history novel *Never Let Me Go* (2005), the story of a generation of clones raised for organ donations. The book's rich metaphorical suggestiveness gestures at issues relatable to the Holocaust, colonial forms of subjugation and a wide range of contemporary atrocities. I argue that Ishiguro's clones are also to be read as embodying British new slaves: subtly turned into ghosts, brainwashed into behaving as such without the use of coercion and unaware of the prisons detaining them, they represent a dystopic version of today's new slaves; I also argue, through reference to Adorno and Fanon, that the artistic, refined education that they are given represents one of the most effective means towards their enslavement. By spectralising both slavery and the camp, *Never Let Me Go* hints at how forms of enslavement can slyly envelop a wider sector of the population than globalisation's migrants; besides, it shows that the concentration camp itself – or its new forms – can be turned into a ghost, thus fusing the two main tropes on which new slaveries are based.

These two points are further elaborated in my Conclusion. Chapter 6.1 returns to Ishiguro's merging of the ghost and the camp through the recurring image of the hooded head in two French movies: Philippe Lioret's feature film *Welcome* (2009) and Sylvain George's arthouse documentary *Qu'ils reposent en révolte* (2010). Both set in Calais (though French, a key location for immigration to Britain), these two works symbolically conflate in this image the migrants' spectral condition, their simultaneous imprisonment and isolation. Furthermore, this merging is shown in its connections to a repeated historical and cultural process of spectralisation of concentration camps, involving the Nazi genocide, British immigration policies and some contemporary cultural theory, as I argue in my critique of Marc Augé's concept of 'non-place'.

Finally, Chapter 6.2 considers how artistic products on British new slaveries question accepted delimitations of postcolonial and Black British studies, given the wide geographical origins of their authors, characters and settings. Inevitably, this involves the debated relationship between globalisation and postcolonial studies: in what ways can the study of new slaveries throw light on it? The dissemination of borders surfacing in this volume is paralleled by a widening of critical confines (a long-standing tendency in postcolonial studies that this book adheres to) and by the need for a renewal of categories. In this regard, I feel very close to David Farrier's multidisciplinary approach in his signal study of asylum seekers: 'investigating the relationship between postcolonial studies and discourses on refugees and asylum seekers has necessitated going beyond the divisions erected between discursive formations, and redrawing lines of engagement' (Farrier 2011: 16). Just like his *Postcolonial Asylum*, this book is meant to be 'an attempt to take this kind of step beyond postcolonial studies – to assess the limits of its application to asylum [in my case, to new slaves'] contexts while remaining faithful to its ethos of dismantling dominant power structures' (Farrier 2011: 20).[50]

In the wake of this renewal of boundaries, in the final part of Chapter 6.2 I make reference to Agamben's call for the rejection of the 'citizen versus migrant' divide. By way of conclusion, I attempt to verify where, in the texts analysed here, this renewal is suggested as a feasible possibility, both individually and collectively. I identify in Albert Camus's *The Rebel* (1951) an inspiring theorisation of how any person's refusal, any individual's 'no', represents a possibility to start such a renewal, to throw a sympathetic bridge towards an Other and thus plant the seeds of a collective action. This kind of gesture is identified in a number of works analysed in the chapters of this book, and also in Monica Ali's *In the Kitchen* (2009). Camus's concept of rebellion is a resistance against complicity, against collaboration with the incessant enslavement of human beings that pervades Britain today – a country where, at the time of the completion of this book, Conservative leaders promised voters the withdrawal of Britain from the European Convention on Human Rights in order to curb the appeals of those who face deportation (Travis 2013: passim).

Notes

1 Young (2001: 194).
2 Anthony Tibbles (2008: 301–2) comments on the British government's ambiguous attitude during the commemorations, and asks himself whether 2007 represented a seized or a missed opportunity to come to terms with Britain's past.
3 Oldfield (2007: 72) also mentions the 2007 setting up of the Wilberforce Institute for the Study of Slavery and Emancipation (WISE), designed as a platform for studying issues of modern human rights, and the 2004 Commons debate on the then forthcoming Bicentenary, when some MPs 'touched on … the need to keep in mind the ongoing struggle against "forced and bonded labour, the worst forms of child labour, child soldiers and early and forced marriages"' (109).
4 Rice quotes Paul Ricoeur's *Memory, History, Forgetting* (Chicago: University of Chicago Press, 2000), p. 88.
5 United Nations, E/CN.4/Sub.2/1981/20, Updating of the Report on Slavery Submitted to the Sub-commission in 1966, Report by Benjamin Whitaker, Special Rapporteur.
6 For a list of international bodies' definitions of slavery, see Kaye (2008: 3); this publication provides a complete survey of forms of slavery throughout the world.
7 In his examination of the legislation on migration in the US, Nicholas De Genova (2002: 438, 429) demonstrates how it is 'deportability, and not deportation per se, that has historically rendered undocumented migrant labour a distinctly disposable commodity … migrants' endurance of many years of "illegality" can serve as a disciplinary

apprenticeship in the subordination of their labour'.
8 See, for instance, Di Nicola (2007: 61–2); Davies (2009: passim).
9 Only at the end of March 2011 did Britain finally agree to sign up to the European plan (Hughes 2011: n.p.), but, even after that, the government failed to implement the EU directive in many ways (*Reporter*, 19:1: 4). Generally speaking, the situation was deemed likely to worsen with the coming of the 2012 Olympics, since the 'mass influx of tourists could fuel a greater demand for cheap, temporary labour in jobs vulnerable to the use of forced labour', as the launch of the new Slavery-Free London campaign showed (*Reporter*, 17:3: 6).
10 Again, in the world of Monica Ali's Labour MP character Fairweather, 'the pressure groups like to call it slavery, sounds more impressive, and we're really world class at that because we've gone so big on deregulation, you see. [...] There's a constant pressure to decrease costs. The old union model of labour is dead and gone. You've got longer and longer chains of sub-contracting and outsourcing, and employers want to buy labour as they buy other commodities – supplies which they can turn on and off as necessary without raising the unit price' (Ali 2010: 326–7, 421).
11 See Bosworth (2007: 162) about UK's 'dubious honour of confining proportionally the most asylum seekers for the longest periods of time in all of Europe'.
12 While this volume was being completed, the Home Secretary Theresa May declared that Britain should be prepared to withdraw from the European Convention on Human Rights, so that the right to appeal against deportation can be restricted (Travis 2013: passim).
13 For a fictional version of this exploitative continuity running between illegal and institutional places of imprisonment, see my analysis of Ian Rankin's *Fleshmarket Close* in Chapter 3.5.
14 'Now for the price of a share everyone can be a stakeholder in immigration control', Steve Cohen writes (2006: 78).
15 See for instance Makenga's poem 'A tale' (2002: 121): 'my papers / It should not be long / in the meantime I can't do anything / there is nothing to be done / other than go round in circles'.
16 For an analysis of this movie, see Loshitzky (2010: 62–76) and Farrier (2011: 107–10). For another case of unallowed work putting asylum application at risk, see Segun Afolabi's short story 'Monday morning', winner of the 2005 Caine Prize (Afolabi 2004: passim).
17 As a world expert on new slaveries, Bales often insists on their distinguishing traits: see, for instance, 2005: 8–9.
18 See also Pai (2008: ix).
19 In this regard, I strongly agree with De Genova's terminological premise (2002: 420, 440): for intellectual and political reasons, he calls for a study into the developments of US legislation on migration, precisely in order to 'denaturalize the reification of' categories such as 'illegals' and expose 'the legal production of "illegality"'.

20 The limits and modalities of this self-identification are discussed in Chapter 4.3.
21 Psycho-social field research on cases of dehumanisation, after all, cannot really touch the core of the victims' situation, for obvious ethical problems (Volpato 2011: 58–9).
22 On how these acts of substitution in Phillips's fiction ('they' are 'us') are at once essential and inadequate, invaluable and limited, see Farrier's analysis (2011: 201–7) of *A Distant Shore*.
23 This implicitly gestures at Bauman's vision of modernity mentioned in Chapter 1.1.
24 See Said (2004: 10, 28, 76).
25 I am indebted to Patrick Williams for emphasising this passage in his paper 'Overlapping intellectuals, intertwined theories' (delivered at the 6th AISCLI conference in Rome, 17–18 January 2013), thus showing the import of Said's book for my research.
26 Fanon himself, after all, closed his *Wretched of the Earth* with a call for a renewed humanism: 'For Europe, for ourselves and for humanity, comrades, we must turn over a new leaf, we must work out new concepts, and try to set afoot a new man' (Fanon 1967: 255). In a way, my efforts may be seen as modestly following in the wake of the literary eclecticism that characterised Said himself: he never affiliated to specific theoretical schools, and combined humanist and post-humanist thinkers in his oeuvre; on the re-evaluation of Said's humanism by the so-called 'post-theory' of the first years of the twenty-first century, see Frassinelli (2014: 33).
27 Baucom's analysis of the transatlantic slave trade also relates to our present globalisation in so far as it is structured, rather than on nation states and centre–periphery dichotomies, on spaces of flows regulating financial circulation, shaping a 'circum-Atlantic archipelago of flow' (Baucom 2005: 36–8).
28 For another study of spectrality in relation to the transatlantic slave trade, see Cimitile 2005.
29 In post-apartheid South Africa (late 1990s), a recent development of this kind of imagery is constituted by the zombie image, associated to the over-exploited workers produced by neo-liberal deregulation (Comaroff and Comaroff 2011: 38–41, 153–71).
30 Durrant quotes Robert Young's *Postcolonialism: An Historical Introduction* (Oxford: Blackwell, 2001), p. 427.
31 The general awareness of this phenomenon among scholars of postcolonial studies, however, has sometimes been surprisingly feeble; the critical collection *Postcolonial Ghosts / Fantômes postcoloniaux* (2010), for instance, includes no essay on the topic of new slaves, despite originating from a very open call for papers from the University of Montpellier.
32 According to Robert Eaglestone (2008a: 74), this field is composed of 'a range of fluid and developing concerns'.

33 See also pp. 59, 71, 82, 99.
34 See Levi (1986: 37, 233, 244). The Appendix to this edition, where Levi answered the most common questions that he had been asked over the years, was later translated as 'Afterword' in Levi 1996.
35 See also Bensoussan (2002: 111).
36 In addition to these theorizations, Olivier Razac's *Barbed Wire: A Political History* (2003: passim) presents an approach to the development of the concentration camp by focusing on one of its emblematic elements, i.e. barbed wire as a means of confinement. Razac considers barbed wire an element of transition toward a political control of space, which has been fading into ever more inconspicuous and virtual versions; he sees new technologies of control as contemporary versions of barbed wire. With the dissolution of barbed wire, I wonder, what sites and cultural imageries can be seen as taking its place?
37 Isin and Rygiel's noteworthy classification of 'abject spaces', which form 'interstitial territories that are literally neither here nor there' (2007: 177), differs from the notion of concentrationary archipelago envisioned in this book, because it is almost completely limited to spaces created by institutions, and neglects the criminal activities imprisoning new slaves.
38 The same need for integration between these two histories is expressed in Paul Gilroy's *The Black Atlantic* (1993: 213), referred to in Chapter 6.2.
39 30 June 2010.
40 This also complicates the debate on the applicability of trauma studies to postcolonial works: if these studies are susceptible to criticism for focusing on the individual, rather than on the collective dimension (Craps and Buelens 2008: 4), what about new slaveries?
41 For an in-depth discussion of this feature in Caryl Phillips's *Higher Ground* and *The Nature of Blood* from the perspective of trauma theory, see Craps (2008: passim). For an analysis of 'the formative role that awareness of the [Nazi] camps played in the realization of both his place as a black man in Europe and his vocation as a writer', see Farrier (2011: 202).
42 *The European Tribe* was published one year after Primo Levi's *The Drowned and the Saved* (1986), which expressed analogous fears about the future of Europe (Levi 1989: 167; see Chapter 1.4).
43 When he associates his father's generation to Othello's misgivings (2011b: 191), Phillips states that 'Nervous hesitation will once again be visited upon the next wave of first generation migrants, wherever they might hail from'.
44 For an analysis of the novel, see Gunning (2011: 143–6, 149) and Farrier (2011: 201–7).
45 I should also mention the elusive and enigmatic character of the Polish girl Danuta in Phillips's novel *In the Falling Snow* (2010).

46 This need for a historically grounded reading of texts, together with my postcolonial critical background, is what makes me see Agamben's works on the concentration camp as central but at the same time incomplete, because limited to a Western perspective centred on classical cultures and languages. Agamben's excessively Eurocentric genealogy would certainly benefit from Rothberg's postcolonial perspective, and from Arendt's colonial genealogy of the concentration camp (Arendt 1958: 185–207). On Agamben's eschewing of the role of colonial history in bio-politics, and of the political specificities of today's refugees, see Rothberg (2009: 62–5, 102) and Farrier (2011: 9, 61, 64). At times, I also sense a limitation in Agamben's typically deconstructive etymological zeal, which I find problematic and anachronistic: see, for instance, his disdainful rejection of the term 'Holocaust' because it used to mean 'pious sacrifice' and carry anti-Jewish connotations (Agamben 1999: 28–31).

47 As the following chapters show, the early 1990s is a crucial period for the surfacing of this phenomenon. Incidentally, the building of new sites to detain foreigners, and the conversion of building into immigrant detention centres, began in 1993 (Bosworth 2007: 162).

48 It is noteworthy that this coincided with the rise and establishment of New Labour, which interrupted Conservative leadership while, unfortunately, aligning – and further enforcing – Conservative policies on immigration control.

49 See Eaglestone (2008b: 35). Chapter 4.3 also refers to the debated relation between postcolonial and trauma studies.

50 Even though Farrier's concept of the 'camp *dispositif*' (2011: 13) only partially overlaps with my 'concentrationary archipelago', *Postcolonial Asylum* studies issues that are extremely significant here, too, such as the questioning of the 'we' (23), the ethics of reading (125), and the implications of responsibility (181–208).

2
Investigating migrant domestic workers

> all the doors were alarmed. So I escaped through the hole in the wall where the pipe from the tumble drier goes. I was very thin because I did not have enough to eat.
> Bridget Anderson, *Britain's Secret Slaves* (1993: 52)

> Immigrants, today's proletarians.
> Étienne Balibar, *We, the People of Europe?* (2004: 50)

2.1 Bridget Anderson's *Britain's Secret Slaves* (1993)

> Slaves cannot breathe in England, if their lungs
> Receive our air, that moment they are free;
> They touch our country and their shackles fall
> (William Cowper, *The Task*, Book II, lines 40–2)

In April 1993, Bridget Anderson's sociological report *Britain's Secret Slaves: An Investigation into the Plight of Overseas Domestic Workers* unveiled the existence of slavery at the end of the twentieth century, informing a shocked public that in many a wealthy house in Britain domestic workers of Third World origin were systematically secluded, abused and beaten – sometimes raped; further investigations and Parliamentary initiatives followed.

In her Introduction, Anderson quotes the famous lines from William Cowper's *The Task* (1785), which can be seen as part of the debate for and against slavery during the Romantic age. As a whole, Anderson's investigation undermines the contemporary validity of this axiom regarding Britain. Her necessary premise, though, starts from the Gulf States, where 1.2 million domestic workers are estimated to live and work; they come from Asian countries such as Bangladesh, Indonesia, India, Korea, Pakistan, the Philippines, Sri Lanka and Thailand. They usually pay huge fees (which they can ill afford) to recruitment agencies in their native countries, by whom they are often promised different jobs from the domestic work they will get, and a higher salary than the money that they will actually receive. This repeated pattern includes the case of Alice, a Filipino woman employed by members of the Kuwaiti royal family (incidentally, the same family for whose sake Western nations engaged in the first Gulf War in 1991). Alice had been promised work as a civil engineer, but, in her own words:

> 'For Filipinas the work here is domestic. No, you cannot phone the agency in Manila, it is too expensive for long distance. Can you pay your airfare back? Can you pay the agency the fees you owe? No? Then you must sign this contract as domestic servant.' ... I was up at 5.30 to make breakfast for the children. I could only go to bed after the adults. ... Midnight was an early night for me. In two and a half years I was working for them I had no day off, no time off. ... The worst time was in the month of Ramadan, when I had to work day and night with no break, only maybe if I could snatch a nap in a chair. It is very hard to attend to the wishes of the parents and the children at the same time. If the father is shouting and I am having to get something for the child he will get very angry with me, and take my shoulders and shake me. ... they will use embarrassing words, and it's no good saying sorry, they just say, 'In what bank are we going to deposit your sorry? We are spending money. We are paying you to do a job.' (Anderson 1993: 13–14)

As Alice's story shows, their situation is particularly harrowing. Their residence permit is linked to their work permit that, in turn, can be managed only by their employer. Their wages vary according to their country of origin, Bangladeshis being the lowest paid. And, above all, in countries where labour organisations are generally illegal, 'the minimum protection granted to workers is not applied to domestic servants, who are explicitly excluded from labour legislation. They are regarded, not as workers, but as members of the household' (Anderson 1993: 20). These are the reasons why they are vulnerable to exploitation, to the point of falling victim to psychological, physical and sexual abuse, much worse than Alice's case. Even when they decide to escape, they are not protected by the criminal legislations of the Gulf States; in some of them, 'posters offering rewards with photographs of runaways appear on billboards and on television' (25). Their only remaining prospect is to obtain a release through a fee paid by another employer (the only way to get a visa) or to fly back home, completely without money, submerged in debts.

'Domestic workers are unique in the Middle East in that it is common for them to travel with their employer': Britain is one of their favourite destinations, for both business and holiday reasons (26). There, the same kind of master/slave relationship is bound to continue. The class origin of the employers is clear: 'I now know that princesses, diplomats, doctors of Medicine and other normally respectable people keep bonded, indentured domestics in virtual slavery,' writes Lord Hylton in his Foreword to Anderson's volume (7); as for their nationalities, beside Gulf Arabs the list also includes Indians, Nigerians and, to the horror of the public, white Britons; many of them are former expatriates who used to live in the Gulf area. As for the nationalities of the servants, there are also some Africans who have arrived via the Gulf or straight from their native countries (42).

Notwithstanding the criminal behaviour of these employers, it would be wrong to put the blame simply on the cruelty of some individuals. *Britain's Secret Slaves* effectively reconstructs the political responsibilities on both a global and a British level. Its second chapter (28–40) focuses on the exemplary case of the Philippines to expand on the connections between world economy and internal and international migratory fluxes, and to establish a cause consequence linkage between national debt and migration, with an ensuing vicious circle: national debt creates crisis, which leads to migration, which causes bondage of human beings, which, in turn, exacerbates the nation's economic and social crisis. 'If Third World Debt is considered a form of debt bondage, then the indebted countries may be considered to be nations in servitude to the rich North' (34–5).

British responsibilities, too, are clearly stated: overseas domestic workers do not have the right to change employers, because:

> they depend for their entire livelihood and immigration status on the employer whose name is added to their passport when it is stamped upon entry to the UK. [...] They are not given an immigration status independent of the household they work for ... [or] treated as members of the household. (Anderson 1993: 11, 45, 46)

They are not even granted leave to stay in Britain in the event that they manage to escape and to start legal action (Anderson 1993: 68): 'I want to stay here legally, but as it is we are not like human beings', says Helen from Nigeria (55). The book's conclusion is obvious: it condemns 'the structural condoning of such practices through the immigration law and rules' (49), which were simply adapted from those of the Gulf States. When tracing the responsibilities generating this international trade in domestic workers, then, Anderson shows how Britain, as a First World country, is to be positioned at the initial and final extremities of this global phenomenon.

Anderson also initiates, though in embryo, a mode of representing new slaveries central to the present book – a mode which will be later followed by other authors, other genres. Assaulted by world economy and British laws, secluded and with no independent status, these migrants inevitably assume a spectral, ghost-like nature. At the time of the publication of *Britain's Secret Slaves*, their number was impossible to determine. This nature also surfaces in the imagery of Anderson's research; when she makes reference to the 1989 *Migrant and Refugee Manifesto*,[1] she writes:

> There is a hidden, thirteenth state in the European Community: the 16 million migrants, immigrants and refugees who live and work in Europe. Together they number more than the combined population of Belgium and Denmark, but they are denied the 'freedom' of the new Europe. (71)

The words 'ghost' and 'spectre' are not mentioned here, but the allusion to Marx and Engels's *Manifesto* cannot be avoided. In the same year as *Specters of Marx*, Anderson makes oblique reference to the *Manifesto*'s famous spectre wandering around Europe and to its contemporary significance for migrant workers. She thus offers an example of Derrida's theory grounded in material reality, as if trying to answer Ahmad's objections to the French theorist's excess of 'metaphoric indirection'.[2]

The urgent question inevitably regards ways to counter the effects of this dehumanising process. On the political level, Anderson's book is an explicit call for the concession of a truly democratic worker status to these migrants: 'change the law' is the watchword.[3] The present book, however, is more concerned with the cultural, rhetorical and literary strategies interacting with all this, for which the ghost undoubtedly represents a major interpretative key. In *Ghostly Alterities: Spectrality and Contemporary Literatures* (2007), Bianca Del Villano examines Fred D'Aguiar's novel *Feeding the Ghosts*, where a slave-witness is 'not heard because she does not exist as a subject in their system' (Del Villano 2007: 21). It is a condition strikingly similar to that of some domestics described by Anderson, unable to continue their legal actions because they are on the brink of deportation (Anderson 1993: 58).

On the other hand, in her analysis of Toni Morrison's *Beloved*, Del Villano emphasises the central role of narration in the reconstruction of a dismembered identity (Del Villano 2007: 55), a fundamental tenet of much postcolonial criticism, which Chapter 1.3 touched upon. An analogous principle seems to uphold Anderson's approach in her reconstruction of these people's lives. She was possibly inspired by the philosophy of the Commission for Filipino Migrant Workers; amongst other things, this UK-based organisation set up regular meetings where women could discuss their individual problems, and thus overcome their trauma through a renewal of their trust in and friendship with others. In one victim's words:

> I went back to normal. Before, when I was alone, I didn't trust anyone. My experience with my employers meant that I couldn't speak up. It makes you silent and not open. When I began to talk to people in similar situations, and I saw that I was not alone, I realised that the problem was not just to do with me, that it was the Philippines and Britain and the government in those countries.

Anderson identifies, in this emotional recovery, a link with urgent, practical matters:

> This sympathy and understanding is crucial in rebuilding the self-respect of women who have been systematically degraded and treated as less than human. It is a process which in turn enables those women to help others. All this gives the women a breathing space, time to recover from their trauma, and importantly, the possibility of making a decision on their next step, informed by sound legal advice. (Anderson 1993: 58–9)

Accordingly, her book often interrupts her analysis with framed case-studies presenting the appalling stories of women, including first-person narrations, for instance: 'The worst thing is I am carrying always the bell. When they call you they just hit the button and you will run. We each had our number of chimes, so we know which one is wanted. Mine was two. So I hear, "Ding! Ding," and even if I am sleeping I must get up and go to them' (Anderson 1993: 22).

Sometimes the victims' voices are interspersed in the main text through a narration (in first or third person, sometimes both) of a case history written in bold type on a framed grey background; these passages are further set off from the main text by their titles, which follow a victim's first name + 'Story' pattern, e.g. 'Roseline's Story' (43). This second technique of conveying their voices is sometimes less directly linked with the issue being tackled by Anderson in the surrounding pages, and thus acquires prominence by its own force. The presence of these voices – or, rather, the lack of it – constitutes precisely what the core of Rendell's crime story is made of.

2.2 Ruth Rendell's *Simisola* (1994)

> Dehumanisation lies at the heart of a democratic modernity that produces the marginalised and the excluded who, being rejected and demonised, sink into the abyss where they have been confined. ... Every extreme oppression makes a savage of its victim, and thus legitimates the recourse to violence against him.
> Georges Bensoussan, *Auschwitz en héritage?* (2002: 110, my translation)[4]

One of the most popular contemporary crime writers,[5] Rendell acknowledges Anderson's research as the source of inspiration for her novel, a bestseller featuring her sleuth Inspector Wexford. It focuses on the murder of an African domestic worker, and Wexford reads passages from *Britain's Secret Slaves* to his colleagues so that they can better grasp this new reality.

The first novel tackling the issue of new slaveries in Britain, then, was a detective story. This should not be surprising, as the chapter on Ian Rankin will also show: a largely unknown phenomenon was there to be investigated by a genre which is typically centred on the figure of the Other – be it victim, detective or culprit (Kim 2005: 1).

In Rendell's story local politics, class barriers, colour fault lines and houses haunted by domestic violence all contribute to the creation of a social setting in a small community in quiet Sussex – the fictional Kingsmarkham, where Reginald Wexford lives and works. Kingsmarkham is a country town only recently touched by multiculturalism, 'becoming more cosmopolitan daily' (Rendell 1995: 32);[6] it functions as a setting where, as in much of provincial England, the few black Britons (and, therefore, colour issues) stand out prominently and are less obfuscated by metropolitan anonymity. One of them, the Nigerian Dr Akande, is also Wexford's GP; the mysterious disappearance of his daughter triggers off the complex plot of this novel, which reaches well beyond the specific case of twenty-two-year-old Melanie Akande.

The third-person narrative perspective often coincides with Wexford's reflective and investigating mind. Wexford is usually considered one of those investigating policemen working as one of a team (Mandel 1990: 77–80). Standing on the shoulders of his more data-collecting subordinates, Wexford

> always delved into human motive and the peculiarities of human nature while Burden concentrated on facts, seldom disputing them however bizarre they might appear. ... Burden thought of something Wexford had once said to him about Sherlock Holmes, how you couldn't solve much by his methods. A pair of slippers with singed soles no more showed that their wearer had been suffering from a severe chill than that he had merely had cold feet. ... With human nature you could only guess – and try to guess right. (Rendell 1995: 152–3)

His subordinates, like Karen Malahyde, know that he 'intuited spectacularly' (41). Such are the faculties through which Wexford starts to delve into ethnic prejudices in Britain, and into his own; he undergoes a process of self-questioning facilitated by his perceptiveness and awareness, a 'detection that violence against blacks exists in a complex continuum with the racist assumptions made partly in ignorance by well-meaning whites' (Rowland 2001: 83). Wexford realises he is being over-kind and over-zealous towards the Akandes; when Melanie goes missing, he starts visiting the Akandes every morning before going to work and senses that this could be a reaction to his generation's engrained racism. At the beginning he frankly admits that white Britons can be 'liberal-minded', but 'we're all racists in this country':

> Without exception. People over forty are worse and that's about all you can say. You were brought up and I was brought up to think ourselves superior to black people. Oh, it may not have been explicit but it was there all right. We were conditioned that way and it's in us still, it's ineradicable.

When Burden suggests that things have changed, he replies: 'No, they haven't. Not much. There are just more black people about', and criticises politically correct language as hypocritical (Rendell 1995: 13–14); ambivalently, Wexford sometimes corrects himself in order not to describe people in racial terms.[7] His ambivalence on colour matters meets a brisk nemesis when, by chance, the corpse of a black woman is discovered, buried in the countryside. It must be Melanie, but, when the Akandes are summoned and they claim that she is not their daughter, everyone is shocked. Mrs Akande's reaction against Wexford rubs salt in the wound:

> How dare you treat us like that? You're just a damned racist like the rest of them. ... You damned hypocrite! You don't have prejudice,

do you? Oh no, you're not a racist, black and white are all equal in your eyes. But when you find a dead black girl it's got to be our girl because we're black! (208)

Wexford takes this humiliation as a 'salutary lesson', conceding to himself that he had neglected normal procedures, to the point of not bothering to reflect on the different heights and supposedly different ages of the two women. From now onwards he seems determined to proceed on the basis of what is most useful to solve the case, eschewing any misleading political correctness and its underlying prejudices (230, 246).

The buried corpse is frightfully beaten up, and ridden with fractures and contusions. It represents a new phase in Wexford's investigations, the first step for taking cognizance of the ghosts of new slaveries. As Derrida writes (2006: 9): 'First of all, mourning. ... It consists always in attempting to ontologize remains, to make them present, in the first place by *identifying* their bodily remains and by *localizing* the dead.' The book's investigation progressively reconstructs the victim's life in Britain as probably based on psychological, physical and sexual abuse by her masters, analogous to the case histories presented by Anderson; Wexford reads from Anderson's volume precisely in order to learn about his country's secret slaves, about whom he knew nothing. The corpse will lead to the core of the plot and show its links with the situation described in *Britain's Secret Slaves*.

Its discovery is introduced through another important facet of Rendell's style, that is to say its intertextuality: mostly thanks to Wexford's erudition, the story is interspersed with references – more or less overt – to world literature and history related to slavery, decisive for the reader to catch the resonance of this book in the context of Black Britain:

> Kingsmarkham lies in that part of Sussex that was once the land of a Celtic tribe the Romans called the Regnenses. To its colonists it was simply a desirable place to live, pleasant to look at and not too cold, the indigenous population regarded only as a source of slave labour. Numerous remains of female infants ... suggest that the Romans practised infanticide among the Regnenses with a view to maintaining a male work force. (Rendell 1995: 195)

After the finding of a small treasure, amateur searchers begin to visit the area, and one of them discovers the woman's corpse. This reference to the Roman conquest inevitably recalls to mind

Marlow's notorious parallel at the beginning of *Heart of Darkness* (Conrad 1987: 28–32). Conrad's plot ended by undermining the stated ethical superiority of European colonialism over that of the Romans; likewise, in Rendell's case this reference seems to suggest that a certain pattern of considering others as work force has, sadly, continued unabated – only to shift its interest on to female (and very private) domestic labour.

On Wexford's initiative, the unidentified corpse is named Sojourner after Sojourner Truth (1797?–1883), the escaped American slave and later Abolitionist, famous champion of civil rights and women's rights:

> 'after Sojourner Truth, the "Ain't I a woman?" poet. And maybe ... well, I somehow see her as impermanent, homeless, alone. "I am a stranger with thee and a sojourner", you know.'
> Burden didn't know. He wore his deeply suspicious uneasy look. 'Sodgernah?' (Rendell 1995: 211)

A name, as Derrida notes (2000: 25), marks the difference between the stranger and the absolute Other. Postcolonial studies have often configured naming as a strategy of resistance: Del Villano, for instance, detects in D'Aguiar's *Feeding the Ghosts* an ethical 'necessity to bring the ghosts back to life and to give them back their names and their identity' (Del Villano 2007: 21).

Depicted as following in the wake of the Roman conquest and the transatlantic slave trade, Sojourner's story is also intricately connected in Rendell's novel with the present state of Britain: she is the product of a very subtly layered social stratification, thanks to the many characters from all walks of life – all of whom, at the same time, can help shed light on her slavery. She certainly occupies the bottom rung of the ladder, whereas Melanie's parents are part of the so-called 'Ebony Elite' (Rendell 1995: 307) and proud to announce to Wexford: 'You may or may not know that black Africans are the most highly educated members of British society. Statistics show that. ... we have high expectations of our children' (23).[8]

Rendell's picture of multicultural Britain exemplified in Kingsmarkham, then, avoids falling into the stereotypes of ethnic essentialism and manichaeism. Colour issues constantly interweave with class issues, in accordance with the view on Black Britain expressed by Stuart Hall in his seminal essay 'New ethnicities' (1988): if black politics could once be taken as a common category based on a shared experience of marginalisation, racism and ensuing resistance, he envisions a second phase principally focused on a critical politics of representation, rather than on a fight for representation in itself, which takes into account the way ethnicity is constantly articulated with other categories such as class and sexual identity (Hall 1988: passim). In other words, Rendell reconstructs the 'stratified map of minoritization'[9] which is part and parcel of today's Britain; seen from this perspective, it seems extremely significant that the real crime and the real victim, unusually, appear only halfway through the novel.

In this regard, another important character is the Lebanese Anouk Khoori, wife of an Egyptian multimillionaire. She is running in the local Council by-elections as an independent Conservative candidate, representing for many the hoped-for resistance against the rise of the xenophobic British National Party. Juana and Rosenda, the Khooris' Philippine domestics, occupy yet another rung of the social ladder, having entered Britain through the same legislation as Sojourner, but without suffering the same abuses. Wexford's talk with Mr Khoori about his domestics is based on one important point from *Britain's Secret Slaves*. The increased restrictions on allowing non-Europeans to enter the country as foreign resident domestics, brought into force from the late 1970s, were overcome thanks to special concessions reserved, on an economic criterion, only for wealthy individuals (like Khoori) and returning British nationals (Anderson 1993: 45). When Wexford mentions this state of affairs, 'Khoori gave a loud braying laugh. "I'm damned if I'd be here if I had to wash my own dishes"' (Rendell 1995: 330). Anderson quotes a member of the government bluntly admitting the economic reason behind this 1990 choice:

> Looking at our national interest, if wealthy investors, skilled workers and others with potential to benefit our economy were unable to be accompanied by their domestic staff they might not come here at all but take their money and skills to other countries only too keen to welcome them.

The status for such workers, then, is practically the same in the Gulf States as in Britain, and 'by their actions, the Home Office are denying the women their most basic rights not only as workers, but also as human beings' (Anderson 1993: 47).[10]

This culminates in cases like Rendell's Sojourner, living with and 'working' for the Ridings – the 'returning British nationals'. Thanks to young Sophie Riding's statement, Wexford finds out in the end that, when they were living in Kuwait, they had bought Sojourner from someone who had previously bought her from her father in Nigeria for £5. She was being beaten and raped by both the respectable paediatrician Swithun Riding and his son Christopher. As Julie H. Kim (2005: 1) writes, 'despite theories about the conservative strain of detective fiction which posit the criminal as the aberrant element to be disposed of ..., many criminals surprise us by being less "other" than one might suppose'.

Sojourner's mystery, then, is represented as the product of a series of concentric exploitative apparatuses, from world economy to British laws to single criminal minds exploiting, in turn, what the system offers them under a semi-legal guise. Her story has many points in common with the case histories of *Britain's Secret Slaves*: she is kept in complete isolation and also mistreated by the youngest members of the family, as Sophie's confession shows:

> 'The bad part – for me, that is – the bad part was that I thought she was stupid and clumsy, I could even see what my mother meant when she said she wasn't fit to sleep in a proper bedroom.'
> The machine went on pause. Wexford went on, 'Psychologists say that someone ugly and dirty is a ready candidate for abuse. That your own abuse has resulted in the ugliness makes no difference. The reasoning behind it seems to be that ugliness deserves punishment and dirt and neglect of personal hygiene even more so. It got to a point where Sojourner was being beaten for every small fault. She worked twelve or fourteen hours a day but that wasn't enough. Susan Riding told me herself they had six bedrooms in that house but that didn't mean they had one for Sojourner. She slept in a small room off the kitchen.' (Rendell 1995: 369)

Rendell introduces here a phenomenon that Primo Levi noticed in the Nazi concentrationary system. In a chapter from *The Drowned and the Saved* (1986) where he tries to find a meaning of the degrading, 'Useless Violence' he witnessed in Auschwitz, he analyses the practice of reducing the prisoners to a subhuman level and to the state of animals through humiliating rules about excrement, nudity and cutlery, in order to have fewer scruples about their elimination (Levi 1989: 83–101). The prologue to this process – culminating in the tattooing of registration numbers – is to be located in Nazi depictions of Jews as animal parasites needing eradication through political hygiene (Bauman 1989: 27), and would continue in the very deportation trains, where no water or container for excrement was supplied; Levi (1989: 88–9) recalls some German passengers at an Austrian station who openly expressed their disgust through the same vicious circle described by Wexford: 'people like this deserve their fate, just look how they behave. These are not *Menschen*, human beings, but animals, it's clear as the light of day.' The chapter closes with a declaration by Franz Stangl, the commander of Treblinka; asked the reason for all these humiliations, given that the prisoners had to die anyway, he replied:

> 'To condition those who were to be the material executors of the operations. To make it possible for them to do what they were doing.'
> In other words: before dying the victim must be degraded, so that the murderer will be less burdened by guilt. This is an explanation not devoid of logic but which shouts to heaven: it is the sole usefulness of useless violence. (101)[11]

In Rendell's novel, when Sojourner's story comes to light, quiet provincial Sussex begins to appear reminiscent of a concentration camp. But in this case, in 1990s Europe, it acquires the features of an inner and fragmented concentration camp, potentially disseminated throughout the respectable houses of Kingsmarkham.[12] The bars at windows[13] become exemplary of this. When Wexford sees bars at the windows of the Ridings' house, he is not surprised: 'Susan Riding was a "Woman, Aware!" woman, one who would no doubt be prudent' (Rendell 1995: 135). Once the case is solved, his views are overturned, because the source of violence was in the inside of the house, and not from the outside: 'All the rooms on the ground floor at the back have bars at the windows, to keep burglars out no doubt, but very convenient if you want to prevent someone escaping' (369).[14] The despondent mood dominating the final part of Rendell's novel may be ascribed to this revelation of a prison potentially existing in every so-called respectable house.

As stated in Chapter 1, the concentration camp and the ghost are the two tropes that I will use to read texts on new slaveries. One of the consequences of this scattered concentrationary system is precisely that these human beings are treated and hidden like ghosts whose existence is denied; in the novel, two peripheral characters are assaulted because they are potential witnesses, having come upon what should not be seen – Sojourner's presence. Even though Sojourner represents the core of the novel, she is the character about whom least is known. In the course of his investigations, Wexford tries to bring her into the light, but very little, almost nothing, can be discovered about her. She has never been recognised as a human subject, therefore her voice has hardly ever been heard, not even in flashbacks; it is reported only once, by another Yoruba migrant whom she meets by chance in an attempt to run away from her prison-like 'home'.[15]

The close of the novel takes readers back to the important role of naming mentioned earlier. While having a drink with Burden and Chief Constable Freeborn (a significant name, here), Wexford concludes the book bitterly: '"If she ever had a surname no one seems to remember it. Sophie never forgot the first name she gave them when she was handed over ..., but the others had forgotten it. She was called Simisola." He got up. "Shall we go?"' (Rendell 1995: 377).

The novel ends with this question. By way of a reader-response-like observation, it could be noticed how the book's title comes up only in its last sentence; it was not mentioned even by Susan Riding. How many readers had forgotten about it while reading, possibly accepting 'Sojourner' as a name, albeit unconsciously? Could this be a crafty way of triggering some sort of awareness in readers, about how (racially) careless one can be about someone else's life?[16]

According to Giorgio Galli, Rendell's work represents a contemporary version of the British classic crime story, full of elaborate human characters but pervaded by an explicit conservative thrust, critical of post-1960s lifestyles (Galli 1990: xviii). But Galli wrote this before the publication of *Simisola*, which seems to undermine this supposed conservatism; rather, it may be associated with the increasing number of thrillers that are based on the illegal nature and leanings of the late twentieth and early twenty-first-century capitalism (Mandel 1990: 152); Rendell herself admits that *Simisola* is 'a deliberate and new direction ... the first of the consciously "political Wexfords"' (Rowland 2001: 193). Order seems far from being restored, as should be the case in a traditional or conservative novel – nay, the powers-that-be are precisely the root of the defeat of order and reason exemplified by Simisola's story. This novel seems to resonate with that kind of detective novel or spy story where the hero assumes tragic connotations, having to work within a system he believes in less and less. Ernest Mandel identifies in this evolution of the genre an ideological shift, whereby the social function of the detective novel changes from an integrating to a disintegrating one, exemplified by the Swiss writer Friedrich Dürrenmatt (Mandel 1990: 171–6) or, one might add, by the Italian Giorgio Scerbanenco.

Since Simisola's spectral identity is enveloped in almost total darkness, it represents a gaping void at the centre of the novel – a void that cannot be filled. According to the standards of canonical crime fiction, the solution is incomplete: by purposely leaving the central character's voice and identity unrevealed, Rendell thus opens a disquieting void at the centre of her book. On the other hand, appalling as it certainly is, this void has drawn Wexford into a process of questioning himself and his own society. As Avery Gordon (2008: 8, 22) writes:

> The ghost is not simply a dead or a missing person, but a social figure, and investigating it can lead to that dense site where history and subjectivity make social life. [...] Following a ghost is about making a contact that changes you and refashions the social relation in which you are located. It is about putting life back in where only a vague memory or a bare trace was visible to those who bothered to look.

Wexford's experience certainly has the potential to communicate some sort of awareness to Rendell's readers. This is probably why Susan Rowland employs the term 'utopian' for this new turn in Rendell's fiction, meaning that it leans towards 'more liberal possibilities [...] a more utopian ethics' (Rowland 2001: 5, 192); accordingly, she sees the novel's ending as reflecting 'Rendell's faith in literature to restore, if not the victim's life, some awareness of her identity which would liberate her from the role of nameless slave' (85).

Rowland's optimism emphasises Rendell's acknowledgement of an issue burning at the heart of British society – a gesture by a mainstream, bestselling writer which might certainly be seen as a landmark, in 1994. Nevertheless, *Simisola* was just as emblematic in the bleak finality of Wexford's closing words, which seal the silent darkness at the centre of the novel. Seen from their perspective, Spivak's problematisation of the subaltern's agency sounds even more urgent:

> Let us now move to consider the margins (one can just as well say the silent, silenced center) of the circuit marked by this epistemic violence, men and women among the illiterate peasantry, the tribals, the lowest strata of the urban subproletariat. According to Foucault and Deleuze ... the oppressed, if given the chance, ... *can speak and know their conditions*. We must now confront the following question: ... *can the subaltern speak?* (Spivak 1995: 25)

Here Spivak seems to foresee one of the main points that this book demonstrates, i.e. how the 'lowest strata of urban subproletariat' will inevitably occupy a 'silent, silenced center' position within the frame of Britain under globalisation – just like Simisola's positioning in Rendell's book.[17] Chapter 3 further discusses the question of the possibility of speaking for new slaves.

Notes

1 Issued by the Refugee Forum and Migrant Rights Action Network, London.
2 See Chapter 1.3 and 1.5.
3 The laws on migrant domestic workers were changed in 1998, allowing them one-year renewable visas and the right to change employer. Nevertheless, their exploitation has continued: the following decade saw the infamous case of Mende Nazer, who described herself thus: 'I was completely isolated and alone. I stayed in the house and worked from early morning to late at night ... trapped in the middle of this strange city [London] that I had been told was dark and dangerous. All I did was work, work, work [...] I started to feel I was no longer alive ... I was just a ghost, floating through life from one day to the next' (Nazer 2003: 277–9). February 2010 was marked by a scandal concerning severe abuse of people working for diplomats (raised by Kalayaan, the same organisation which co-published Anderson's book). Autumn 2011 saw several protests against the coalition government's plans to remove the right to change employer (*Reporter*, 17:3: 4). Not only was the right eventually removed in April 2012, but in June 2011 the government also abstained from voting on the ILO Domestic Workers Convention (*Reporter*, 19:1: 5). For significant data on the effects of this 2012 change on migrant domestic workers' lives (in terms of wages and exploitation), and for some exemplary personal stories, see Donovan (2013: 10).
4 This is my translation from the Italian edition.
5 She also campaigns on such issues in her capacity of member of the House of Lords (Rowland 2001: 5).
6 In this sense, the novel continues a tradition of 'multiracial' British crime fiction which began in the 1950s and often expressed 'an anxiety about national identity' (Kim 2005: 3).
7 More generally, this novel tackles, amongst its themes, prejudices of all sorts, including those about women, old age and blue-eyed beauty.
8 Accordingly, they show a palpable snobbery about Melanie's former boyfriend because he is West Indian (Rendell 1995: 27).
9 This is Michael Rothberg's definition (taken from Susan Koshy) of Caryl Phillips's *The Nature of Blood* (Rothberg 2009: 167). In the following decade, Stephen Frears's film *Dirty Pretty Things* will efficaciously represent a similar 'hierarchy of migrants' (Loshitzky 2010: 68).
10 Suzanne Penuel (2005: 63–6) detects in Rendell's novel anti-Muslim and anti-Arab sentiments, neither contextualising it in the frame of

globalisation and new slaveries nor considering the import of Anderson's book as template to Rendell's story. By passively applying the category of Said's Orientalism to a much-changed context, Penuel turns it into the dead critical instrument pointed at by Said himself through his concept of Traveling Theory (see Chapter 1.5).

11 In her research on the female body in the Nazi concentrationary system, Alexia Giustini (2010: 48–9) highlights how it was reduced to a mere object deprived of any humanity, will and dignity, thus legitimising the violence being committed against it.

12 Concerned with a similar issue, Adele Ward's poem 'Next Door' begins with the lines 'wasn't quite what I expected / from leafy Golders Green' (Ward 2011: 32).

13 Sometimes described in *Britain's Secret Slaves*, too (Anderson 1993: 48, 50). See also the introductory epigraph to Chapter 2, quoting the testimony of Alice from the Philippines.

14 Malia, the protagonist of the award-winning TV drama *I Am Slave* (based on the famous autobiography by the Sudanese Mende Nazer), finds herself enslaved as a migrant domestic worker in a wealthy British house, which is described through a pervasive horror atmosphere. Very soon in the narration, she tries to leave the house in secret in the dead of night, but her plan fails when the burglar alarm goes off. On the following day, her mistress's ambiguously threatening words ('Someone … tried to break in … I should probably take your passport, for safe-keeping') highlight the change in accepted standards as far as the house security system, and security in general, is concerned: it is supposed to keep slaves in, beside keeping burglars out. The need to break *out* of an imprisoning house also marks the ending of Whittaker Khan's play *Bells*, which deals with sexual slaves in a British brothel flat (Whittaker Khan 2005: 194–6).

15 This Yoruba woman is assaulted by the novel's culprit because she is a potential witness of Sojourner's existence. When questioned by Wexford in her hospital bed, she says: 'a girl come along and stop in front of me, right on the pavement, right in front of me, and she talk to me in Yoruba. I am so surprise that you could knock me over with a feather. I never hear Yoruba in twenty years but from my sister and she too proud for it. But this girl is from Nigeria and she say to me in Yoruba, what way is it to where they give you jobs? *Mo fé mò ibit'ó gbé wà* I want to know where it is' (Rendell 1995: 272).

16 And how careless were the publishers of the Italian edition of this novel when they changed its title into *La leggerezza del dovere* (literally, *The Lightness of Duty*), thus completely missing the above-mentioned effect?

17 Spivak expressed an analogous preoccupation, concerning the possibility of retrieving the subaltern's view, in her *In Other Worlds* (1988: 203–4).

3

The ghost and the concentration camp in the twenty-first century

> The New World. A twenty-first century world. A world in which it is impossible to resist the claims of the migrant, the asylum seeker, or the refugee.
> Caryl Phillips, *A New World Order* (2001b: 5)

Wexford's final words might also be seen as an ominous anticipation of the relative silence which enveloped new slaveries in the second half of the 1990s, after Anderson's and Rendell's pioneering works. As the following chapters show, the issue resurfaced in cultural productions in the first years of the twenty-first century, in works where the ghost and the concentration camp reappeared, even more solidly, as key images.

A sign of the literary re-awakening towards the plight of undocumented migrants came with Benjamin Zephaniah's novel for younger readers *Refugee Boy*, published in 2001. Set around the turn of the millennium (1999–2000), it is the story of fourteen-year-old Akem. Being of Ethiopian father and Eritrean mother, he is persecuted in both countries. Zephaniah develops a well-structured plot, smoothly flowing with clear dialogue, with the obvious intention of making his young readers identify with Akem's ordeals in a children's home and a welcoming foster family, supported by the Refugee Council in his legal fight against the typically confrontational attitude from the Home Office. Akem is no new slave, and his story is not to be compared with the gruesome narrations of bondage described in the present book. Curiously enough, though, *Refugee Boy* was later selected for the project 'SMALL ISLAND READ 2007 ... linked to the 2007 commemorations of the 200th anniversary of the Slave Trade Abolition Bill – a year that is being used *to explore the legacy of slavery and its continuing impact upon modern Britain*' (Zephaniah 2001: Appendix; italics mine). Arguably, this is symptomatic of an urge to relate transatlantic slave trade issues to today's migrants, as discussed in Chapter 1.1.

Almost contemporaneously with *Refugee Boy*, two visual projects expressed analogous fears about the state of human rights in Britain at the beginning of the twenty-first century. The first is Kay Adshead's *The Bogus Woman* (2001), a one-actress play that received critical acclaim and was repeatedly staged until at least 2010. Written as a shocked reaction to how the New Labour government was scapegoating asylum seekers and migrants during the late 1990s,[1] it is the ghastly story of an African human rights journalist who survives a political gang rape and the extermination of her family. Her asylum-seeking period in England prefigures many issues that the following chapters will delve into: the inhuman conditions of British detention centres, marked by sexual abuse (Adshead 2001: 27, 64)[2] and persecution of various kinds (23–4, 32–8, 55); the insensitively accusatory attitude of asylum proceedings and interrogations (14, 79–82, 84–8); and the destitution manufactured by the living conditions imposed on her when she is temporarily released, driving her to prostitution out of desperation (123).

Something similar befalls Tanya, the protagonist of Pawel Pawlikowski's film *Last Resort* (2000): having applied for asylum by mistake, she is trapped in a coastal town with her son while her case is being processed: she nearly falls into cyber-porn business and she once sells her blood as a way to escape her institutionally imposed destitution.[3] Filmed on location in Margate, *Last Resort* came out in the year following the national dispersal policy, which had a great impact on southern costal towns.[4] Out of Margate's decadent landscape, Pawlikowski conjures up a visionary town turned into detention centre, which is tightly controlled (by CCTV, fences, barbed wire and patrolling policemen with dogs) while at the same time letting Tanya roam about, not to mention her going to the local bingo place where Alfie works. While not a very realistic setting, it prefigures suggestively how the problem of new slaves (with its entailing co-existence of illegal activities and institutional policing) was bound to spread throughout the country, shaping the concentrationary archipelago that the following chapters focus on.[5]

3.1 Recovering the voices and beyond: Louisa Waugh's *Selling Olga* (2006) and Rahila Gupta's *Enslaved* (2007)

The social cohesion and inclusion debate does not even begin to touch their [new slaves'] lives. They no more scratch at our consciousness than rats living below the floorboards, reminding us of their existence by their occasional scratching noises and their footprints in our flour. ... some slaves are truly invisible.

Rahila Gupta, *Enslaved* (2007: 4, 5)

Like them immigrants they also have asylum-seeker eyes; them eyes with the shine that come about only because of a reptile kind of life, that life of surviving big mutilation in the big city and living inside them holes.

Brian Chikwava, *Harare North* (2010: 2)

the notion of the testimony thus turns out to be tied up, precisely, with the notion of the underground.

Shoshana Felman, 'Education and crisis' (1995: 21)

While Anderson's 1993 research focused on Britain, nearly a third of it was dedicated to the analysis of international migrations; discussing a phenomenon like this inevitably calls for a global perspective that should take into account the obnoxious effects of economic globalisation. The same goes for two more recent publications, Louisa Waugh's *Selling Olga: Stories of Human Trafficking and Resistance* (2006) and Rahila Gupta's *Enslaved: The New British Slavery* (2007).

Waugh's volume is structured precisely on her international investigations into the roots of some forms of new slaveries (mostly sex slaves), which took her to Moldova, Bosnia, Albania, Kosovo and Italy. The geographical thread of *Selling Olga* is compounded with her feelings, thoughts, travels and interviews with a good number of people involved. Her meetings with NGO workers and police officers certainly help readers understand the complexity of the 'trade', but the most striking difference from *Britain's Secret Slaves* is the prominence given to the victims' voices – a feature that further develops a strategy initiated by Anderson, and shared with Gupta's book. Neither Waugh nor Gupta quotes these voices as detached interpolations which simply exemplify the observations of the text. The first-hand accounts are pushed to the forefront, assuming a fundamental role in their books, thus conveying a sense of human suffering which represents a step further from the renditions of sociological reports. They are likely to touch readers, and to lead them to experience the tragedy lying behind the narrations, thus exemplifying the primary role of literature for the analysis of new slaveries, touched upon in Chapter 1.2.

To this end, these ghostly humans are given flesh and blood by Waugh's and Gupta's stylistic priorities and choices of presentation. First of all, names play a primary role, just as they did in Anderson (who used them as titles for her framed case histories) and in Rendell. At the beginning of their interviews, Waugh (2007: 15, 145, 160) and Gupta (2007: 9, 61) must often check whether they can use the victims' real names or must have recourse to pseudonyms. The role of names in their cases can imply a humanising drive close to Wexford's, or a way to maintain a protective anonymity. In Naomi, who is pregnant, both options seem valid:

> *Renaming herself becomes wish-fulfilment, as if another name would magically whisk her to another life. When ... I discover how utterly alone she is in this world, I ask her why she wants to be anonymous.*
> 'What if I go ahead with my life and one day my baby buys the book? It might be that when I have the baby, I won't tell him how he came.' (Gupta 2007: 110; italics in the text)

Secondly, both authors take great care in reconstructing the context of their interviewees: a socio-economic and historical depiction of their country of origin, their personal and family background, and the practicalities surrounding their meeting, such as having to sign 'a confidentiality waiver, agreeing not to publish anything that will personally identify my interviewee' for safety reasons (Waugh 2007: 15). Waugh and Gupta seem intent on noting the corporeal expressiveness associated with these voices, in an effort to carry the full impact of their oral testimonies. Annette is a young African who 'looks very young, and her clenched body language spells out reticence and resignation', and who speaks 'avoiding any eye contact' (Waugh 2007: 44). Gupta (2007: 61–2) similarly describes Natasha: '*She does not make eye contact except fleetingly – she says it is a habit she developed when working as a prostitute. She hated the clients so much she never looked at them and now she has trouble looking anyone in the eye.*' Subtle vocal nuances, too, are registered: when Naomi recalls her homeless days in Sierra Leone, Gupta's observation in italics (116) provides a fuller picture: 'Maybe somebody will leave food on their plate. I will take it and eat (*She says the word 'eat' with real passion.*)'.

This tactful attention to the fragility of their interviewees calls for a substantial presence on the authors' part – a remarkable difference from Anderson's approach. Gupta (2007: 109) records her own doubts concerning her questions to illiterate Naomi (*'But it suddenly occurs to me that perhaps she cannot read or write. I stop myself.'*) and consequently helps her calculate the dates and periods of her life (117, 121). The human bond between interviewer and interviewee sometimes involves translators (61, 68) and/or other people present, such as social workers, thus creating a less tense atmosphere which is more conducive to free talking:

> 'Yes! I bet you were!', '*Pravda!*', 'How dare he, the bastard!' All four of us are suddenly shouting, gesturing, and laughing out loud together, like four women anywhere sharing an outrage between them. The painful tension in the room ruptures. ... It feels bizarre to laugh at this, but it is a tremendous relief for all of us. It is as though between us we have finally jeered at this bar-owning pimp with no name. Olga sits back in her chair, stretches and exhales, and for a moment her face looks almost serene. Then she takes us all by surprise by suddenly recalling a local Kosovan who used to [visit her] ... quite regularly just to chat her up. (Waugh 2007: 23)

This quotation suggests another important feature of these narrations: they are sometimes transcribed as they were delivered, i.e. without respecting a strict chronological order, especially in Gupta's *Enslaved*. For instance, when the Russian Natasha narrates being driven from Frankfurt to Brussels and is finally told that she is expected to work as a prostitute, she recalls her shock and her thoughts of escape, immediately starting a ten-page-long digression on her childhood escapes and her problematic family (Gupta 2007: 67–77). Thanks to its free-flowing progress, her narration depicts the complexity of a full picture by connecting past with present, Russia with Western Europe, family alcoholism and beatings with her escape toward exploitation. Apart from a short introduction and two concluding chapters where the phenomenon is analysed, Gupta's book is structured on five case histories (one for each chapter) reporting the victims' narrations of their trials. In each chapter, Gupta's italics are limited to providing an opening context and interspersing the main narrations with clarifying digressions on several issues such as current immigration laws or the narrator's emotional state and body language. In their centring of these voices, the main chapters of Gupta's volume acquire a more fictional nature.

The journalistic-investigation plot of *Selling Olga* seems to invite more controlled narrations. Nevertheless, Waugh's perceptiveness emphasises a connection between traumatic memories and non-chronological narrative development; when the Moldovan Anna describes her trials in Bosnia as 'a bad dream', Waugh (2007: 33) writes:

> She seems to enter an almost hypnotic state of shock as she moves her story back and forth between countries, colouring in details seemingly at random, honing in on particular awful moments and then leaping towards the next crisis. ... It is impossible to track the sequence of events, and after a while ... I realise that I am missing the point. This chaos is Anna's story. She sounds as though she is reliving individual moments that then ignite other memories and hurtle her off on a tangent.

Gupta's and Waugh's efforts to communicate this trauma-induced chaos lie at the core of the narrative stylistic choices supporting their non-fiction;[6] this linkage between trauma and literary structure will be further analysed in Chapter 4.3.

By and large, in their volumes the victims' attitude towards their own narratives appears to swing between two extremes. On one hand, one might detect a hint at the therapeutic value of speaking it out, already present in Anderson's book; one case in point might be Olga's fleeting serenity mentioned above. From a medical perspective, this might be associated with the so-called 'narrative therapy' theorised by Michael White and David Epston (1990: 13–15), which lays emphasis on the storying of one's experience in place of the constraining versions imposed by others, as a way to trigger new meanings and possibilities for one's life. As a consequence, and interestingly for the present chapter, White and Epston configure this kind of therapy as more oriented toward a narrative, rather than logico-scientific, mode of thought (White and Epston 1990: 77–83).[7]

On the other hand, and more evidently, researchers inevitably stumble on the difficulty of finding willing narrators. Anna's halting start exemplifies both feelings:

> Natasha [the translator] and I sit opposite Anna, who begins to speak and tremble at the same moment. She also begins to weep quietly, wiping her eyes with her trembling hands as she resolutely continues.
>
> 'Anna, we don't need to do this,' I say to her. But she shakes her head and turns towards Natasha.
>
> 'I want to tell you,' she says. 'This is my story, and I want to tell you.' She begins again at the beginning, breaks down once more and

then repeats, 'I want to tell you my story.' And on this third attempt when she launches herself into her story, it seems as though she is suddenly almost in a rush to expel it, like a toxin. (Waugh 2007: 30)

Before the passage from oral to written presence, then, one must acknowledge a preceding step – the wall of silence surrounding the exploited victims: 'I'm uncomfortably aware that everything I've heard about the British sex industry so far has been second-hand information, as opposed to first person', writes Waugh (2007: 142). This wall is a mixture of embarrassment, shame, pain in reliving one's trauma, fear of reprisals. At rending moments of recollection, it reappears in telling silences and elusions that the authors respect: '*Naomi goes into a long and deep silence*' (Gupta 2007: 125); 'it is the things that she does not talk about that become more and more apparent to me, until the air in the room feels heavy. ... Annette's experience has been almost unspeakable, and it seems in many ways as though much of it still is' (Waugh 2007: 147).

In some cases, this barrier is made yet more formidable by linguistic problems, which might require a translator's help. Gupta (2007: 111) makes an effort at reproducing non-standard Englishes, too: pregnant Naomi from Sierra Leone says about her child: 'When he grow up, I will be there strong to tell him the history of what happened.' Naomi's illiteracy is an extreme case which exemplifies the link between linguistic difficulties and an increased sense of isolation and vulnerability for new slaves in Britain, a sense which 'create[s] barriers to them accessing knowledge about their rights or where to go to' (Craig et al. 2007: 17).[8] She presents striking similarities to Rendell's Simisola, completely cut off from her surroundings because of her illiteracy. Naomi cannot read signboards, mail or official documents regarding her status: in a written-culture-based country, she is often too scared to ask for help, and cannot develop any sense of independence and self-dignity: she 'has developed a habit of not asking questions because she feels, as a result of her experiences, that it is not her place to do so. In the most simple ways, this impacts on her life and her ability to take control of it' (Gupta 2007: 126): her recollections and daily movements are impaired by this, because she lacks concrete data (117). On the other hand, she expresses an encouraging wish to learn: 'When you go to school, you learn to ask questions. Before I do something, I want to know why and what is that?' (134). The role of education as a way to repossess one's life is even more prominent in other interviewed victims, whose college attendance is seen as a hopeful sign of future integration, as in the cases of Somali Farhia (43, 47, 59) and Russian Natasha (106).

This barrier prior to the level of orality calls for a rethinking of some critical categories in the context of British new slaveries. 'Subaltern' is a case in point. The field of subaltern studies has been extensively problematised, and some of the crucial points in this debate may be useful in enriching the study of new slaveries. Can the subaltern objectively speak, and with whose voice? Would not scholars risk committing what Spivak (1995: 24) would call 'epistemic violence', when essentialising an extremely heterogeneous community (Loomba 1998: 239–41) – a heterogeneity at its utmost in the hyper-fragmented and hyper-multicultural phenomenon of new slaveries in Britain, as shown in the present book?[9] The question is still very much open, and is further explored in Chapter 6.2. Suffice here to say that the scenario of new slaveries in contemporary Britain seems to exemplify perfectly Spivak's statement: 'one must nevertheless insist that the colonized subaltern *subject* is irretrievably heterogeneous' (1995: 26). Similarly to Spivak's notion of subaltern, one may 'read the retrieval of subaltern consciousness as the charting of what in post-structuralist language would be called the subaltern subject-effect: ... that which seems to operate as a subject may be part of an immense discontinuous network' (Spivak 1988: 204).

The issue of sources is equally controversial, and the subaltern studies historian often 'makes direct reference or alludes to the sheer difficulty of gaining access to the sources of subaltern history' (Said 1988: vii).[10] This involves the supposed opposition between orality and official histories, too, a pervasive presence in postcolonial studies as a whole. Ania Loomba (1998: 231) states that 'such questions are not unique to the study of colonialism but are also crucial for any scholarship concerned with recovering the histories and perspectives of marginalised people'.

In the case of new slaveries, however, some further problematising layers need to be added at an earlier stage. Even though their victims belong to the here and now, the very seclusion and spectralisation that they undergo represent a formidable obstacle in *finding* their voices, and in finding basic data about their spectralised lives, as already said in Chapter 1.1. Who are they? Where do they live, where are they imprisoned and exploited? How many of them? In Britain, the number of undocumented workers ranges between 700,000 and one million (Pai 2008: 9, 246), but this is usually believed to be a conservative estimate. This is one of the reasons why these migrants are frequently described as spectres,[11] or, as in the three epigraph to this chapter, associated with the underground.[12]

Even when these undocumented migrants are physically present, even when they have obtained their freedom from their hidden prisons, an earlier problematic stage should be tackled: they are not willing to speak out, out of fear or shame at their brutalisation. Between 2007 and 2008 Operation 'Pentameter 2', for example, led to more than five hundred arrests and the rescue of 167 victims, including sixteen children, across the country, but:

> Although the Home Office claims that Pentameter 2 is 'the most successful of its kind', one major challenge is encouraging the victims to speak out against the traffickers and accept assistance and support from the authorities. Home Office Minister Vernon Coaker said that many victims, particularly children, resist help and refuse to speak out. (*Reporter*, 16:3: 4)

Beside the above-mentioned emotional difficulties in narrating their stories, one practical reason to account for this is to be found in institutions, which have been extremely (and suspiciously) late in tackling the phenomenon.[13] Only in December 2009 did the UK ratify the European Convention on Action against Trafficking in Human Beings. Around the same time, the London Metropolitan Police Human Trafficking Team faced closure owing to lack of funding, but this was averted thanks to pressure from humanitarian organisations (*Reporter*, 15:1: 5). Moreover, as mentioned in Chapter 1.1, institutional policies still tend to treat victims as illegal immigrants: a notable case in point is the Vietnamese trafficked children exploited on cannabis farms in suburban homes, who face arrest for drug offences (*Reporter*, 16:3: 4).

On a higher, political level, the criminalisation of migrants was also effected through the infamous national dispersal scheme, which began at the start of the twenty-first century and denied asylum seekers the right to choose where (and with whom) they live (see Mynott 2002: passim). This policy of scattering migrants throughout the country is emblematic of how institutions do not always work against (to speak euphemistically) the atomised exploitation of undocumented migrants. Only if they agreed to be dispersed could applicants receive the very controversial allowance in vouchers.[14] Not only did the scheme trap migrants like animals; as discussed in Chapter 3.5 through an analysis of Rankin's *Fleshmarket Close*, it also contributed to their spectralisation: 'In practice, many applicants just *disappear* – giving up the supposedly lavish benefits from the public purse – rather than be separated from friends and relatives. Once *disappeared*, they can become *ordinary* illegal migrants, able to look for work and thus much better off than when trapped in the misery of asylum-seeking' (Harris 2002: 39; italics mine).

Institutional persecution of migrants, then, is to be seen as triggering another kind of silence – not simply the result of traumatic events, shame and/or self-defence from criminal harassment. In a seminal essay on this topic, Dave Gunning identifies in some literary characters (all of them asylum seekers in Britain)[15] a retreat into silence and disappearance. Faced with inhospitable institutions that tighten borders and demonise them, they are 'granted rights that other illegal immigrants are denied, but they perhaps cannot be seen as *human* rights. Rather, they are the rights of the less-than-human: infrahuman rights' (Gunning 2011: 144). These characters, then, willingly embrace silence and disappearance for reasons which could be likened to those leading to escape from dispersal schemes: as a sort of protection of their 'deeper sense of personhood' against institutional expectations whereby 'only the [unwelcome] fact of needing, and deserving, refuge can be stated' (145).[16] Once again, Avery Gordon's insights on spectrality in contemporary society prove extremely useful; when tackling 'the intricacies of the dialectic of subjection and subjectivity ... of domination and freedom' (Gordon 2008: 8), she observes:

> It has always baffled why those most interested in understanding and changing the barbaric domination that characterizes our modernity often – not always – withhold from the very people they are most concerned with the right to complex personhood. (Gordon 2008: 4)

Denied to Simisola and to the victims described by Anderson, Gupta and Waugh, the 'right to complex personhood' is a key concept that the present volume is designed to emphasise.[17]

In his essay, Dave Gunning comes to the poignant conclusion that 'silence is an unwieldy tool of resistance', and that

> the place of absolute otherness is not one that can comfortably be held by a person for long. The subjectivity of the infrahuman must be rejected, but not in favour of possessing no subject position at all. The flourishing of humanity and welfare of the refugee demands more. Ultimately, someone must listen to, someone must recognize the refugee. (Gunning 2011: 147, 149)[18]

To return to British new slaveries, this is probably why Waugh's and Gupta's most obvious aim is to raise public awareness and ignite counter-actions to this relatively new and unknown phenomenon.[19] Both authors could be likened to the ambivalent attitude that Loomba (1998: 234) identifies in Gayatri Spivak (and could well embody the attitude ingrained in the writing of the present book): 'a philosophical scepticism about recovering any subaltern agency with a political commitment to making visible the position of the marginalised'.[20]

The political value of Waugh's and Gupta's transcribed examples of oral testimonies is further enhanced by their representing potential instruments to tackle the coldly bureaucratic reports and their supposed objectivity. When Farhia Nur's application for asylum is rejected, Gupta (2007: 48–9) comments that

> *Much of the judgement deals with the issue of credibility. It is easy to see why parts of Farhia's story may sound implausible without the detail to flesh it out and the nuances that get lost in translation ... without the benefit of a fuller narrative. ... These reports have come in for extensive criticism for the partial and often misleading way in which they quote from source material in order to support a particular view. Unfortunately for people like Farhia, ... tribunals rely heavily on them.*

Here it is of interest to make reference to Bohmer and Shuman's *Rejecting Refugees: Political Asylum in the 21st Century* (2008). Its authors, a lawyer and a folklorist, focus on the stories asylum seekers tell to British and American authorities, and on 'the process of translating those trauma stories into a document that will be recognizable by the authorities' (Bohmer and Shuman 2008: 2). Unfortunately, the gap between their stories and bureaucratic reports often looks formidable, involving the above-mentioned issue of trauma.[21] Bohmer and Shuman take, as one point of departures for all these cases, the Post Traumatic Stress Disorder (PTSD) resulting from persecution, exploitation and/or enslavement.[22] One therapist is quoted as describing a victim of torture as follows:

> She has flashbacks, dissociates ...; we had to teach her techniques to keep her grounded. We were very concerned about her chances in court, because she was not able to be an effective witness. I had to explain how her memory had been affected by the torture experiences – she had dissociated during the experience – how the impact on her memory could complicate the ability to remember some of the details. (Bohmer and Shuman 2008: 128–9)

The therapist's concerns are well founded: the book describes at length how these applicants for asylum are often received with Byzantine, Kafkaesque bureaucracy and methods of interrogation (Bohmer and Shuman 2008: 47, 56–7, 267), prompted by a general policy of determent:[23] an applicant 'can't win an asylum case unless the [her or his] story has the three C's: corroboration, consistency, and chronology' (115), whereas '[s]tories of the horrors of persecutions are by definition implausible, trauma is defined as out of the ordinary and a disruption of everything ordinary' (153).[24] Interestingly, PTSD is described by some researchers as involving an ambivalent attitude that swings between, once again, wanting and not wanting to speak:

> Patients ... appeared to alternate between re-experiencing, and then avoiding, their traumatic memories. ... These two tendencies, argued the psychiatrist M. J. Horowitz in the early 1980s, the tendency to complete what was missing and the tendency to repress, led traumatised people to oscillate. It was when they proved incapable of processing the traumatic material ... that chronic post-traumatic reactions followed. (Moorehead 2006: 216)

Once again, the pressing need seems to be to help break this stalemate, and help the uniqueness of these people's humanity to surface: as David Farrier writes (2011: 158), 'narrative is also the means by which the sovereign exclusion can be challenged'. What comes again to mind here is the method of 'narrative therapy': its privileging those 'aspects of lived experience that *fall outside of the dominant story*' (White and Epston 1990: 15; italics mine) offers, in the context of new slaveries, a way to counter the infra-human expectations of institutions.[25]

PTSD (employed as a key concept in Chapter 4.3) and the desperate need to make one's full presence be heard may both account for the extreme acts of self-affirmation that some new slaves resort to, like the protagonist of Chris Abani's novel.

3.2 From speaking to inscribing: Chris Abani's *Becoming Abigail* (2006)

> For these people we were no longer men; with us, as with cows or mules, there was no substantial difference between a scream and a punch.
>
> Primo Levi, *The Drowned and the Saved* (1989: 70)

As in Rendell, Abani's novel significantly bears its central character's name in the title. In this case, the suffering involved in her negated identity is unravelled lyrically. Chris Abani's *Becoming Abigail* traces the thoughts of its fourteen-year-old protagonist in the third person. The book alternates 'Now' chapters, where Abigail sits near the sphinxes and Cleopatra's Needle by the Thames meditating on her life, and 'Then' chapters, where events from her past are approached directly; all in all, the protagonist's thoughts (mixing pain, loss and melancholy) dominate the narration without chronological order, where 'she wasn't always able to tell how much she was inventing and how much was real' (Abani 2006: 40), thus echoing Waugh's words about the shocking experiences behind her interviewee's chaotic narration.

In order to reconstruct her tragedy, Abani blends socio-political, gender and personal factors. Nigeria is a country 'where the dead littered the streets of big towns and cities like so much garbage' (55).[26] In a way, here Abani represents the fictional equivalent of Anderson's, Rendell's, Waugh's and Gupta's efforts to trace the global roots of new slaveries in Britain.

Abigail's identity has always been marked by absence. Her mother died in giving birth to her; the book opens with her suggestive memories of her mother's burial: 'Even this. This memory like all the others was a lie' (17). Abigail had to live with a father who never ceased to mourn his wife's loss; an affectionate man, but carrying the 'shadows under the smiling eyes that said over and over – you killed her. You. Why her? I loved her' (44). On one hand, Abigail is caught in her painful loss, leaving her thirsty for detailed stories about her mother: 'it was hard to do anything but try to fill the [her mother's] hollowed-out shape'; on the other hand, there inevitably ensues an inability to shape an autonomous personality for herself, to move away from a deceased woman who bore the same name:

> She was more ghost than her mother, however, moving with the quality of light breathing through a house in which the only footprints in the dust were those of her dead mother. ... She tried to talk to her father about this need to see herself. ... She couldn't be the ghost he wanted her to be. (Abani 2006: 44, 45)

Abigail's ghostly identity is also shaped by her relationships with men, who had never really 'seen her' (Abani 2006: 26). Abani conveys this through a metaphor reminiscent of the postcolonial 'female-body-as-conquered-land' trope (Loomba 1998: 151–2), thus fusing the personal, gender and political roots of Abigail's ordeal: 'She was a foreign country to them. One they wanted to pass through as quickly as possible. ... And though there had only been a few men, sometimes she felt like there had been whole hordes' (Abani 2006: 27). Consequently, her reaction towards men calls to mind the victims interviewed by Gupta and Waugh in Chapter 3.1, who avoided eye contact.

With the consent of her father, who will hang himself shortly before her departure, she is taken to London by their relative Peter, thanks to forged documents. Her move to Britain thus articulates her original ghostliness into the phenomenon of new slaveries. She becomes one of the thousands of trafficked West African minors, a wide-scale plague within that part of Africa from the 1990s (Dottridge 2007: 39), presumably connected with the mysteriously unknown whereabouts of many African children in Britain (Left 2005: passim).

She resists a first rape attempt which was designed to reduce her to prostitution, but cannot do anything against the violence of Peter, who chains and harnesses her to the doghouse in his yard ('You want to bite like a dog? I'll treat you like a dog', Abani 2006: 89), leaving her in the freezing weather for days:

> Filth. Hunger. And drinking from the plate of rancid water. Bent forward like a dog. Arms behind her back. Kneeling. Into the mud. And the food. Tossed out leftovers. And the cold. And the numbing of limbs that was an even deeper cold. (Abani 2006: 91)

After being made a ghost in more than one way, Abigail is further degraded through this animalisation; something of this sort is already present in the books by Anderson, Gupta and Waugh, where the dehumanising experience undergone by the victims is often described through hints, direct references or imagery related to animal conditions: in Bexleyheath, Helen 'was forced to sleep outside the back door, even in winter, and was dressed only in rags', and 'her food consisted mainly of unripe apples and pears from the garden' (Anderson 1993: 55); a group of Greek migrants on a daffodil farm in Cornwall were given cans of dog food to eat (Waugh 2007: 90); Rendell's Inspector Wexford says of Simisola's respectable gaoler's wife: 'She let her sleep on a mattress on the floor in the "dog's room" because she's that sort of woman, the kind that used to talk about the poor keeping coal in the bath if you gave them bathrooms' (Rendell 1995: 373).

The animalisation of the prisoner's body introduces, once again, some recurrent tropes from the area of Holocaust studies. Deprived of any quality apart from her bare body, Abigail is to be construed in the light of Giorgio Agamben's concept of 'naked life' or 'bare life'. Agamben (2000: 41) writes:

> Inasmuch as its inhabitants have been stripped of every political status and reduced completely to naked life, the camp is also the most absolute biopolitical space that has ever been realized – a space in which power confronts nothing other than pure biological life without any mediation.

Significantly for the study of *Becoming Abigail*, Alexia Giustini's perceptive analysis of women's testimonies from Nazi concentration camps deals with the specificity of the body, degraded to a larval state, to an 'animal, instinctual, primal body, easily manoeuvrable and manipulated' (Giustini 2010: 49, translation mine), to the point of becoming mute (45).[27] Women's femininity was ridiculed and humiliated through nudity (39–40); Primo Levi's words (1989: 90) intensely convey the import of this practical detail, striking the body to annihilate the soul:

> Now a naked and barefoot man feels that all his nerves and tendons are severed: he is a helpless prey. Clothes, even the foul clothes distributed, even the crude clogs with their wooden soles, are a tenuous but indispensable defence. Anyone who does not have them no longer perceives himself as a human being, but rather as a worm: naked, slow, ignoble, prone on the ground. He knows that he can be crushed at any moment.

Women were thus reduced to sexless, grotesque, skeleton-like figures (Giustini 2010: 18, 26); this may seem a marked difference from the sexual exploitation operated by new slaveries, but in Nazi camps women were regularly exploited by persecutors through rapes, camp-brothels (*puppenhäuser*) and medical experiments (47, 42).

Abani's Abigail seems to incarnate this degrading process to its extremes: she is spat on, peed over, fed with rotten food and rancid water if not urine, repeatedly raped into submission (Abani 2006: 89–93). Or, at least, that is supposedly Peter's aim, because at some point Abigail attacks him exactly as if she were a dog, thus leaning on her bare animality as a final resort. In doing so, she wins her own freedom: 'Fifteen days, passing in the silence of snow. And she no longer fought when Peter mounted her. *Wrote* his shame and anger in her. Until. The slime of it threatened to obliterate *the tattoos that made her*. Abigail' (95; italics mine).

This quotation shows the decisive factor behind her reaction, linked to a crucial element in her search for an identity. In various ways, Abigail has used her body as a writable surface since she was a child: first lightly, as a way to recapture her mother: 'Sated [with stories about her mother], she traced their outlines on her skin with soft fingers, burning them in with the heat of her loss, tattooing them with a need as desperate as it was confused' (45). Her confusion later manifested itself in more pain-inflicting practices:

> With the tip of a wax crayon she would write 'me', over and over on the brown rise of [her growing breast] .... With time came finer lines, from needles, marking an improvement. But there were also the ugly whip marks of cigarette tips. Angry. Impatient. And the words: Not Abigail. My Abigail. Her Abigail? Ghosts. Death. Me. Me. Me. Not. Nobody. (Abani 2006: 26–7, 33–4)

Deprived of voice and agency, Abigail has resorted to this extreme form of self-affirmation. Significantly, Abani attributes a similar attitude to some of his fellow detainees in his poetry collection *Kalakuta Republic*, concerning his own imprisonment under Nigeria's military regime in the late 1980s:

> Invisibility
>
> stalks our every step. Some men brand,
> with cashew sap, their names on buttocks, stomachs,
>
> Hidden
>
> from view. A welt to remind them of
> who they really are, their past, their only hope.
> ('Tattoo'; Abani 2000: 49)[28]

The centrality of the body as a site of both oppression and reaction is yet another issue where postcolonial and Holocaust studies converge. 'The body itself has also been the literal "text" on which colonization has written some of its most graphic and scrutable messages. ... The body, too, has become then the literal site on which resistance and oppression have struggled' (Ashcroft et al. 1995: 322). In Nazi camps, too, women began to practise some forms of resistance precisely from their degraded bodies, for example by simply taking care of their appearance (Giustini 2010: 58–60).

Abigail's passion for maps (another typically postcolonial site of oppression and resistance)[29] may be analogously construed as a sublimated search for permanence through written signs, merging her fleeting past with her wished-for future:

Not all maps. Old ones. ... That unrolled with all the crackling promise of a flying carpet warming up. ... pretending that here, at least, on the flat spread of the map, it was possible to have any kind *of dominion over a landscape. Over things*. And sometimes the alchemy of her stare transmuted the parchment into her mother's skin. ... This was how Abigail spent many rainy afternoons, the cartographer of dreams. Of ghosts. (Abani 2006: 71–2; italics mine)

Abigail, then, writes on herself as if she wanted to become her own map, in an attempt to conquer a form of agency. Her reaction against Peter is obviously triggered by his threat against her identitarian bodily marks.

Her escape leads to her custody with social services, and to her love for the social worker Derek: 'And Abigail was giving. For the first time, she wasn't taken. ... Abigail, this Abigail, only this Abigail, always this Abigail, felt herself becoming, even in this moment of taking' (Abani 2006: 52). On one hand, such moments of happiness seem to offer her a way to affirm a respected identity – something she cannot help recording on her skin (53); on the other hand, her relationship with adult and married Derek is legally unacceptable, so he is fired and tried for abusing a minor. She finds herself invisible again, under the care of institutions that have taken away her only free choice and therefore the voice, the agency and the identity that she briefly glimpsed:

> But what are the limits of desire? The edges beyond which love must not cross? Those were questions she had heard others discuss in these last few days. Discuss as if she was a mere ghost in their presence. Called this thing between Derek and her wrong. How could it be? (Abani 2006: 79)

Through this delicate and debatable situation, Abani expresses a complex perspective on the relationship between Abigail and Derek, beyond an expectable moral judgement – a perspective obviously related to the institutional denial of agency and full personhood, as described in Chapter 3.1.

Abani's novel thus offers a lyrical, psychological and, some would say, controversial version of the trap which victims of new slaveries find themselves in (see again Chapter 3.1), once they manage to escape their torturers. British legislation and institutions are seldom prepared to offer real help for the recovery of self-dignity, and they are therefore criticised at length by Anderson, Waugh, Gupta and Rendell, who all lay bare their limited (if not counter-productive or connivant) effect of further marginalising and spectralising new slaves. These writers all report stories by or about people who feel, in one way or another, 'let down by immigration services' (Waugh 2007: 159).[30] In one case, Bridget Anderson (1993: 51) used the title 'Trapped' for one of her case histories, to refer to the legal dead-end that escapees find themselves in, owing to their unrecognised status. The assumed opposition between ghostliness and institutional legality will be further exposed in the following chapters.

Abani's Abigail is taken by this current of events to the Needle, a monument symbolic of her failed body-writing attempts at self-affirmation; there, where she imagines 'she could see all the ghosts of those who had also ended it there' (Abani 2006: 26), her tragic end is consummated. Rendell's and Abani's endings are not so distant, after all. Both writers close their novels with a victim sacrificed to the mechanisms of new slaveries in contemporary Britain. Nevertheless, their narrative perspectives mark a decisive difference in emphasis: Simisola's unvoiced, gaping, spectral void at the centre of Wexford's investigation, opposed to Abigail's conspicuous, masochistic, desperate form of writing, as an attempt to fill a similar emptiness.

3.3 Enslaved childhood and the concentrationary system of detention centres: Chris Cleave's *The Other Hand* (2008)

It is a striking coincidence that Little Bee, the protagonist of Chris Cleave's *The Other Hand*,[31] finds herself at the same spot where Abani's Abigail is, the so-called Cleopatra's Needle by the Thames:

> A million people were all around me. Their faces hurried past. I looked and looked. I never saw the faces of my family but when you have lost everyone, you never lose the habit of looking. My sister, my mother, my father and my uncle. Every face I see, I am looking for them in it. If I did meet you then the first thing you would have noticed would have been my eyes staring at your face, as if they were trying to see someone else in you, as if they were desperate to make you into a ghost. If we did meet, I hope you did not take this personally.
>
> I hurried along the river embankment, through the crowds, through my memories, through this city of the dead. Once, beside a tall stone needle engraved with strange symbols, ... I stood still for a moment and the dead flowed around me, like the muddy brown Thames flowing around the pillar of a bridge. (Cleave 2008: 121–2)

The London described by Little Bee is certainly reminiscent of T. S. Eliot's famous picture of London Bridge in *The Waste Land* (I: 61–2): 'A crowd flowed over London Bridge, so many / I had not thought death had undone so many'. In Little Bee's specific case, these beings are turned into ghosts as a result of her violent past. Abani's Abigail and Little Bee are both from Nigeria, and both moved to Britain at the age of fourteen, but Little Bee's story is quite different: after two years spent in a detention centre, she is now sixteen; as this chapter shows, the process of spectralisation that she has been undergoing was exacerbated by an institutional form of confinement, not only by a private and criminal one.

Another similarity with Abigail's story is related to gender oppression and sexual exploitation. Little Bee had to run away from her home village during one of those undeclared, little-spoken-of wars scarring the Niger Delta. All her friends and relatives were massacred by ruthless gangs so that the subterranean oil could be extracted without having to bother with the local community. After a long escape, her sister Nkiruka was eventually raped and butchered. This is why, during her two years in the Black Hill Immigration Removal Centre (Essex), Little Bee lives under a constant terror of men, erasing her gender: 'I made myself undesirable. I declined to wash, and let my skin grow oily. Under my clothes I wound a wide strip of cotton around my chest, to make my breasts small and flat' (Cleave 2008: 9). For the same reason, she wears baggy clothes and has her hair cut very short. Little Bee's story resembles many others, in that detention centre: 'All the girls' stories started out, *the-men-came-and-they-*. And all of the stories finished, *and-then-they-put-me-in-here*' (16). And her own personal way of coping with her fears is heart-rending:

> There are things the men can do to you in this life, I promise you, it would be much better to kill yourself first. Once you have this knowledge, your eyes are always flickering from this place to that, watching for the moment when the men will come.[32]
>
> In the immigration detention centre, they told us we must be disciplined to overcome our fears. This is the discipline I learned: whenever I go into a new place, I work out how to kill myself there. In case the men come suddenly, I make sure I am ready.... Some of the others that were detained with me, they really did these things. The detention officers sent the bodies away in the night. (Cleave 2008: 67–9)

Being detained by British institutions, rather than by criminals in a private house, does not seem to change the heart of the matter, when it comes to sexual exploitation. This chapter employs *The Other Hand* as a way to reflect on the continuity between illegal and legal places of imprisonment, which has been already mentioned in Chapter 1.1, and which will be further considered in the pages on Ian Rankin (Chapter 3.5) and in other following chapters. At the beginning of *The Other Hand*, Little Bee finds herself suddenly free to leave after two years of detention, together with three other girls. Only later will she discover what her Jamaican friend, the rumbustious Yevette, had to do in order to be set free:

> 'Me swear to you, dat man's ooman mus of kept her legs cross for de las ten year, de way he took me up on me offer. An it wasn't just on de one day, mind. It took de man *four interviews* fore he was certain me papers was in order, yu know what I'm sayin?'
> I stroked her hand. 'Oh, Yevette.'
> 'It was nuthin, Bug. Compare to what dey do to me, if I be sent to Jamaica? *Nuthin.*'
> Yevette smiled at me. The tears flowed from the corners of her eyes and around the curve of her cheek. (103)[33]

Alongside the issue of sexual exploitation, what Cleave's novel brings to the fore is another ghastly facet of new slaveries in Britain, namely detained children. Rendell's Simisola was in her late teens, Abani's Abigail is fourteen, but it is in *The Other Hand* that the awareness of these new slaves' minority is fully conveyed.[34] This is effected by Cleave in two ways. Firstly, he emphasises the British policy towards minors through the institutionally detained condition of Little Bee, whose stay in Britain begins and ends in a detention centre.[35] Since 2001 refugee children, both with and without a family, can be detained under the same policy as adults. Similarly to the general phenomenon of new slaveries, figures are extremely hard to determine (Crawley and Lester 2005: 5; ECPAT 2011: 6), even though we are dealing only with institutional places. British institutions have not been conspicuous for their care of undocumented minors, and the lack of educational facilities is a case in point (Crawley and Lester 2005: 14). More recently, the flaws of the British government's new trafficking strategy has also raised concerns 'that trafficked children will be left particularly vulnerable because of the lack of guardian scheme or detail on preventing children from being trafficked from the UK' (*Reporter*, 17:3: 4).[36]

Secondly, Cleave makes the issue of minors central to his novel through its peculiar voice. *The Other Hand* is narrated in the first person by Little Bee and, in alternating chapters, by Sarah, the white British citizen who befriends her after the detention centre. When it comes to the chapters narrated by Little Bee, the author contrives the voice of a girl who must have recourse to her imaginative faculties in order to cope with the terrible ordeals she has been going through and with a host country she must make sense of. Thus he confers on his story a quality of lightness in the midst of suffering: differently from Abani's crude physical pain, Little Bee also expresses hope and humour, and her voice and thoughts fill half the novel to the brim.[37] Her fervent imagination even manages to highlight unconsciously the amusing facet of her suicidal obsession:

> I began to eat the meals they brought me. I thought to myself, you must keep up your strength, Little Bee, or you will be too weak to kill your foolish self when the time arrives.... Which will make me stronger for the act of suicide? The carrots or the peas? ... I worked out how to kill myself under Labour and Conservative Governments, and why it was not important to have a plan for suicide under the Liberal Democrats. I began to understand how your country worked. (Cleave 2008: 70–1)

As often happens with children's narrations, Little Bee's imaginative musings hint at deeper truths. *The Other Hand* opens with the protagonist who thinks 'Most days I wish I was a British pound coin instead of an African girl' (Cleave 2008: 1), fancifully translating the dominating role of money in the circuits of globalisation:

> A pound coin can go wherever it thinks it will be safest. It can cross deserts and oceans and leave the sound of gunfire and the bitter smell of burning thatch behind. ... This is the human triumph. This is called, *globalisation*. A girl like me gets stopped at immigration, but a pound can leap the turnstiles, and dodge the tackles of those big men with their uniformed caps, and jump straight into a waiting airport taxi. *Where to, sir?* Western civilisation, my good man, and make it snappy. See how nicely a British pound coin talks? It speaks with the voice of Queen Elizabeth the Second of England. (Cleave 2008: 2)

Having spent two years of detention perfecting her Queen's English, Little Bee can also show a penchant for an utterly conscious (and bitter) humour. One case in point concerns the detention centre's therapy room:

> they gave us poster paints and brushes and they told us we must express ourselves. I used a lot of red paint. When the therapeutic assistant looked at what I painted, she said it would be good for me to try to *move on*. I said, *Yes, madam, it will be my pleasure, if you will just open a little window for me, or even better a door, I will be*

happy to move on right away. [...] At five p.m. they tell you to move on and at six p.m. they lock you back in your cell. (202, 209)

Refugee children are described as subject to a 'triple vulnerability – as children, as detainees, and as asylum-seekers or otherwise uprooted children. ... the greatest negative impacts appear to be in terms of mental health' (Crawley and Lester 2005: 13).[38] This can perhaps account for what one psychiatrist tells Little Bee during her detention: '*Psychiatry in this place is like serving an in-flight meal in the middle of a plane crash. If I wanted to make you well, as a doctor, I should be giving you a parachute, not a cheese-and-pickle sandwich.*'[39] Little Bee closes this convincing observation with her own comment, saying 'To be well in your mind you have first to be free, you see?' (Cleave 2008: 210)

Nevertheless, the events of the novel partly prove her wrong, because when she is inexplicably and illegally free to leave together with three other girls, as a consequence of Yevette's sale of her body, the four of them come face to face with the ghostliness inherent in their condition. The long scene when they try to phone for a taxi (14–23) is, again, subtly balanced upon comedy and tragedy: they do not know exactly where they are, some of them are illiterate – in other words, they are almost cut off from any bearings. Some of them do not even know the name of the centre detaining them. According to the geographer Tim Cresswell (2004: 9), 'Naming is one of the ways space can be given meaning and become place': Little Bee's fellow detainees are to be seen as spectrally afloat in space, within the country which has been holding them for two years and denying them a place.

Eventually Little Bee's Queen's English manages to convince a cab to come along, but the full import of her situation is made clear when they finally leave the barbed-wired walls behind them. After Yevette has proudly declared 'We going *dere, in England*', and the taxi driver has refused to take them on board, the four girls feel at a loss about what to do, and where to go. This is poignantly expressed by Mr Ayres, the kind outspoken farmer who finds them wandering aimlessly: 'The government doesn't care about anyone. You're not the first people we've seen, wandering through these fields like Martians. You don't even know what planet you're on, do you? Bloody government' (Cleave 2008: 88).

In the context of new slaveries in Britain, this appears to be a fairly recurrent situation.[40] In the already mentioned TV drama *I Am Slave*, one day, the gates of the house imprisoning Malia are surprisingly left open, and she runs away; she finds herself helpless, not knowing where to go and whom to talk to, with no other options than to go back to the house: she too is a ghost in Britain.⁴¹ In another popular TV drama, Abi Morgan's *Sex Traffic* (2006), the Moldavian protagonist Elena manages to escape from the London house where her sexual exploitation is to take place: in a suburban area devoid of any sign of life, she is chased and beaten up by her trafficker in broad daylight. It is a gruesome scene which astonishes for the utter lack of any awareness from the neighbourhood and, more symbolically, from British society at large.⁴² The presence of these new slaves is not acknowledged in the least, thus magnifying their ghostliness.

In *The Other Hand* Yevette realises the risks of their new situation: 'Mebbe dis is de hardest part, now dey is letting us out. In dat detention centre dey was always telling yu, *do dis, do dat*. No time to tink. But now dey all ovva sudden gone quiet, no? Dat dangerous, me tellin you. Let all the bad memory come back' (Cleave 2008: 97). That is precisely what will happen. Now that they are exposed to a world which hardly acknowledges their existence, the scars of past traumas burst, and one of the two Asian girls starts panicking and hallucinating: 'Make them stop coming! They will kill us all, you girls do not understand! ... Look! Look! My child!' (106–7).⁴³ Little Bee, Yevette and the third girl humour their ailing companion: 'We divided the food into five portions, and we gave the biggest helping to the daughter of the woman with no name, because she was still growing' (110). Having ghosts from their own past to deal with, they quickly adjust themselves to living in the midst of spectres – and thus one may account for Little Bee's description of London that opened this chapter.

In the night, the deranged girl hangs herself. Little Bee is first tempted to acquire her identity, because she carried a collection of official papers which could testify to a credible story for the immigration authorities, but she changes her mind:

> I started to read the story of the girl with no name.
> *The-men-came-and-they*... I was still crying, and it was difficult to read in the dim light from the moon.... A story is a powerful thing in my country, and God help the girl who takes one that is not her own. I left it on the girl's bed, every word of it, including the paper-clips and all the photographs of the scar tissue and the name of the missing daughters, and all of the red ink that said this was CONFIRMED. (Cleave 2008: 113–14)

What could be superficially interpreted as superstition should be seen as Little Bee's proud refusal to become a willing actor in her own process of spectralisation, unlike the protagonists of Broomfield's film *Ghosts* who precisely assume false identities to be given a job (see Chapter 4.1). Faced with this suicide, Little Bee decides to abandon her companions, reaffirming the fragmentary condition of new slaves: 'Truly, there is no flag for us floating people. We are millions, but we are not a nation. We cannot stay together' (Cleave 2008: 114–15).

The one solid human tie that Little Bee manages to establish in Britain is represented by Sarah Summers, editor of a fashion magazine. Two years earlier, when Sarah and her husband Andrew O'Rourke rashly visited Nigeria for a holiday which was meant to 'save' their marriage, they came across Little Bee and her older sister Nkiruka running away from the thugs who had just exterminated the inhabitants of their village to make room for the oil companies.[44] Andrew could not comply with the request from the thugs' leader, whereas Sarah courageously amputated her finger in order to save Little Bee's life. Two years later, Little Bee shows up at Sarah's door on the morning of Andrew's funeral (he could not bear his sense of guilt at what happened in Nigeria and has therefore hanged himself). The relationship between Sarah and Little Bee carries important implications that will be discussed in Chapter 6.2. Sarah feels determined to help Little Bee out of her predicament as an undocumented immigrant, but the following conversation between the two characters represents a significant comment on the British system of immigration control:

> 'Why did they let you out of the detention centre, if you're not allowed to stay?'
> 'They made a mistake. If you look good or talk good, sometimes they make mistakes for you.'
> 'But you're free now. They couldn't just *come for you*, Bee. This isn't Nazi Germany. There must be some procedure we can go through. Some appeal. I can *tell* them what happened to you over there. What will happen to you if you go back.'
> I shook my head. 'They will tell you Nigeria is a safe country, Sarah. People like me, they can just come and drive us straight to the airport.' (Cleave 2008: 196)

In spite of the deep bond developed between them, things eventually take exactly the course predicted by Little Bee, and not the one expressed by Sarah's ingenuous idealism. Her comparison with

Nazi Germany resonates again profoundly when a frightened Little Bee fetches a police car because of the disappearance of Sarah's son, Charlie:

> If this policeman began to suspect me, he could call the immigration people. Then one of them would click a button on their computer and mark a check box on my file and I would be deported. I would be dead, but no one would have fired any bullets. I realised, this is why the police do not carry guns. *In a civilised country, they kill you with a click.* The killing is done far away, at the heart of the kingdom in a building full of computers and coffee-cups. (Cleave 2008: 335–6; italics mine)

Little Bee's observation might be felt as overly self-conscious and slightly inconsistent with her spontaneously imaginative tone of narration.[45] Remarkably, however, it gestures at the debate around the uniqueness of the Nazi extermination of the Jews. In his *Modernity and the Holocaust* (1989), Zygmunt Bauman rejects the approach that had dominated the field of sociology, that is to say the vision of the Holocaust as the exceptional cancer, the isolated, irrational failure (circumscribed in space and time, and exclusively pertaining to specific monster-like peoples versus their victims) of a modern social organisation which could otherwise be deemed to be rationally humanising (Bauman 1989: viii–5). Bauman conceives of the Holocaust, rather, as a 'product' (5), a 'paradigm' (6) of modernity, resulting 'from an impeccable, faultless and unchallengeable rule of order' (151). Analogously, in his *Auschwitz en héritage* (1998) the historian Georges Bensoussan (2002: xi) emphasises how technical progress and barbarity are not the two opposite poles of our modernity, but they lie one inside the other, and therefore the *Shoah* could be seen as the emblem of our times. For both writers, the modern technology of industrial production and the bureaucratic structure behind the Nazi regime are to be seen as the main factors behind the exceptionality of the attempt at the extermination of European Jews. Bauman (1989: 13–19) retraces in detail how the so-called final solution was, most of all, the result of a bureaucratic straining after efficiency based on feasibility, costs and budget balancing; not only are the rules of instrumental rationality, he claims, incapable of preventing phenomena like the Holocaust, but they are the very terrain where such tragedies breed, inherently capable as they are of involving morally principled individuals in their immoral procedures. Bensoussan (2002: 67) describes these ordinarily complicit individuals as bureaucrat-killers – 'good' workers whose very sense of duty constitutes the guarantee of criminal efficiency, wheels in a huge mechanism that dilutes any individual sense of responsibility. As Primo Levi's famous statement goes, 'love for a job well done is a deeply ambiguous virtue' (Levi 1989: 98).[46] One first important theorisation of the figure of the desk killer is Hannah Arendt's report on the trial of Adolf Eichmann, where she expressed her surprise at discovering that he was no monster, no fanatic, but a mediocre, dutiful bureaucrat (Arendt 1964: 28–33).[47] Eichmann's lack of exceptionality was particularly evident in his use of cliché-ridden, bureaucratic stock phrases (55, 86, 109), which reflected a kind of reasoning limited to instrumental rationality.[48] According to Arendt, his problem was an 'inability to *think*, namely, to think from the standpoint of somebody else' (49),[49] a statement echoing the function of literature envisaged in Chapter 1.2. She therefore concluded that Eichmann represented a 'word-and-thought defying banality of evil' (252). In light of this, she foresaw the emergence of a new type of criminal capable of committing 'administrative massacres organized by the state apparatuses' (294), a 'terribly and terrifyingly normal' criminal acting 'under circumstances that make it well-nigh impossible for him to know or feel that he is doing wrong' (276).[50]

In *The Other Hand*, this figure is embodied in one policeman arguing with Lawrence (Sarah's lover) during Little Bee's quick second detention, prior to her deportation:

> 'But surely you can give us a bit of time to make a case. I work for the Home Office, I can get an appeal together.'
>
> 'If you don't mind my saying so, sir, if I worked for the Home Office and I knew all along this lady was illegal, I'd keep my mouth shut.'
>
> 'Just one day, then. Twenty-four hours, please.'
>
> 'I'm sorry, sir.'
>
> 'Oh for fuck's sake, it's like talking to a robot.'
>
> 'I'm flesh and blood like you, sir. The thing is, as I say, I don't make the rules.' (Cleave 2008: 342)

A similar pride at this kind of role, combined with a good dose of asylophobic (and circular) rhetoric, seems to exude from the policewoman driving Little Bee to the airport, surprised at the Nigerian girl's impeccable English:

> 'I thought if I learned to speak like you people do, I would be able to stay.'
>
> The officer smiled.

The ghost and the concentration camp   75

'It doesn't matter how you talk, does it?' she said. 'You're a drain on resources. The point is, you don't *belong* here.' ...
'But please, what does it mean?' I said. 'What does it mean, to belong here?'
The female officer turned to look at me again.
'Well, you've got to be British, haven't you? You've got to have our values.' (Cleave 2008: 344–5)[51]

The majority of those in the immigration control system, though, are not likely to come across their victims in person, just like the modern bureaucracy described by Bauman as the main factor behind the Holocaust; Bauman gives prominence to Lachs's concept of 'mediation of action'[52] in modern societies as erasing the conflict between personal morality and the immoral social consequences of one's action (Bauman 1989: 24–5). In our hyper-technological age, this mediation of the action is steadily increasing – 'they kill you with a click', as Little Bee said above.[53] Bauman's analysis of the Holocaust rests on Kelman's theorisations on moral inhibitions being eroded in the presence of three factors: when violence is authorised, when it is routinised and when its victims are dehumanised (Bauman 1989: 21)[54] – three factors which are clearly present in today's Britain, as this volume shows.[55] Both Bauman and Bensoussan, then, argue that modern societies are structured in such a way that social organisations work toward the elimination of personal responsibility (Bauman 1989: 163; Bensoussan 2002: 75): in Milchman and Rosenberg's words (1992: 221):

> the quintessential features of the modern high-level bureaucrat are precisely those which characterise the desk killer: technical expertise, obedience, the implementation of policies with the same diligence as if they conformed to one's most profound convictions, the predominance of functional reason ... to the exclusion of reflective judgement or qualitative reason, 'thoughtlessness', and the impoverishment of language and the inability to speak in anything but 'Officialese'.

Compared with the importance of state bureaucracy in these theoretical readings of modernity originating from the field of Holocaust studies, Cleave's *The Other Hand* brings to the fore the key role played by private companies. The private guard who escorts Little Bee during her deportation flight sounds precisely like the individuals who took part in the Holocaust machinery according to Bauman's and Bensoussan's view: a friendly, kind-hearted fellow, completely detached from the moral consequences of his actions, and speaking through stock phrases not dissimilar from Eichmann's language described by Hannah Arendt.[56] He reveals something significant about his job:

> 'Course the people who really make the money are the big contractors. The ones I'm working for now, Dutch firm, they run the whole show. They run the detention centres and they run the repatriations. So they're earning either way, whether we lock you up or whether we send you back. Nice, eh?'
> 'Nice,' I said.
> The man tapped his finger against the side of his head.
> 'But that's how you've got to think, these days, isn't it? It's the global economy.' (Cleave 2008: 349)

Chapter 1.1 of this volume already mentioned the disquieting possibility for every 'respectable' citizen, as stake-holder, to participate in (and capitalise on) this institutionally operated side of the imprisonment and spectralisation of new slaves.[57]

The following two chapters deal with two examples of genre fiction on contemporary new slaveries in Britain, almost contemporaneous with Cleave's book. They are to be seen as closely related to *The Other Hand* in so far as they develop two of its important facets: the (quite unexpected) possibility of describing this appalling phenomenon through the lenses of levity and humour (Lewycka) and the continuity between institutional and criminal forms of exploitation (Rankin).

3.4 United bloody Nations: Marina Lewycka's *Two Caravans* (2007) and humour

> They gave you a pink form to write down what had happened to you. This was the grounds for your asylum application. Your whole life, you had to fit it onto one sheet of paper. There was a black line around the edge of the sheet, a border, and if you wrote outside the line then your application would not be valid. They only gave you enough space to write down the very saddest things that had happened to you. That was the worst part. Because if you cannot read the beautiful things that have happened in someone's life, why should you care about their sadness?
> Chris Cleave, *The Other Hand* (2008: 315–16)

Lidia De Michelis (2011: 286) aptly identifies in this passage a key moment for *The Other Hand*, where Little Bee confronts the claustrophobic, constraining narrations imposed by the powers-that-be on migrants' lives. The 'border' can be seen as containing, both on the page and on British soil, the much-feared overflowing of the migrant's subjectivity. Dave Gunning (2011: 145) similarly sees, in the migrants' narrations he analyses, a desire to shelter their 'deeper sense of ... personhood'[58] in the face of institutional expectations dominated by infra-human rights, whereby 'only the [unwelcome] fact of needing, and deserving, refuge can be stated'.

In addition, Little Bee's claim to a full story including the 'beautiful things' of her life therefore resonates with meta-literary implications around the genre and tone of *The Other Hand*, and the value of lightness and humour for narrating new slaveries – in spite of their apparent inappropriateness for such a tragic phenomenon. The characters of Marina Lewycka's *Two Caravans* (2007) compose a multifarious group of migrant workers, coming from Ukraine, Poland, Moldova, Malawi, Malaysia and China. They live in two caravans provided by the farmer Leapish, and for a living they pick the strawberries in his nearby fields. The beginning of the novel presents readers with a bucolic picture:

> There is a field – a broad south-sloping field sitting astride a long hill that curves away into a secret leafy valley. It is sheltered by dense hedges of hawthorn and hazel threaded through with wild roses and evening-scented honey-suckle. In the mornings, a light breeze carries up over the Downs, just enough to kiss the air with the fresh salty tang of the English Channel. In fact so delightful is the air that, sitting up here, you might think you were in paradise. And in the field are two caravans, a men's caravan and a women's caravan. (Lewycka 2008: 1)

The reality of these people's lives, however, contrasts sharply with the dream-England they had formed in their imagination. Lewycka provides abundant details about the business. Pickers are paid 30p a kilo before deductions – meaning that 'half you [the farmer] fork out in wages you can claw back in living expenses'. These living expenses (accommodation, food, transport, amounting to £99 a week) are managed by a separate company set up by Leapish's wife, Wendy: 'that's how you get round the red tape that restricts how much you can deduct from wages' (Lewycka 2008: 31–4). In contemporary Britain, agriculture is one of the sectors (together with care, construction and contract cleaning) where forced labour constitutes a particular concern, where the problem of gangmasters is widespread, and with a high rate of fatal injuries (Anderson and Rogaly 2005: 11, 22, 33):[59]

> Press coverage has identified a range of food production, horticulture and agriculture outlets that supply some major supermarkets and food outlets, which depend on migrant workers who are being paid less than £3 per hour for 72–hour weeks and living in substandard housing conditions. (Craig et al. 2007: 42)

In *Two Caravans*, the image of the English countryside as a pastoral paradise is further undermined when unfortunate circumstances scatter the characters into several places and jobs. The Pole Tomasz finds himself on a poultry farm where forty thousand chickens are crammed:

> a thick carpet of white feathers; ... so tightly packed you can't make out where one chicken ends and the next begins. And the smell! ... a rank cloud of raw ammonia that makes his eyes burn and he coughs and backs away from the door, his hand over his mouth. He has seen paintings of damned souls in hell, but they are nothing compared with this. (Lewycka 2008: 120)

The wished-for paradise, then, turns into a hell where chickens sizzle in their own excrement, burning their buttocks and legs.

The ideal Britain undermined by the encounter with reality is not an image exclusive to literature about contemporary new slaveries. Black British literature had already presented it as a recurrent trope confronted by first-generation immigrants, whose experience was historically rooted in the educational structures of the colonial enterprise and their exaltation of British values (Dawson 2007: 2). Salman Rushdie (1991: 259) defines the image he grew up with as a Bombay child as 'dream-England':

> I can't escape the view that my relatively easy ride is not the result of the dream-England's famous sense of tolerance and fair play, but of my social class, my freak fair skin and my 'English' English accent. Take away any of these, and the story would have been very different. Because of course the dream-England is no more than a dream. Sadly, it's a dream from which too many white Britons refuse to awake.

The clash between those two modes is one of the main sources of humour in *Two Caravans*, as in Tomasz's ordeal: it surfaces in his exchanges with his teenage colleague, the white British Neil. Their linguistic misunderstandings play on the ambiguous similarities between intensive poultry raising and British mainstream life and low-brow popular culture:

'Don't you know Big Brother? What do they have on telly where you come from? It's where they lock 'em all up together in a house, and you can watch 'em.'
'Chickens?'
'Yeah, yeah, just like chickens. I like that.'
...
'They [the farmers] keep the light on low, so they never stop for a kip – just keep on feeding all night. Bit like eating pizza in front of the telly.' (Lewycka 2008: 121–2)

Dream-England receives its final blow when the Ukrainians Irina and Andryi accompany the Malawian Emmanuel to Richmond Park to visit Toby McKenzie, a young, pot-smoking Brit whom Emmanuel saved from incarceration during his gap year in Malawi. Toby's father, a wealthy businessman, is a whisky drinker: after a few glasses, he sets his unhappiness loose with a nostalgic, whimpering tone verging on the ridiculous, and reminiscent of Rushdie's words on indigenous Britons refusing to awake:

'Can you take me with you, young man? When you go camping? Down in Kent? Hunting in the woods, with the dog? I'm quite handy with a shotgun, you know. Hares. Rabbits. Pigeons. I can skin a rabbit. I've still got my Swiss army knife. Fetching wood. Making the fire. Damp matches. Smoke everywhere. Kettle boiling. Tea in enamel mugs. Baked beans. Burnt toast. The whole lot.' He looks up at Andryi, his eyes watery and sad. 'I wouldn't get in the way.' (Lewycka 2008: 187)

Against the background of Black British literature, *Two Caravans* brings to the fore the continuity of the expectations raised by dream-England in the lives of those contemporary economic migrants who do not necessarily come from former British colonies. This continuity can be accounted for by the lure exercised by Western culture, especially in former Communist countries.

The gangmaster Vulk is explicit as soon as he fetches Irina at Dover: 'England is not like in you school book' (Lewycka 2008: 7). Irina's expectations about England had indeed grown from her studies at home, building an ideal landscape merging with culture:

In fact I was particularly looking forward to meeting a gentleman in a bowler hat like Mr Brown in my *Let's Talk English* book, who looks supremely dashing and romantic, with his tight suit and rolled-up umbrella, and especially his intriguing bulge in his trouser-zip area, which was drawn very realistically in black ink by a previous owner of that textbook. Who wouldn't want to talk English with him?! Lord Byron looks romantic, too, despite that bizarre turban. (Lewycka 2008: 20–1)

A miner's son, Andryi is much less cultured if compared to Irina, but he too has a model to dream of: a 'blond-haired *Angliska rosa* ... packed with high-spec features ... And a rich pappa' (Lewycka 2008: 17). When he is unexpectedly and briskly seduced by a woman closely fitting that description, she turns out to be the farmer's wife, thirsty for revenge on her husband for his adultery:

> 'What the hell ...? You bitch! You bloody bitch!'
> The farmer strides towards them. The *Angliska rosa* looks up over Andryi's shoulder and with her free hand, not the one that is fumbling with his fly zip, she gestures at the farmer with two fingers. Andryi tries to seize the moment to escape, but the blonde holds him fast, and now the enraged farmer runs forward with a roar, and flings himself onto Andryi's back. Holy whiskers! This is not turning out at all according to plan. He is trapped between the two of them like the meat in some mad sandwich. (Lewycka 2008: 49)

In the ensuing brawl, the woman runs over her husband with her car and the whole group of foreign workers will consequently have to leave for fear of trouble with the police, thus reaffirming the process of spectralisation underlying new slaveries.

As for Tomasz's fantasising, he dreams of ideals of freedom instilled in him by his passion for Bob Dylan's songs, which led him to come to the West. In the context of British new slaveries freedom may mean having to stifle one's identity, and through Neil's words the case of Tomasz's fellow-workers is turned into a Kafkaesque situation:

> Yeah, mad, innit? Yer see Brazils are illegal, so they get in by saying they're Portugeezers. But the Portugeezers are legal now, wiv that Europe like marketing fing, and some of 'em've been making trouble, so nobody wants to take 'em on any more. ... trade unions. Minimum wage. Elf and safety. Brazils don't cause trouble, see, 'cause they're illegal. So if the Portugeezers want a job, they have to pretend to be Brazillers – Portugeezers pretending to be Brazillers pretending to be Portugeezers. Mad, innit? (Lewycka 2008: 127)[60]

During breaks, Tomasz is half-horrified and half-amused when his Portuguese-Brazilian colleagues squeeze chickens in order to hit one another with spurts of excrement. When the workers start playing football with a chicken as ball, he grabs it, runs to the fence, puts it down, sees it go away and explains to his puzzled fellow workers: 'Rugby. I score' (Lewycka 2008: 131). The following day, he will notice the same chicken squashed on the road. This experience triggers some bitter reflections:

[Titchington, near the poultry farm] turns out to be no more than a cluster of quaint steep-gabled cottages with gardens full of roses, clustered around a pretty medieval church. He wonders whether the villagers know the horror that is happening on their doorstep. It was said that the villagers who lived near Treblinka had only a hazy idea of what was happening behind the barbed wire fence a few kilometres away. They, like the villagers of Titchington, must have been bothered by the smell when the wind blew in a certain direction.[61]

[...]

Is he freer here in the West today than he was in Poland in the years of communism, when all he dreamt of was freedom, without even knowing what it was? Is he really any freer than those chickens in the barn, packed here in this small stinking room with five strangers, submitting meekly to a daily horror that has already become routine? Tormentor and tormented, they are all just damned creatures in hell. There must be a song in this. (Lewycka 2008: 132, 134)

All in all, Tomasz's thoughts reinforce the main assumption behind this book: namely, the presence of a palimpsest constituted by concentration camps beneath the forms of imprisonment to which new slaves are subjected. Moreover, this passage is laden with thematic issues that are crucial to new slaveries, proving once more how misleading the apparent simplicity of humorous literature can be. The most obvious theme is the processes by which new slaves are animalised, dehumanised as a necessary step towards their exploitation (as the previous chapters have shown). Secondly, Lewycka hints at the recurrent parallel between the Nazi concentrationary system and the brutalisation of animals.[62] Thirdly, there may be a biographical side to this, since Marina Lewycka was born in a refugee camp in Germany at the end of the Second World War: this is something which surfaces in her debut novel *A Short History of Tractors in Ukrainian* (2006: 268–73, 309–11) as a sore, grief-laden issue for the narrator's father and sister.[63]

In this intricate context, Lewycka struggles to maintain the balance between tragedy and humour, and she is often successful. Much also depends on who is speaking: there is one brilliant passage (amongst others) where the sarcastic cynicism of an employer succinctly conveys all the exploitative attitude ingrained in the British economic system, and the particularly wrenching ordeal of Chinese migrants, who occupy the bottom rung of this new slave society:

six quid an hour. The other hour is voluntary, like I said. You don't have to do it. There's always plenty that do. Ukrainians, Romanians, Bulgarians, Albanians, Brazilians, Mexicans, Kenyans, Zimbabweans, you lose track. Jabber jabber jabber round here. Day and night. It's like United bloody Nations. We used to get a lot of Lithuanians and Latvians, but Europe ruined all that. Made 'em all legal. Like the Poles. Waste of bloody time. Started asking for minimum wages. Chineesers are the best. No papers. No speekee English. No fuckin' clue what's goin' on. Mind you, some folk do take advantage. Like them poor bleeders down at Morecambe. Jabber jabber jabber into the mobile phone, tide comin' in, and nobody's got a clue what they're on about.[64] What's the point of having foreigners if you got to pay 'em same as English, eh? That's why we went over to the agency. Let them take care of all that. (Lewycka 2008: 117)

'United bloody Nations': the speaker's half-voluntary humour replicates in embryo the general strategy on which the irony of the whole novel is based, that is to say the contrast between the ideal and the real. In this case, these two poles hint at equality versus slavery, universal rights versus total lack of rights.

The novel's final chapters, a long on-the-road escape from those who want to turn Irina into a sexual slave, are probably the part where the reader tends to be doubtful about the effectiveness of the medium of humour for the narration of new slaveries.[65] On the other hand, thanks to its picaresque plot and collective cast, *Two Caravans* incisively marks a scattering of the spaces of imprisonment for the literature about new slaves. The fiction analysed so far is mostly centred on either hyper-private (houses) or hyper-public (detention centres) spaces. Lewycka's novel opens the field (literally, too), because it develops its plot in many sites of exploitation constituting a 'human wasteland' (Lewycka 2008: 172): cultivated fields, farms, factories, restaurants,[66] old people's homes where African nurses work.[67] The gruesomeness of the sex trade is probably most representative of this wasteland reducing humans to commodities or, again, to beasts; when chased by the pimp and would-be rapist Vulk, Irina feels like 'a hunted animal' (61).[68]

It is a landscape which forms, as I argued in Chapter 1.4, what may be called 'Britain's concentrationary archipelago'. The novel's dynamic plot effectively conveys the ever-shifting positions of these locations of enslavement, a crucial feature of British new slaveries that is also well exemplified in Nick Broomfield's film *Ghosts*, examined in Chapter 4.1.

3.5 Chasing the overworld: Ian Rankin's *Fleshmarket Close* (2004) and the crime story

Chapter 2.2 on Ruth Rendell has shown how detective fiction is a natural vehicle for discussing the literary representations of new slaveries, given their frequently criminal nature. Ian Rankin's novel, though, unravels its investigations into the institutional sphere exacerbating new slaveries, similarly to Chris Cleave. *Fleshmarket Close* (2004) is a crime novel which alludes to new forms of slavery right from the double meaning of its title.[69] When the corpse of an unidentified immigrant is found stabbed, DI John Rebus gets involved in a complex investigation, leading him also to wonder about his own Polish ancestry, of which he knows very little. He happens to work side by side with the black Immigration Official Felix Storey from London, who illustrates the bigger picture to the inexperienced Rebus:

> My own parents arrived here in the fifties: Jamaica to Brixton, just two among many. A *proper migration* that was, but dwarfed by the situation we've got now. Tens of thousands a year, coming ashore illegally... often paying handsomely for the privilege. Illegals have become big business, Inspector. Thing is, *you never see them* until something goes wrong. (Rankin 2004: 210; italics mine)

Similarly to Rendell in *Simisola*, then, Rankin does not elude – indeed, he makes explicit – the continuities and discontinuities between new slaveries and the issues characterising Black British history, something reflected on in Chapter 6.2 of this volume.[70] Moreover, Storey's last sentence is yet another reference to contemporary enslaved migrants as invisibles, as ghosts; Rebus, too, realises: 'I haven't seen any of these people, the people everyone is so angry at' (Rankin 2004: 68). Not differently from Rendell's Wexford, the first big obstacle for Rebus consists in identifying the corpse found in the ghetto of Knoxland, in the western outskirts of Edinburgh. The place is composed of high-rise blocks '[r]eaching skywards with all the subtlety of single-digit salutes' (4). It is

> a dumping ground for tenants the council found hard to house elsewhere: addicts and the unhinged. More recently, immigrants had been catapulted into its dankest, least welcoming corners. Asylum-seekers, refugees. People nobody wanted to think about or have to deal with. Looking around, Rebus realised that the poor bastards must be left feeling like mice in a maze. The difference being that in laboratories, there were few predators, while out here in the real world, they were everywhere. (Rankin 2004: 5–6)

Rankin's description through Rebus's thoughts clearly points at the responsibility of political authorities who place foreigners in a prison-like, or jungle-like, nightmarish environment, turning them into prey; here, Rankin's animal imagery echoes with Levi's and Abani's. This is to be seen as part of the 'national dispersal scheme' commented on in Chapter 3.1; more specifically, Rankin's Knoxland seems to be inspired by the aftermath of the dispersal scheme which took place in Glasgow in 2001, when a great number of asylum seekers were housed in Sighthill, 'one of Scotland's "sink estates" [...] the poorest constituency in Scotland, the second most unhealthy in Britain [... with] the highest male unemployment rate in Britain' (McGhee 2005: 82–5), 'the poorest areas with high levels of empty housing stock' (Mynott 2002: 119–22; Robinson et al. 2003: 166).[71] Such operations were bound to spur asylophobia, fear and hatred of asylum seekers, and racist violence, resulting in stabbings, angry demonstrations by the immigrants and counter-protests by rampaging far-right movements (McGhee 2005: 85; Moorehead 2006: 141). Institutions sent immigrants to these kinds of areas although they were well aware that anti-refugee violence rates are higher there (Bosworth and Guild 2008: 705);[72] this represents one of the clearest examples of the punitive attitude towards migrants:[73] 'To be a refugee, it seems, may be to have access to important rights, but woe betide those who arrive in Western states claiming to be a refugee.'[74]

In Rankin's Knoxland, where a 'venerable piece of graffiti had been altered from JUNKIE SCUM to BLACK SCUM' (Rankin 2004: 61), the so-called natives resort to angry protests, the lawyer Mo Dirwan gets beaten up and asylophobic questions abound, even from some of Rebus's colleagues (61, 115). Highly perplexed at the course of events, Rebus silently questions the state of contemporary Scotland as a whole, hinting again at the invisible nature of his case through a sarcastic reference to Shakespeare's *Tempest* and Huxley's *Brave New World*:

> 'What in Christ's name is happening here?' he found himself asking. The world passed by, determined not to notice: cars grinding homewards; pedestrians making eye contact only with the pavement ahead of them, *because what you didn't see couldn't hurt you. A fine, brave world* awaiting the new parliament. An ageing country dispatching its talents to the four corners of the globe ... unwelcoming to visitor and migrant alike. (Rankin 2004: 204; italics mine)

Surrounded by a wall of 'white' resentment and fear, Rebus is unable to discover the victim's real identity until a call comes from Whitemire, an old prison in West Lothian recently converted into a so-called 'Immigration Removal Centre' (as fictitious as Knoxland, but based on the real Dungavel). The speaking voice belongs to someone working at the Centre who has recognised the photo of the victim because his wife and children are held in Whitemire. She is calling anonymously, a detail which casts doubts on the legal activities in Whitemire from its very first appearance in the novel (as happens with many structures of detention and deportation, Whitemire is run by a private security company).

During his visits there, DI Rebus sees for himself the appalling state to which its guests are reduced: 'families, individuals scared out of their wits ... people who know that to be sent back to their native land is a death sentence' (Rankin 2004: 124). In Whitemire, inmates are not given a humane environment, but are kept with 'a bare minimum of education and nourishment' (167), and cannot even take food to their rooms (139).[75] Rebus encounters harrowed, hollowed-out human beings, one of them resorting to a suicide attempt (247–9);[76] they clearly suffer from 'barbed-wire disease', a syndrome that medical science identified in enemy aliens' internment camps in Britain during the First World War.[77]

Whitemire has not lost its prison-like nature, and is described by Rankin in these terms, with its 'twelve-foot perimeter fence ... augmented by runs of pale green corrugated iron' (132), uniformed guards with sets of keys, tight security measures and regulations (134, 139). Rankin's setting is obviously based on real places. Lindholme Removal Centre, for example,

> holds up to 112 men ... staff routinely impose random strip-searches after visits. Detainees are also strip-searched on admission to the centre as a matter of routine, without any reason given. Staff at this former prison treat detainees as offenders, though they have not been convicted of any crime. There is a prison atmosphere with detainees being made to wear prison clothes. (Cohen 2006: 97)[78]

In Britain, a major expansion of detention centres was announced by the government in the year 2000. 'Some 15 per cent of applicants (of about 10,000 per year) are currently detained, or 700–1,000 at any one time.... The leader of the [right-wing] opposition went one step further, to prove he could be more vicious in his compassion than the government, and promised that all asylum-seekers would be detained if he came to power,' writes Harris (2002: 39).

In Whitemire, Rebus bears the bad news to Mrs Yurgi and her two children. Their story exemplifies the way families are often treated by the immigration control system:

> The family did not want to leave Sighthill. They were beginning to be happy there. The children made friends ... they found places in a school. And then they were thrown into a van – a police van – and brought to this place in the middle of the night. They were terrified. (Rankin 2004: 246, original ellipsis)

They will all be driven to the mortuary, children included, to identify the body of Stef Yurgi (a human rights Kurdish journalist persecuted by Turkish authorities);[79] they are taken in a custodial blue van 'with bars on its windows, a toughened grille between the front seats and the benches in the back' (Rankin 2004: 175–6).

For his part, Rebus is made increasingly suspicious by the barely suppressed lack of collaboration from the Centre's manager. Eventually, the full picture will prove his doubts to be well founded. On one hand, authorities stack immigrants in God-forsaken ghettos where they become easy prey to slavers and exploiters.[80] On the other hand, Whitemire's officials allow these slavers to bail immigrants out for their criminal purposes, and thus help them strengthen their empire with the bonus of the perfect blackmail: 'Any of them complain, Whitemire's hanging over them like a noose' (423): this is what Stef Yurgi discovered, and the reason why he was killed.[81] In other words, Rebus's investigation discloses how closely the two supposed opposites on the legal/illegal axis, the ghetto of Knoxland and the Whitemire Centre, are connected, to the point that criminal dens of enslavement and official sites of removal inevitably blur, becoming indistinguishable. Aghast at the sheer inhumanity of the living conditions in Whitemire, Rebus tries to respond to the similar frustration of one of his colleagues:

> 'That's the problem though: who is it I *am* pissed off with?'
> 'The people in charge?' Rebus guessed. 'The ones we never see.' He waited to see if she'd agree. 'I've got this theory,' he went on. 'We spend most of our time chasing something called "the underworld", but it's the *overworld* we should really be keeping an eye on.' (Rankin 2004: 142)

Here it seems appropriate to return to the final considerations on Rendell's *Simisola* in the context of crime fiction (see Chapter 2.2), given that Rankin shows an analogous distrust of the 'system' by making underworld and overworld indistinguishable. According to Ed Christian (2001: 3), one of the recurrent features of postcolonial detective fiction is to show 'how such things as a totalitarian or racist regime, a strong army, or *police and political corruption* interfere with the detective's search for justice' (italics mine). Rankin certainly brings some of these elements to the fore in his reconstructions of British new slaveries. In comparison with Rendell, he also sounds much more disruptive, because his critique involves police forces, too. Felix Storey and Rebus gaol the whole criminal organisation, but only (Rebus finds out) thanks to anonymous tips coming from an even more powerful slaver and migrant-smuggler (Rebus's arch-enemy Caffery) who managed to use the Immigration Service[82] to get rid of his rival in crime. Rebus concludes to Storey:

> 'But here's the thing – all the glory you're going to get, it adds up to the cube of bugger-all, because what you've done is smoothed Caffery's path. It'll be *him* in charge from now on, not only bringing illegals into the country, but working them to death too.' Rebus paused. 'So thanks for that.' (Rankin 2004: 475)

As far as the complementariness of the institutional and criminal dimensions is concerned, then, the ending of *Fleshmarket Close* is unsparing.[83] In addition, the merging of institutional and criminal persecution of migrants takes place on a palimpsest constituted by some of Edinburgh's tourist attractions – in this case, Gothic and historical tourism. Two skeletons, a woman and an infant, are found buried under a concrete cellar floor in a street called Fleshmarket Close. They are soon revealed to be old specimens which had disappeared from the Faculty of Medicine. Nevertheless, in a very short time, thanks to the sly promptness of the cellar's owner who is turning his pub into a 'theme bar' (Rankin 2004: 173), the place is included in the city centre ghost tour along the 'Royal Mile'. The same skeletons, however, were being shown by the migrant smugglers as if they were recent victims of slaughter, to threaten any exploited migrant who turned rebellious. Whether fake or ancient, they were at the same time part of the terrifying atmosphere on which new slaveries work.[84]

Through this narrative turn, Rankin seems to be implying a number of important points. First of all, even though Knoxland and Whitemire are two liminal places far from the bustling city centre, tourist Edinburgh is certainly involved in their suspension of human rights; thus, the supposed liminality associated with new slaveries is shown as more and more dispersed, hard to locate[85] – a key concept for the present volume.

Secondly, Rankin links new slaveries in contemporary Edinburgh to the serious issues from Scottish history underlying today's Scottish tours. One of the two skeletons might be that of the eighteenth-century Mag Lennox – a woman accused of witchcraft and burnt by citizens (78). Her descendant Judith Lennox works as a ghost-tour guide and as a consultant to the bar owner (173). Here, Rankin walks again in Rendell's footsteps, this time regarding her use of Roman history in Britain as a palimpsest for new slaveries. In Rankin's case, the implication is obvious: who are the witches being burnt *today* by respectable citizens? At Whitemire, when told that Stef Yurgi's family is to be deported because 'they hadn't proved they weren't economic migrants', Ellen Wylie replies: 'Tough one. ... Like proving you're not a witch ...' (137, original ellipsis).

One final detail from *Fleshmarket Close* proves to be an important link with the following chapter on Nick Broomfield's film *Ghosts*: the presence of new slaves from China. Rebus witnesses a raid by Storey's immigration squad against a group of Chinese labourers cockling on a beach, who give vent to their desperation at being caught:

> 'They don't want to be sent home.'
>
> Rebus looked around. 'Can't be any worse than this, can it?'
>
> The officer's mouth twitched. 'Forty kilo sacks ... they get paid maybe three quid for each one, and it's not as if they can go to an employment tribunal, is it?'
>
> 'I suppose not.'
>
> 'Slavery's what it boils down to... turning human beings into something you can buy and sell. In the north-east, it's fish-gutting. Other places, it's picking fruit and veg. The gangmasters have a supply for every possible demand.' (Rankin 2004: 357–8, original ellipsis)

Rankin's novel came out in 2004, the year when a group of Chinese cockle-pickers drowned while labouring in Morecambe Bay – whether the book was prophetic on this, or simply very up to date, it is pointless to try to determine here. On that tragedy Broomfield's *Ghosts* is based.

Notes

1 'and more shocking in the first year under a Labour Government for which I had waited eighteen years!' (Adshead 2001: 9)
2 For the prominence of issues related to the woman's body in this play, see Farrier (2011: 102–4).

3 When she discusses her lack of money with her British friend Alfie, he proposes that she should sell one of her kidneys – a joke with ghastly undertones, reminiscent of Frears's later film *Dirty Pretty Things* (2002).
4 For the issue of the coastal town as a liminal place in relation to this film, see Farrier (2011: 77–85) and Andrews and Roberts (2012: 4–5).
5 Possibly it might be seen as a prophetic film in light of Margate's 2003 turbulent events concerning asylum seekers (Andrews and Roberts 2012: 3), too.
6 Compounded by the inherently digressive nature of oral literatures (Okpewho 1992: 96–7).
7 I am grateful to my former student Bianca Bressy for directing my attention towards White and Epston's work.
8 For two specific examples of linguistic isolation and its consequences, see the case of the Guinean Suleiman Dialo (Moorehead 2006: 129–31), and Nazer (2003: 315).
9 In his 2004 essay exploring the limited category of refugee *artist*s, for instance, Alex Rotas (2004: 51) wonders if 'this marginalization of individuals who have already endured not inconsiderable trauma might lead to a sense of solidarity-in-adversity amongst them, with the emergence of a sense of a separate community'.
10 See, for example, Pandey (1988: 89–92).
11 At the end of the TV drama *I Am Slave*, one caption reads: 'Inspired by the life of Mende Nazer, and those slaves who *still cannot speak*' (italics mine).
12 A thinly disguised incarnation of the new slave as underground creature is present in Monica Ali's *In the Kitchen* (2009), where a member of staff of a London hotel restaurant is found dead in the kitchen basement, where he had secretly set up his residence.
13 See Chapter 1.1.
14 On the issue of clustering and dispersal, see also Robinson et al. (2003: passim); McGhee (2005: 68–71); Moorehead (2006: 138–9).
15 Gunning analyses three key novels from the first decade of the twenty-first century, as far as the topic of subalternity is concerned: Abdulrazak Gurnah's *By the Sea* (2001), Caryl Phillips's *A Distant Shore* (2003) and Manzu Islam's *Burrow* (2004). Incidentally, the protagonist of Gurnah's novel, on his arrival at Heathrow, pretends he speaks no English – precisely like the protagonist of Karim Haidari's short story 'The journey' (2005: 100): 'Oh, my first conversation started with a lie. How many lies should I tell before I could prove the truth? Why do reasons fail against the system?'
16 In this regard, the words by Gurnah's protagonist are arrestingly suggestive: 'I am a refugee, an asylum-seeker. These are not simple words, even if habit of hearing them makes them seem so' (Gurnah 2001: 4).
17 See what the protagonist of Chikwava's novel *Harare North* (2010: 82)

says on the subject: 'You see me stepping down them pavements from graft [work] with hands in my pockets and you think you know me? ... You lick ice-cream, I bite mine and you laugh because you think you know my arse better than your mother's petticoat?'

18 The protagonist of Gurnah's novel likens himself to Melville's Bartleby. Hardt and Negri (2002: 202–3) exalt the figure of Bartleby (and Coetzee's Michael K.) as embodying the refusal of authority, but their conclusion is not different from Gunning's: they 'may be beautiful souls, but their being in absolute purity hangs on the edge of an abyss. Their lines of flight from authority are completely solitary, and they continuously tread on the verge of suicide. What we need is to create a new social body, which is a project that goes well beyond refusal.' On this need, see the ending of Chapter 6.2. For the importance of Bartleby for the study of asylum seekers, see Farrier (2011: 125–7, 131–52, 175–9).

19 In order to counter, in Kirmayer's words (1996: 192), 'the failure of the world to bear witness'.

20 An analogous leaning might be detected in the contested relationship between two well-established notions pertaining to trauma studies, with regard to the assumed unspeakability of trauma versus narrative as a therapeutic way of overcoming it. Between these contradictory tendencies, Irene Visser (2011: 274) holds the latter as 'a more sustainable perspective for trauma studies ... because it allows a historically and cultural specific approach to trauma narratives'.

21 See also Farrier (2011: 157–60).

22 The first-person voice of Brian Chikwava's novel *Harare North* (2009) is a narrative example of how one's mind can fall to pieces; he comes from a Zimbabwean background of war, and has to bear with institutional criminalisation and labour exploitation in London. See Paola Splendore's perceptive reflections (2011: passim), which place this book within the context of Black British writing; Splendore likens Chikwava's London to Foucault's concept of heterotopia: I take exception to that, since heterotopia is conceived by Foucault (1986: 24; this essay is quoted in Chapter 1.4) as a secluded place 'outside of all places', whereas British new slaveries (as discussed in Chapters 1.1 and 1.4) develop in close proximity to mainstream society.

23 See Moorehead (2006: 136). On how this policy was implemented and later reinforced by the 2007 New Asylum Model, see Farrier (2011: 157–66). For a telling, dramatic example of such methods, see Adshead's *The Bogus Woman* (2001: 86–7): 'Why did they rape you? / And not kill you / ... / Generally it is reported / that / a woman / in the situation / you describe / from the area / you claim / to come from, / would more likely / be raped / *then* killed.' For an example of the arbitrary management of credibility by asylum institutions, see Ali (2010: 153).

24 See, for example, the incoherence of Lena, former sexual slave in London, in Monica Ali's *In the Kitchen* (2010: 199). See also Kay

Adshead's *The Bogus Woman* (2001: 40): 'I will tell you my story / some bits you won't believe. / Here and there, a day, a week / goes missing / sometimes the pictures shiver, / and the voices shriek, / in my head. / sometimes they shred.' In *Holocaust Testimonies: The Ruins of Memory* (New Haven: Yale University Press, 1991, pp. 174–5), L. L. Langer propounds a view which might explain these chronology-related difficulties: 'Witnesses are both willing and reluctant to proceed with the chronology; they frequently hesitate because they know that their most complicated recollections are unrelated to time. ... [Trauma] stops the chronological clock and fixes the moment permanently in memory and imagination, immune to the vicissitudes of time. The unfolding story brings relief, while the unfolding plot induces pain' (quoted in Van der Kolk and Van der Hart 1995: 177).

25 'For him [the refugee] ... his story is a treasured possession. For true, it is the most important thing he owns' (Ali 2010: 380).
26 A description very close to Bauman's analogy between rubbish and wasted lives (see Chapter 1.1).
27 Testimony by L. Beccaria Rolfi, from Beccaria Rolfi and Bruzzone (2003: 92).
28 Francesca Giommi (2011: 178) recognises an analogous tendency throughout Abani's oeuvre.
29 'The prevalence of the map topos in contemporary post-colonial literary texts, and the frequency of its ironic and/or parodic usage in these texts, suggests a link between a de/reconstructive reading of maps and a revisioning of the history of European colonialism' (Huggan 1995: 407).
30 See also Craig et al. (2007: 31).
31 Published in the US with the title *Little Bee*.
32 Nowhere have I found this impending menace of wolfish, preying men as pervasive as in Warsan Shire's collection of poems *Teaching My Mother How to Give Birth*, where the two-line closing poem simply goes 'To my daughter I will say / "when the men come, set yourself on fire"' (Shire 2011: 34).
33 For another case of sexual exploitation in the context of detention centres, see Adshead's *The Bogus Woman* (2001: 27, 64).
34 This is what this novel shares with Zephaniah's *Refugee Boy*, mentioned at the beginning of Chapter 3 as the novel which signalled a renewed interest in the issue of refugees and new slaveries at the beginning of the 2000s. It should also be noted that cruelty to children (including forced separation from parents) was central to the abolitionist debate in the eighteenth and nineteenth centuries (Equiano 2001: 43, 82; see also John Wesley, 'Thoughts upon Slavery', in *The Works of the Reverend John Wesley*, vol. xi, 1872, p. 76, quoted in Knox-Shaw 1993: 303). Besides, it was one of the most terrifying aspects of the Nazi genocide (Giustini 2010: 50–2). For the break-up of families in ancient, classical slavery, see Finley (1983: 76).

35 'I was fourteen years of age when I came to your country but I did not have any papers to prove it and so they put me in the same detention centre as the adults' (Cleave 2008: 9). Quoting interviews with Cleave, De Michelis (2011: 274) notices that Cleave volunteered in an Immigration Removal Centre in Oxfordshire. For a collection of short stories concerning asylum-seeking children (written by asylum seekers or people who worked with them), see Bradman 2007.

36 Although the UK is classified by ECPAT among those countries that have made 'notable efforts' against child trafficking, the same organisation highlights the incomplete implementation of ratified conventions, in aspects such as special protection measures, creation of nationwide specialist police team, legal prosecution of children forced into criminal activities, and support services (ECPAT 2011: 11–13). To quote more specific cases, the Children's Commissioner for England has uncovered how trafficked children were sent straight back to France under a '"gentleman's agreement" ... returned to France within 24 hours if they did not immediately apply for asylum. ... seven Vietnamese children, who had been trafficked into Britain to work as "gardeners" in cannabis factories in 2010, ... were sent back to France. Kent social services said they knew nothing about these children' (*Reporter*, 18:1: 5). Another blatant case of institutional neglect was the 2004 law (dropped in 2006) that 'included provision ... to withdraw the welfare support given to failed asylum-seekers and, where they refused to leave the UK voluntarily, to remove their children into care' (Farrier 2011: 88). In September 2013, the Home Secretary Theresa May, when declaring that Britain should withdraw from the European Convention on Human Rights, also blamed migrants' abuse of article 8 (right to family life) in order to justify their deportation.

37 And more warmly so, if compared with Zephaniah's third-person story, more neutral in tone (although this could with some justification be seen as a way to make *Refugee Boy* more approachable for teen readers).

38 See also Moorehead (2006: 116).

39 For a similar observation by Australian doctors working in detention centres, see Moorehead (2006: 115).

40 Zephaniah's *Refugee Boy* describes yet another escape (Alem's running from the children's home where he is being bullied): after a whole night's running, he dismally realises that '[h]e had done nothing but go around in a large circle' (Zephaniah 2001: 82); this chapter is significantly entitled 'The Road to Nowhere'.

41 When Malia was enslaved as a girl in a wealthy private house in Khartoum, she was kicked out of the house and left standing in the middle of the street: 'You see?' her mistress said triumphantly. 'Without me, you don't exist.' An identical scene takes place in the play *Roadkill* (Bissett and Smith 2011: 50), examined in Chapter 4.3.

The ghost and the concentration camp 93

42 Not that a security system would help much. In Adele Ward's poem 'Next Door' (2011: 33) an analogous scene is observed: 'And all the time the red light blinking / on the Orthodox Jewish Primary School / security camera, peering left and right / at the sheer improbability'.
43 The relationship between trauma and new slaveries will be further studied in Chapter 4.3 on drama. Suffice it here to quote Moniza Alvi's poignant short poem 'Candle': 'The fresh wound is a candle / lighting steps down into the caves. / / Among stalagmites and stalactites / the old wound crouches low' (Alvi 2008: 16).
44 Little Bee comes from one of those areas that Achille Mbembe's Foucauldian elaboration would qualify as ruled by 'necropolitics' (2003: 30, 40), where wars and militias are tightly connected with the economy of resource extraction, and lead to the formation of 'deathworlds' populated by 'living dead'. On the importance of instability and civil strife for new forms of imperial monopolies, see also Brennan (2005: 144–5).
45 De Michelis (2011: 278) quotes reviewers writing that Cleave's intentions are sometimes too explicit.
46 For a powerful dramatic elaboration of this concept, see Caryl Churchill's 2000 play *Far Away* (Churchill 2008: 129–59).
47 See also Arendt (1964: 48–9, 134–5, 145, 151–3).
48 For an analysis of this functional rationality, of how it was elaborated by Weber, Heidegger, Marcuse and Adorno, and of its relations to the desk killer, see Milchman and Rosenberg (1992: 214, 222–4).
49 See also Arendt (1964: 288).
50 See also Arendt (1964: 273).
51 The policewoman's reply hints at the new kind of racism characterising Hardt and Negri's 'empire': different from the old, biological one, this is a cultural racism that is presented as an effect of socio-historical conditions (rather than a cause), while establishing 'an equally strong theoretical ground for social separation and segregation' (Hardt and Negri 2000: 192). On this kind of racism, see also Chapter 6.2. For a similar example of cultural racism, see Gurnah's *By the Sea* (2001: 12); when the Gatwick immigration officer says 'You don't belong here, you don't value any of the things we value, you haven't paid for them through generations, and we don't want you here', the asylum-seeking protagonist thinks: 'But the whole world had paid for Europe's values already, even if a lot of the time it just paid and paid and didn't get to enjoy them.'
52 Lachs (1981: 12–13, 58).
53 '[I]t could be said that the more modern a society, the greater the reliance on desk killers in planning and carrying out policies of genocide' (Totten and Bartrop 2008: 111).
54 Kelman (1973: passim).
55 On a lexical level, this structural constant between the Nazi Holocaust

and contemporary new slaveries in Britain is reinforced by the very definition of 'desk-killing': if the *Dictionary of Genocide* (Totten and Bartrop 2008: 110–11) identifies its origins with Eichmann, Dan Gretton applies the same concept to present-day transnational corporations in his book *I You We Them: Thirty-three Journey into the Mind of the Desk Killer* (forthcoming), which deals, amongst other things, with the oil companies that have been pillaging the Niger Delta – the cause of Little Bee's ordeal.

56 As Primo Levi (1996: 396) writes, 'monsters do exist, but they are too few in number to be truly dangerous. More dangerous are the common men, functionaries ready to believe and to act without asking questions, like Eichmann'; Levi also projects his vision into the postwar decades, mentioning Hoss, Stangl, the French military in Algeria and the Khmer Rouge.

57 On the role of private companies in the detention centres system, see Bosworth (2007: 165, 172–3).

58 Here again, one is reminded of Avery Gordon's emphasis on the 'right to complex personhood' (2008: 4).

59 For a descriptions of individuals harshly exploited in this sector, see Pai (2008: 120–57); in the same pages, the author narrates the weeks she spent undercover, pretending to be an undocumented agricultural labourer.

60 In 1943 Hannah Arendt (1995: 116) noted with bitter sarcasm how the European Jews had tried to adapt to all the countries where they were grudgingly given shelter: 'Our identity is changed so frequently that nobody can find out who we actually are.'

61 In some cases it has been demonstrated how the world of the Nazi camp was not neatly separated from ordinary society; see Bensoussan (2002: 7), where he refers to Gordon Horwitz's *In the Shadow of Death: Living outside the Gates of Mathausen* (1990).

62 This is not the place to open a discussion here on such a complex topic, also involving specism; see, for example, Alessandra Meoni's essay on Coetzee (2011: passim).

63 The father of her first novel briefly reappears in *Two Caravans*, as one of the inmates of the old people's home (2008: 47–62).

64 The novel is dedicated to 'the Morecambe Bay cockle-pickers' who drowned in 2004. On the presence of Chinese migrants in the wider picture of British new slaveries, see the next chapter on Ian Rankin, and my analysis of Nick Broomfield's film *Ghosts* in Chapter 4.1.

65 De Michelis (2011: 276), too, notices the dissatisfaction expressed by some readers about the ending of *The Other Hand*. Possibly, narrating new slaveries through humour does pose a great problem as to how to end the story.

66 Working as a kitchen hand is described by Andryi as 'being a slave with ten masters' (2008: 212).

The ghost and the concentration camp 95

67 'BBCs – British Buttock Cleaners', as the protagonist of Chikwava's *Harare North* calls them.
68 See also 179. Two oriental girls who are originally part of the group are sent to Amsterdam to work – in theory as nannies, but ending up in the prostitution market (2008: 83–4, 90–5, 228); the rest of their story is not narrated, leaving a gap analogous to Simisola's story in Rendell's novel (Chapter 2.2).
69 'More than one kind of flesh market' is DS Siobhan Clarke's comment after a visit to a lap-dance club (Rankin 2004: 157).
70 See Agbaje (2009: 241) for a bitter confrontation between a Black British citizen and a 'new' immigrant, who will try to have her brother released from a Detention Centre by acceding to the sexual demands of a Home Office clerk (253–5).
71 According to a World Health Organization report (August 2008), there is a twenty-eight-year gap in life expectancy between the poorest and the richest suburbs in Glasgow; available at www.who.int/mediacentre/news/releases/2008/pr29/en/index.html (accessed 1 February 2011). Arriving in so run-down an area is likely to shatter idealistic expectations in many a migrant's minds (see Chapter 3.4); Moorehead (2006: 130, 141) describes some asylum seekers' astonishment when they were sent to the Byker area of Newcastle.
72 Bosworth and Guild (2008) refer to 2005 Home Office research.
73 More generally, McGhee (2005: 65–77) argues that from 1998 the Labour government policies constantly introduced an attitude of deterrence which was bound to create an atmosphere of suspicion and prejudice towards asylum seekers (for an account of how the nine British bills issued between 1997 and 2007 increasingly criminalised migrants by presenting them as a danger, see Bosworth and Guild (2008: passim)).
74 M. J. Gibney (2006), 'A thousand little Guantanamos: western states and measures to prevent the arrival of refugees', in K. E. Tunstall (ed.), *Displacement, Asylum, Migration* (Oxford: Oxford University Press), p. 141 (quoted in Gunning 2011: 143).
75 For the lack of educational and medical facilities in detention centres, see Crawley and Lester (2005: 14).
76 Moorehead explores in depth the issue of suicides among refugees in Britain (2006: 128–36). For a satirical depiction of a suicide in a detention centre, see Hope (1997: 43).
77 In 1919 the syndrome was described as a consequence of the unreal life led in camps, driving internees to erase the external world from their consciousness, to become unable to deal with any concrete issue whatsoever, and to live in a world of shadows (A. L. Vischer, *Barbed-Wire Disease: A Psychological Study of the Prisoner of War* (London, John Bale & Sons & Danilesson, 1919), p. 146, quoted in Pietro Di Paola's introduction to Rudolf Rocker (2006: 19); in this book about

his time as an interned enemy alien, Rocker describes instances of this syndrome). See also Yarnall (2011: 163).

78 For details concerning the prison-like aspects of detention centres, see Bosworth (2007: passim); Farrier (2011: 35–6).

79 'Kurds from Turkey have a very hard time convincing the authorities that they are persecuted' (Bohmer and Shuman 2008: 16). 'Turkey is a difficult country. The evidence of torture is notorious, but Turkey is a friend, a member of NATO, a potential member of the EU. The claims of those in flight from Turkey, mainly Kurds, are treated with suspicion' (Harris 2002: 38).

80 The immigration raid, carried out in a Knoxland block, will discover a huge number of undocumented people stashed on a single floor (Rankin 2004: 387–90).

81 Unfortunately the TV drama based on the novel (2005) erased this part of the story, reducing the crime to a personal blackmail affair; the import of Whitemire was greatly downsized.

82 Although they 'wielded more power than the police' (Rankin 2004: 387).

83 Brian Diemert (2005: 180) identifies this 'hard-boiled theme' of the 'criminal complicity of the socially respectable' in many novels by Rankin. Diemert also considers the Rebus–Cafferty enmity as a manifestation of the 'monstrous double of Gothic horror fiction [...] the textual manifestation of a hidden self discerned in the Calvinist's extreme self-examination'. The theme of the Gothic double will be examined in Chapter 4.1, with reference to Nick Broomfield's *Ghosts*.

84 The TV version of the novel completely erased the skeletons. One wonders why the title was maintained, since 'Fleshmarket Close' is completely absent.

85 This is possibly why Rankin declared that 'the real mystery' of his Rebus series 'isn't the crime … [U]nderneath, the real mystery is Rebus coming to terms with Edinburgh'; see 'Gothic Scot: Ian Rankin talks to Robert McCrum', *Guardian Unlimited (The Observer)*, 18 March 2001 (quoted in Diemert 2005: 164).

4

The British concentrationary archipelago in cinema, photography and drama

4.1 Cinema: Reshaping the Gothic in Nick Broomfield's *Ghosts* (2006)

In your country, if you are not scared enough already, you can go to watch a horror film. Afterwards you can go out of the cinema into the night and for a little while there is horror in everything. ... Horror in your country is something you take a dose of to remind yourself that you are not suffering from it. ... But the film in your memory, you cannot walk out of it so easily. Wherever you go it is always playing. So when I say that I am a refugee, you must understand that there is no refuge.

Chris Cleave, The Other Hand (2008: 65–6)

Morecambe, half-resuscitated, half choked on the karma of the drowned Chinese cockle-pickers, was an unresolved argument between entropy and aspiration.

Iain Sinclair, Ghost Milk (2012: 260–1)

At the end of Ian Rankin's *Fleshmarket Close*, a gap is evident between the frivolity of 'ghost tours' and the harsh reality of new slaveries: in the face of the two skeletons and of how they were employed, these tours become a mere gloss for the depth of enslavement – a gloss which hides the real ghosts, the real skeletons, the real fleshmarkets of our age.[1] It is the same irrelevance of horror art for those who experience horrific events every day that is candidly expressed by Little Bee in the introductory epigraph above. The expected paradigms of the Gothic, then, need revision in the light of the context provided by new slaveries. So far, detective stories have been considered a privileged genre for the literary unearthing of new slaves' invisibility. As one of the ancestors of crime fiction,[2] the Gothic is worth equal attention.

The following pages focus on Nick Broomfield's film *Ghosts* (2006), which reconstructs a true story – the tragedy of the twenty-three Chinese cockle-pickers who drowned in Morecambe Bay in February 2004 'because they didn't know about the treacherous local tides and no one had told them' (Waugh 2007: 189). *Ghosts* is not the only film dealing with new forms of slavery in Britain, but part of a 'recent wave of movies attempting to address the issues of political and economic asylum and illegal immigration' through 'an alternative discourse to that proliferated by politicians and the media' (Tan 2008: 303). One might think of Stephen Frears's *Dirty Pretty Things* (2002) and Ken Loach's *It's a Free World …* (2007), much more popular and successful than Broomfield's movie. Alongside its artistic merits, *Ghosts* is here studied because of its emphasis on the *spectral* lives of new slaves. Broomfield's movie offers interesting opportunities to elaborate on the relations between discourses on new slaveries and the Gothic genre.

The adjustment of established Gothic paradigms to so recent a phenomenon should not come as a surprise. Fred Botting defines the Gothic as an extremely protean mode:

> Many of the anxieties articulated in Gothic terms in the nineteenth century reappear in the twentieth century. Their appearance, however, is more diverse, a diffusion of Gothic traces among a multiplicity of different genres and media. … [Gothic is] a mode that exceeds genres and categories … a hybrid form, incorporating and transforming other literary forms as well as developing and changing its own conventions in relation to newer modes of writing. (Botting 1996: 13–14)

What follows focuses on Broomfield's contribution to the contemporary development of this mode, as an exemplary case of the general features described by Botting and other critics.[3] This examination, developed with the help of some theorists' contributions on the characteristics of the Gothic, is designed to bring to the fore Broomfield's peculiar employment of Gothic elements, which can be fully understood only in the light of the features of new slaveries in contemporary Britain; as Misha Kavka aptly writes (2002: 212), 'the Gothic is mutable [also] because it is bound to the historical moment, constantly reworking the material of the past in terms of the cultural fears of the present'.

Before moving on to the analysis of the film, some data about the presence of Chinese immigrants in Britain are in order. In many cases, they embody to the extreme the fragility and helplessness of new slaves. They leave their country because of conditions of extreme poverty; around one per cent of them for political reasons.[4] They are recruited by highly organised criminal groups like the Snakeheads, whose networks are 'particularly impenetrable' (Waugh 2007: 198); these organisations have strong links with the provincial government, where corruption is said to run amok (Gupta 2007: 186, 145, 147). Their journey often becomes an odyssey which can last from three to six months, crossing countries by all sorts of means of transportation, even trekking over snow-covered mountainous borders without sufficient clothing and equipment (153–5).[5] These trials can leave permanent traces on their bodies and minds, as in Keung's case: after travelling for three months to reach England, he was diagnosed with schizophrenia, and his wife had to undertake the same journey in order to join him, take care of him and work to repay both his and her debts to the Snakeheads (Waugh 2007: 196).

This general picture accounts for the particular vulnerability of Chinese immigrants, 'the bottom layer ... of the UK workforce' (Pai 2008: xix), who are further isolated by their usually insufficient knowledge of the English language, and thus rarely able to escape their predicament.[6] The atmosphere of constant, impending menace, represented by Chinese authorities, Chinese criminal organisations and finally British authorities in search of undocumented immigrants,[7] maintains a sort of permanent anguish, if not terror, reminiscent of the eighteenth-century Gothic mood inspired by 'tortuous, fragmented narratives ... horrible images and life-threatening pursuits' (Botting 1996: 2).[8] The Morecambe Bay cockle-pickers, on whom the story of *Ghosts* is based, are described by researchers as follows:

> Their documentation was removed from them, they lived in appalling conditions and were transported in closely supervised vehicles to their place of work, they worked in equally appalling conditions and for pitifully small 'wages', and they had no opportunity to protest their circumstances. As much evidence shows, those who have protested such conditions may be beaten, abused, raped, deported or even killed. (Craig et al. 2007: 12)

This atmosphere is reproduced in Broomfield's film, which makes clear how its characters have no alternative, once they are caught in the Snakeheads' web. In one case, one of them gives vent to his desperation when he is told that his mother has been threatened by his money-lenders back in China: 'I shouldn't have left. I wanted my mum to have a better life.'

According to the 2002 UK Census, some 250,000 ethnic Chinese live in Britain, but unofficial estimates almost double their number (Waugh 2007: 189); some figures assess 170,000 to 200,000 undocumented Chinese workers (Pai 2008: 252). They mostly come from the poor south-western province of Fujian:[9] from that area came both the so-called Dover 58 (who were found suffocated in a tomato lorry in June 2000)[10] and the twenty-three victims of the Morecambe Bay 2004 tragedy. Ai Qin, the protagonist of Nick Broomfield's *Ghosts*, is a single mother abandoned by her husband. She decides to leave Fujian in order to support her child financially, and contracts a debt of $25,000 dollars in order to be smuggled into Britain.

From its very beginning, Ai Qin's journey is marked by a succession of claustrophobic spaces, inevitably reminiscent of the suffocating and menacing settings of Gothic writing (Kosofsky Sedgwick 1986: 5).[11] On her sad departure from home, she anxiously tries to open her coach window and to say goodbye to her family and baby son, but she is not successful. This is the emblematic beginning of a six-month journey, during which she is pushed into all sorts of situations and means of transportation, and her existence becomes increasingly hidden and, in many cases, spectral.

Broomfield's camera conveys all this in two ways. First, he dwells on factual details, such as Ai Qin being closed in a small, coffin-like box that is screwed shut in the back of a truck (see Plate 1).

The scene brings to mind the African slaves amassed in ships' holds during the Middle Passage, or the Second World War deportation trains. More specifically, it is not far from first-hand accounts of the appalling ways in which Chinese migrants are smuggled into Britain:

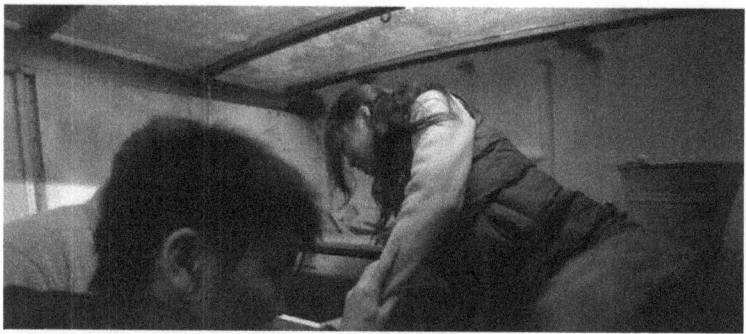

1 Ai Qin is made to hide in a box in the back of the smuggling truck.

We were asked to transfer to a waiting container full of cartons and people. ... We had to climb on top of the cartons and crawl to the far end in the dark where there was a gap between the cartons and the wall dividing us from the driver's cab. There was a 2 ft gap between the top of the boxes and the roof of the lorry. We guessed that there were washing-machines in the boxes. There was a wooden shelf halfway down this narrow space. People could stand below the shelf and others could stand or sit on the shelf.

When my eyes got used to the dark, I could see that we were all tightly packed together. There were sixteen of us in all. It was really cold. ... It was a twenty-hour journey and no toilet stops. There was such a dank and mouldy smell in the container already that even if people pissed inside the truck I wouldn't have been able to smell it. (Gupta 2007: 174)

Secondly, Broomfield employs less realistic, more suggestive images, as when Ai Qin and her fellow undocumented bordertrekkers are projected as transparent figures on to the map which re-traces their journey through Eastern Europe: as a consequence of this visual choice, the texture of these characters acquires an ethereal, ghost-like presence, intensified by their surroundings of misty mountains.

Ai Qin's stay in Britain, characterised by a succession of menial, exploitative jobs, is presented as having analogous features through a directorial wealth of details accompanied by some symbolic images. In the company of her fellow undocumented migrants, Ai Qin lives a life cut off from the rest of British society, a life mostly

2 Ai Qin at the window.

spent in shabby, overcrowded houses and unsafe working places. Window panes (shown from both the inside and the outside) are a recurrent element in the film, a transparent barrier separating this group of people from the rest of society: on one occasion, Ai Qin writes something on one of them with her finger (see Plate 2), signifying the nebulous, precarious trace left by her presence.

For a while she works in a meat-processing factory, stunned by the endless rows of carcasses and the deafening noise. The overall effect induces a comparison between the meat and the workers, which becomes inescapable when a truck is shown entering the factory: the camera dwells on the caged animals it is transporting, thus hinting at the journey previously undertaken by Ai Qin and her fellow migrants. Similarly to Lewycka's poultry, then, this part of the film traces an animal meat/human flesh parallel, related to the animalisation of new slaves.

Broomfield's work poignantly conveys one typical feature of the phenomenon of new slaveries (which stands in relief in Lewycka's *Two Caravans*, too): if undocumented migrants can be described as modern ghosts haunting the complacent conscience of British society, their haunting is not limited to specific, circumscribed spaces. They are potentially everywhere, disseminated throughout the country: Broomfield is at a remove from most contemporary European cinema on migrants, which has used the city as its privileged setting (Loshitzky 2010: 45). In *Ghosts* any building may host some of these contemporary spectres, be they factory, agricultural, domestic or sexual workers. Any factory, building site, means of transportation, cultivated field or house is potentially included in the British concentrationary archipelago, and can contain, hide and exacerbate the suffering of these exploited people.

In the film, Ai Qin refuses the non-coercive offer to work in a 'massage place'; hence, the movie does not broaden its perspective on the sex trade. According to Hsiao-Hung Pai's investigations, this reality is sometimes marked by a constant mobility which makes the overall picture of the concentrationary archipelago even more complex: to pander to customers' taste for variety, 'the Misses get rotated each week, sent to different parlours. They have to perform well in their week's slot in each parlour, to make sure they'll be invited back again. ... Swapping, I discovered, is standard practice in the sex trade' (Pai 2008: 172). One might expect a disorienting effect arising from this. And one might wonder whether a similar effect is produced by the transfers among various detention centres set up by the British authorities which independent sources describe as 'unexpected, unexplained and sometimes frequent', causing 'distress, disorientation and loss of contact between detainees and their families, friends and legal representatives' (Crawley and Lester 2005: 20). Incidentally, the Nazi concentrationary system likewise moved its victims from one camp to another according to workforce needs; this happened especially from 1942, when the war effort made the economic exploitation of prisoners more pressing (Giustini 2010: 36).

The presence of new slaveries, then, permeates British society so much that it goes well beyond claustrophobic interiors. This is well exemplified by the final part of the tragedy of the film's characters, set in the Morecambe Bay area. Their arrival is welcomed by a view of the bay crowned with a rainbow; when Ai Qin says 'I hope this is a new beginning', her best friend Xiao Li replies: 'I think that rainbow is a good omen. It announces a new beginning.' Unfortunately, this seemingly idyllic landscape is soon shattered by the harsh reality of their lives. After being insulted and beaten up by white British cockle-pickers who do not want them to intrude in their best picking spots (when shooting the film, Broomfield's crew were similarly driven away by local cockle-pickers, as shown in Hoeferlin's 'The Making of *Ghosts*, 2006), their boss decides that they will go there anyway, at night. At this point, in a sort of circular structure, the film goes back to where it started, to the

3 The group of Chinese cockle-pickers on the roof of the van, surrounded by the rising tide.

scenes on the beach that anticipated the film's tragic ending: the audience is again given some dialogue heard at the beginning before the scenes set in China, and can make much more sense of it. The characters find themselves on the roof of their van, surrounded by the rising tide, secluded not by walls now, but by the sea, and most of them will soon drown (see Plate 3).

They can use technology to call for help, but they cannot locate themselves, even vaguely, so that it is as if they were not there at all: Xiao Li is shown while he is phoning for help without being able to explain where they are.[12] Mobile phones are described by Bonini (2010: 73–4, 81) as functioning like mobile homes for migrants, as vital links with their families and work opportunities. Their uselessness in Broomfield's film is significant of how these migrants move spectrally in the British landscape without occupying any place, like Little Bee and her fellow inmates when leaving the detention centre (see Chapter 3.3). The ending of *Ghosts* follows Ai Qin, luckily saved from drowning, who is finally flown back to China. At her arrival, she tearfully asks her son 'Don't you recognise mummy?', as if afraid that she will not be acknowledged even by the person dearest to her after almost a year of spectral, hidden life.

The suggestions evoked by the drowning scenes are many. First, the sea points back to the history of slavery and its horrors, to the bodies of African slaves thrown overboard during the Atlantic trade. Secondly, this is reminiscent of the classic 'sea-Gothic' literature from the Romantic period, inspired by the horrors of the sea.[13] Thirdly, their separation from the rest of British society is again emblematic of how varied the typologies of their spectral presence can be, far from being simply limited to indoor spaces. According to Hazel Andrews and Les Roberts (2012: 3–4), British coastal areas have been particularly affected by the 'liminal experience of migrancy', not least because their concentration of hotels and guest houses met the requirements of the national dispersal policy; commenting on the specific area of Morecambe Bay and its 2004 tragedy, they evoke the contrast between two different kinds of spatial identity:

> the precarious and un-navigable landscape of Morecambe Sands becomes a metonym for the increasingly destabilising landscapes of trans- or post-national capitalist mobility. Moreover, the settlement of asylum seekers and refugees in UK coastal resorts ... has exposed the underlying tensions and social divisions between representations that play on the ludic, touristic heritage of these resorts and

those which address the marginality and exclusion that characterises the other set of mobilities and meanings evoked by these spaces. (Andrews and Roberts 2012: 6)

This confrontation between two identitarian positions is an issue in Broomfield's *Ghosts*, too, beginning from its very title (another aspect which confers a Gothic quality on this movie). Partly because of what has been said so far, before watching the film anyone with even a vague knowledge of new forms of slavery, or of the Morecambe Bay tragedy, or of the film's plot, is likely to associate its title with the lives of its Chinese protagonists. Moreover, the first sentence uttered in the film by the group's boss while he is driving the van on the beach through the howling wind ('Ghosts won't come out when it's like this') calls to mind some Chinese superstitions, perhaps unveiling some sort of prejudice on the audience's part.

As the film proceeds, the reference contained in the title proves both expectations to be ill founded. In Chinese, 'ghosts' is the polite word for 'foreign devil' or 'evil foreigners' (Gupta 2007: 159, 161). Realisation of this is likely to come slowly, on the occasions when white Britons are referred to as such: 'It's all you need. Ghosts don't care', it is said about a forged worked permit; when Ai Qin protests that the name printed on it is not hers, implicitly affirming her identity, her boss replies 'It doesn't matter. ... I'm selling it cheap.' Thus, 'ghosts' can indicate both the Chinese migrants and the white Britons who exploit them or occupy those countless intermediate positions which Primo Levi would have called the 'grey zone'.[14]

My point is that this linguistic ambivalence can offer some insights into the import of Broomfield's story, and into the implications of new slaveries in Britain. By shaping a specular relationship between citizens and undocumented migrants or new slaves, who can both be seen as spectres, *Ghosts* certainly hints at one classic Gothic trope – 'the monstrous double signifying duplicity and evil nature' (Botting 1996: 2) – and at contemporary and successful Gothic movies like M. Night Shyamalan's *The Sixth Sense* (1999) and Alejandro Amenábar's *The Others* (2001), where the supposed difference between humans and ghosts is surprisingly reversed. Nevertheless, *Ghosts* points to these literary and filmic Gothic models while departing from them at the same time. There is no literal double here, or an unexpected final denouement about the difference between the living and the spectres. Rather, *Ghosts* reformulates the ways in which nineteenth-century fiction 'projected the darkness of Gothic fears and desires on to other cultures, peoples and places' (Botting 1996: 154). The crucial difference here, rather than between the dead and the living, seems to be between those who are dehumanising and those who are dehumanised. Even when they go out to buy (mostly unaffordable) food,[15] Ai Qin and her mates do not mix with the local population, who hardly take any notice of them[16] – not to mention some instances of crass racism, or when they are targeted by police raids. As both are associated with the film's spectral title, the ensuing implication is that the dehumanising ones are in the end dehumanised themselves.

In the history of the relationship between Gothic and slavery, this Janus-faced structure is nothing new. Historicising interpretations of *The Rime of the Ancient Mariner* have raised a similar point. Raimonda Modiano, for instance, examines Coleridge's interest in the figure of Cain, whereby Cain becomes a ghostlike slave who mirrors his brother's spectrality for the very reason that he killed Abel. Modiano connects him with the Ancient Mariner who, in killing the Albatross, becomes both tormentor and victim; he

> instinctively destroys this very assumption of brotherly love and unity for which he finds no immediate corroboration in the ice-bound and distinctly hostile environment around him, nor for that matter did Coleridge find much evidence of it in his world, where the daily traffic in slaves and slaughter of human beings not only in France, ... but also in African countries by Africans themselves, offered a demoralizing picture of 'humanity cannibalizing itself'. (Modiano 1999: 209)[17]

A similar kind of binding relationship was extensively discussed in Western philosophy (by Rousseau, Hegel and Montesquieu) around the nature of the master–servant dynamics and the abolitionist debate: the master, so the argument goes, was bound to become a dehumanised tyrant to himself, and therefore a slave (Knox-Shaw 1993: 299–300).[18] Holocaust studies, too, has produced reflections of this kind: the dehumanisation of perpetrators was expressed by Primo Levi in his historic *If This Is a Man* (1958), where he described all those who took part in the genocide as sharing 'a uniform internal desolation' (1996: 127–8).[19] Significantly, in the edition Levi himself edited for secondary schools he added a footnote (1986: 161, n. 1) stating that this very passage encloses the deepest meaning of the novel, i.e. how the concentration camp denies humanity and human dignity 'in both victims and oppressors' (translation mine).

What is new in Broomfield's *Ghosts* is, of course, the changed context. The film can be interpreted as an indictment of the deep ethical crisis that pervades British society at the beginning of the third millennium. As remarked above (and suggested by Sinclair's epigraph to this chapter), it is a crisis involving not only those who directly persecute new slaves but Western society as a whole, what Primo Levi called 'the grey zone'. According to him, 'the ill-defined area of ambiguity and compromise to be born from political coercion' created a generation marked by a fragile moral conscience, 'But how strong is ours, the Europeans of today? How would each of us behave if driven by necessity and at the same time lured by seduction?' (Levi 1989: 51–2) In the film there are exceptions, of course, as for example when the Chinese migrants are offered tea by a kind woman for whom they have been picking apples, or when Ai Qin chats in friendly manner with a British fellow worker. In other words, these exceptions seem to have welcomed Avery Gordon's call (2008: 196): 'It is essential to see the things and the people who are primarily unseen and banished to the periphery of our social graciousness. At a minimum it is essential because they see you and address you.' Accordingly, Broomfield moves closer to Gerry Turcotte's view of the Gothic and its attempt to penetrate 'the outskirts, the excluded, often to show (either intentionally or not) how inextricably related is the margin to the centre, thereby blurring the very basis upon which such fraudulent polarities are established' (Turcotte 2009: 22);[20] it is a way to overcome Derrida's 'visor effect', where the spectre 'looks at us and sees us not see it even when it is there. A spectral asymmetry interrupts here all specularity' (Derrida 2006: 6). This communicative possibility will be further explored in Chapter 6.2.

The Gothic as a genre, then, needs adjusting under the pressure of new slaveries. *Ghosts* clearly belongs to the territory of realism. Broomfield's camera pays minute attention to details, especially those regarding the working activities of the exploited migrants, such as the raking and sifting of the beach mud in order to collect the cockles. As the final credits say, inspiration was taken from the *Guardian* articles by Hsiao-Hung Pai: 'the Norfolk house in which Ai Qin and her co-workers live was very similar to the one in Liverpool uncovered by Hsiao-Hung Pai and was filmed exactly as Broomfield and his crew found it' (DVD booklet).[21] Remarkably, however, it is a peculiar kind of realism: naturalism is broken several times by estranging effects, such as the use of maps to explain the route taken by the migrants, or subtitles providing important data like Ai Qin's daily earnings in China, the duration of her entire journey and her working hours in England. All these practical details contribute to the formation of a 'low-key realist aesthetic that frequently operates at the intersection between fact and fiction' (DVD booklet).[22] This aesthetics bears a notable resemblance to Michael Winterbottom's *In This World* (2002, winner of the 2003 Berlin Festival's Golden Bear), where the protagonist's travel routes can also be followed on a map. Sissy Helff (2008: 289) calls Winterbottom's technique 'mockumentary': according to her, 'in a Brechtian sense' it 'reminds the audience of its own constructedness' and 'visualises the "realness" of refugees' journeys'.[23]

Broomfield's form of realism constitutes a markedly distinguishing feature that makes *Ghosts* stand out from the main bulk of the Gothic tradition. When observing how 'Gothic elements have crept into filmic genres from science fiction to film noir and from thriller to comedy', Heidi Kaye (2000: 180) does not seem to include movies like Broomfield's. Eighteenth-century Gothic fiction, too, is usually defined through coordinates which have little, if anything, to do with *Ghosts*' language: 'a writing of excess' (Botting 1996: 1), 'sublime ... associated with grandeur and magnificence' (3),[24] where the presence of romance is never ousted by the predominance of the novel (24, 128), 'exciting rather than informing ... fed uncultivated appetites for marvellous and strange events, instead of instructing readers with moral lessons' (4). When it comes to non-Western, postcolonial cultures and their relationship with the Gothic, Lucie Armitt (2000: passim) identifies the mode of *magical* realism as a privileged site.[25]

Ghosts, however, seems again to fit a different model. There seems to be a historicist 'counter-tradition' in Gothic studies much closer to the language and sensibility of *Ghosts*. Chris Baldick and Robert Mighall highlight a kind of critical approach based on historical and literary research, on the links between the eighteenth-century Gothic and bourgeois realism, Protestant scepticism, modern rationality and Whiggery. They claim that these links have been increasingly marginalised from the 1930s onwards, by a dominant tradition which has privileged the anti-Enlightenment, anti-realist, spiritual, oneiric and later psychological strain of the Gothic (Baldick and Mighall 2000: 211–18). As for nineteenth-century fiction, the same approach has led to the 'anxiety model', i.e. to interpreting Gothic works as the embodiment of the (repressive) Victorian bourgeoisie's fear of the (liberating) Other: 'the bourgeoisie paralysed by dread ... everything is a source of fear except perfect stasis'.[26] Baldick and

Mighall (2000: 226) propose a different, more Marxist-oriented reading that can with some justification be applied to the context of *Ghosts*, if adapted to Broomfield's wider frame dominated by twenty-first-century world economy:

> If one approaches the bourgeoisie from a different starting point though – from the stock exchange rather than from the psychiatric couch – one is likely to be led to the opposite conclusion: that everything is a source of profit except perfect stasis. At least in Marx's account, the bourgeoisie is the most restlessly dynamic and iconoclastic class in history, driven as it is to embark upon ceaseless transformation and innovation. ... [T]he true bourgeois can afford to regard his 'Others' not with terror but with equanimity or even delight, because, from opium fiends in China to wielders of 'Pink Dollars' in California, they represent what he loves best – a new market.

If one engaged in a search for a suitable ancestor for works like Broomfield's, then one should turn to William Godwin's *Caleb Williams* (1794), where the eponymous protagonist is relentlessly pursued, gaoled and persecuted by the representatives of an unfair system. Incidentally, the novel's original title (*Things as They Are; or, The Adventures of Caleb Williams*), with its profession of truth and realism, reinforces this claim. Analogously to this, what *Ghosts* is supposed to inspire in its white British audience is not terror but a sort of ethical awareness.[27] The above-mentioned choice of documentary realism may be accounted for by the need to picture the complex, ever-changing face of the British concentrationary archipelago as fully as possible, within a context of global economic forces which is just as complex. In a way, then, fear is exactly what *Ghosts* does not aim at. Far from indulging in the obscurity, irrationality and unrepresentability of the whole phenomenon, to unveil the reality and to clear the mystery around these migrants can be seen as a necessary step to spark awareness, in order to avoid breeding the monstrous fears (such as asylophobia) which always tend to run counter to multiculturalism.

Through the techniques outlined above, *Ghosts* intends to present as much as possible of this picture: the poverty in Fujian, the well-organised people-smugglers, the appalling travelling conditions and, later, the conditions of living and working in Britain. The film contrives to show how whole sectors of the British society are involved more or less directly in this system of exploitation, from factories to agriculture, retailers, employment agencies. Ai Qin's boss calls cigarettes 'ghost food at the employment agency. With this, you can get a good job from them.' And when Ai Qin asks 'Ghosts take bribes?', he replies 'Who doesn't?'[28] As Avery Gordon (2008: 169) writes about the import of the capitalist market on contemporary forms of haunting, this 'is a market where exchange relations continue to transform the living into the dead, a system of social relations that fundamentally objectifies and dominates a putatively free society'.

Unfortunately, the institutional assault on migrants is not destined to stop even in the face of tragedies like the Morecambe Bay one. The family of those cockle-pickers and of the so-called Dover 58 never succeeded in receiving just compensation from the British authorities (Gupta 2007: 187; Pai 2008: 255). As its final credits say, *Ghosts* was also designed to be a fund-raising project to cover the families' remaining debts.[29]

In the wake of this tragedy the British government issued the Gangmaster Licensing Act. According to Monica Ali's MP character Fairweather:

> The GLA set up an authority that is tiny and self-funding, it will hardly scratch the surface, but I guess as long as we don't have more mass drownings or other *spectaculars*, then nobody's really going to notice or mind. Nobody's in favour of raising food prices, you know. (Ali 2010: 327)

That the tragedy had little effect is also proved by the fact that the Morecambe Bay cockle-pickers were replaced very soon by other Chinese migrants desperate for work, and only one week after the tragedy forty migrant workers found themselves dangerously stranded there (Waugh 2007: 190, 192).

4.2 Photography: Behind a screen in Dana Popa's *Not Natasha* (2009)

The photographic exhibition *Disposable People: Contemporary Global Slavery*, which toured Great Britain between 2008 and 2010, arose from the dissatisfaction with the celebrating mood dominating the 2007 anniversary of the abolition of the slave trade, examined in Chapter 1.1. As its curator Mark Sealy said, the 'national focus on the 1807 Act had the effect of glossing over the political realities and legacy of slavery today' (Sealy 2008: n.p.).

Sealy was also involved in another project more apposite to the scope of this volume: the award-winning exhibition *Not Natasha*, by the Romanian photographer Dana Popa, which toured England

4 Maria behind a window.

in 2009–2010.³⁰ *Not Natasha* is concerned with sexual slaves in Britain, and touches on tropes and key images similar to those analysed so far. 'Natasha is a nickname given to prostitutes with Eastern European looks', says the first of Popa's short captions which alternate with the photos in the exhibition catalogue (Popa 2009: 6); the following one adds 'Sex-trafficked girls hate it' (8). The volume also contains longer captions (such as a victim's description of a gruesome gang rape, 18) and a final two-page report; but the short captions prove, I think, extremely effective in their horrifying swing between hinting and hiding. See, for instance, '"I was twelve years old. I don't want to talk about it." Alina' (32).

In a way, their form may be seen as reflecting the fragmentary nature of the pictures: these enslaved women are often portrayed as veiled, screened, filtered by cracked window-panes, half-covered in darkness or showing a limited part of themselves, with their faces turned or hidden (see Plate 4).

When Rahila Gupta (2007: 61–2) interviewed another 'Natasha', she noticed: '*She does not make eye contact except fleetingly – she says it is a habit she developed when working as a prostitute. She hated the clients so much she never looked at them and now she has trouble looking anyone in the eye.*'

Popa's approach to her subjects conveys several facets of new slaveries discussed in this volume: the hidden, ghostly existence of new slaves; their claustrophobic sites of exploitation[31] – sometimes represented without their victims in all their desolation, at other times taking the outside view from the window, as in a Soho street where businessmen are strolling (Popa 2009: 10–11).

5 Elena's face covered by her wig.

The women's broken, hard-to-recompose personalities are made emblematic by a close-up of Clarisa's forearm covered in self-inflicted scars (26–7). Page 67 shows Elena's long hair combed forward to cover her face; it is a wig which her pimp allowed her to wear (see Plate 5).

Next to it, on page 66, the caption says only 'Why do you have to dig up my life again?' This suggests the more practical reason behind Popa's particular strategy, namely the need for extreme delicacy towards women who, after having been reduced to an inhuman state, are scarred by shame and fear of reprisals: 'I had to be both discreet and protective,' the author writes (91). The extreme difficulty that she encountered when trying to narrate, 'dig up', recompose the victims' lives is shared with some authors discussed in Chapters 2 and 3.

Another facet that Popa shares with most of the authors studied in this volume is the desire to describe the geographically wide, globalised frame of the new slave trade, which includes Soho, and Britain generally, only as a destination point. In the same way as Waugh began her investigation in Chisinau, Popa visited and photographed Moldova, 'the poorest country in Europe, and the main exporter of sex slaves for the whole continent' in 2006 and 2007 (90). There she captured 'the *ghostly emptiness* of the places where a while ago the missing women used to be a natural presence' (91;

6 Poverty and absence back in Moldova.

italics mine), with their dignified, albeit crumbling, poverty (see Plate 6).

As Mark Sealy writes, in *Not Natasha* viewers are faced with 'the ongoing misery of those who have been left behind to wait'; where the violence of poverty meets the violence of exploitation,

> it is not enough to talk about the actual victim .... None of this makes sense unless we take time to analyse the cultural and economic conditions that make it possible for women's lives to be seen only in terms of their potential for exploitation. (Sealy 2009: n.p.)

Not Natasha proves photography to be as effective as literature to achieve this aim.

4.3 Drama: Traumatic deconstructions of the stage in Clare Bayley's *The Container* (2007), Cora Bissett and Stef Smith's *Roadkill* (2011), Abi Morgan's *Fugee* (2008) and Lucy Kirkwood's *It Felt Empty When the Heart Went at First but It Is Alright Now* (2009)

> No one leave home unless home is the mouth of a shark. ... They ask me *how did you get here*? Can't you see it on my body? The Libyan desert red with immigrant bodies, the Gulf of Aden bloated, the city of Rome with no jacket. I hope the journey meant more than miles because all of my children are there in the water. ... I want to make love, but my hair smells of war and running and running. I want to lay down, but these countries are like uncles who touch you when you're young and asleep. Look at all these borders, foaming at the mouth with bodies broken and desperate. ... I spent days and nights in the stomach of a truck; I did not come out the same. Sometimes it feels like someone else is wearing my body.
>
> Warsan Shire, 'Conversations about Home (at the Deportation Centre)' (2011: 24–5)

What follows focuses on four plays concerning new slaveries. In order to stage the forms of physical imprisonment involved, they envision and employ dramatic spaces in very characteristic ways, indicative of a highly creative conception of drama. This is one of the reasons why the so-called verbatim theatre and its testimony-based plays[32] are here taken into consideration only through passing references. Alongside stylistic reasons, this choice has to do with the issue of agency: verbatim theatre has been taken to task for foregrounding the victims' passivity (Farrier 2012: 433),[33] whereas at the end of this chapter I will contend that these playwrights' non-naturalistic representations confer on their protagonists a more active subjectivity.

Clare Bayley's play *The Container*[34] is set in a freight container driven from north-western Italy to the north of France. Two Somali women, a middle-aged Afghan businessman, a young Afghan woman and a young Kurd are the undocumented immigrants travelling inside it. They share a wish to reach England and begin a new life, but they are utterly at the mercy of the Turkish 'agent'. As far as the whereabouts and progress of their journey are concerned, they are completely helpless:

> AHMAD. Can you hear something?
> *JEMAL listens.*
> JEMAL. Nothing. I can't hear anything.
> *A pause. JEMAL gives up and sits down.*
> FATIMA. Why have we stopped?
> *Nobody answers her.*
> You. Rude man. Why have we stopped?
> JEMAL. I'm not the fucking tour guide, am I? I don't fucking know why we stopped.
> FATIMA. Don't listen to him, Asha. You see? Always so rude. And bad language, too.
> *The doors are opened. The sudden light is dazzling. They all melt back into their hiding places.*
> *MARIAM enters.*
> *She stands, trying to see in the darkness, her hand over her mouth and nose, because of the smell in there. She retches. The doors are closed behind her. AHMAD emerges.*
> AHMAD. Where's the agent?
> FATIMA. Where's the food?
> JEMAL. Do you know where we are?
> *The truck starts moving.*
>
> (Bayley 2007: 4–5)

One encounters here the disorientation discussed in Chapter 3.3 about Cleave's *The Other Hand* – though, in this case, related to the journey *towards* Britain. During his research in Sangatte detention centre, Tony Grisoni (scriptwriter of Winterbottom's *In This World*) was told by one refugee: 'you don't know what country you're in;[35] you just want to get it over with. It [the journey] was something to be forgotten' (Tan 2008: 305).[36] The quotation above shows how the characters' situation is bound to create tensions, which in the course of the play are further raised by the pregnant Mariam being sick again, by everybody's inevitable need to empty their bowels inside the container (Bayley 2007: 11) and by the secrets each of them hides (Mariam's pregnancy is not the only one). During their impassioned exchanges, they sometimes reveal parts of their personal stories, signalling a background of poverty, violence and war not far from Popa's photographic subjects: Mariam's husband was a teacher beheaded by the Talibans in front of his class of girls (31);[37] Somali Fatima and Asha crossed the Mediterranean by boat and lived in a refugee camp (12–14). The Kurdish Kemal's story is significant of how Kafkaesque the life of an undocumented migrant can be, as shown in Chapter 3.4 on Lewycka's *Two Caravans*:

> FATIMA. What did you do that they made you leave England? Eh? You a man with bad secrets. You said it yourself. You a liar.
> JEMAL. Yeah, I'm a liar.
>
> I come from Turkey. My parents ran away from Turkey when I was a little kid. They ran away because the Turkish police came to get my dad one day. ... We managed to get to England. I grew up there. I went to school there. I met my wife there. But she's not British either.
>
> Then suddenly the British say, it's safe to go back to Turkey now. Turkey is safe for Kurds, they say. Turkey is almost Europe now.
>
> But the prisons are still full of Kurds. ...
>
> I fought it. I fought it all the way to the High Court. My wife was nine months pregnant and I lost my case. They took me from the court and put me in the detention centre.
>
> And they sent me back.
>
> But this time, I'm going to lie. I'm going to get back into that country any way I can.
>
> I'm going to say I'm from Iraq. I've come all the way from Baghdad, non-stop travel. Clever lying, you see.
>
> I'll keep trying until I get there.
>
> (Bayley 2007: 43–4)

The emotional climax of the plot is reached when the agent claims that the truck's driver wants more money. Mariam cannot pay, so sexual exploitation comes into play again, when the agent claims that she can pay the driver only in kind. The moral crux of the matter becomes how much characters can (or are willing to) risk in order to prevent a pregnant woman from being raped (Bayley 2007: 32–40). *The Container* represents yet another powerful reminder of the British concentrationary archipelago also including means of transportation, which 'become mobile prisons within a foreign landscape' (Loshitzky 2010: 17). It should also be noted that institutional practices transport migrants in not so different ways. In the words of Daren, sixteen years old:

The British concentrationary archipelago   117

I stayed in Dungavel about two weeks. One early morning they woke me up. They said I was going. They put us in a van. They told me the place where we were going but I didn't know the name. The van went from early morning to 11 at night. I needed to pee but they said no, can't stop. They stopped the van to change drivers, but not to let us pee. We had a bottle of water – we threw out the water and peed in the bottle. We were six in the van. We arrived at night. They took us to one place, but they couldn't open the gate, so we went off again … to Oakington. (Crawley and Lester 2005: 21)[38]

One cannot help thinking of Levi's descriptions of the trains that crossed Europe taking prisoners to the camps (Levi 1989: 85–9). According to the historian Carlo Greppi (2012: 19), this is a part of Holocaust history that, in spite of its importance, has not been studied in depth. Amassing people in sealed wagons with very little air, food and water implied a degradation of their human nature, a 'precocious dehumanisation' (91, translation mine) preparing them for what was to come – not much differently from some new slaves' stories, where terrifying journeys are followed by labour exploitation on British soil.

As said above, *The Container*'s spatial frame constitutes one of its main assets. A note to the text says that the 'play was written to be performed in an actual container' (Bayley 2007: 2).[39] I had the privilege of being in the (necessarily restricted) audience of one performance[40] of *The Container* directed by Tom Wright at The Young Vic. It took place *in front of* The Young Vic, where an actual container occupied one half of the main road called The Cut. The audience was made to sit inside on makeshift seats, their backs against the walls, extremely close to the actors – never further than approximately four metres from them, and from the physical and psychological suffering being performed. The proximity to the action was magnified by long spells of complete darkness, so that the characters were literally left in the dark about their journey; the only natural light came with the rare openings of the container's back door, and lighting was provided by the characters moving their torches, which contributed to conferring an aura of ghostliness on to the characters themselves.

From the perspective of naturalistic verisimilitude, it might be objected that stowaways are usually hidden behind goods that occupy most of the space in the containers (Gupta 2007: 174; Waugh 2007: 195). All the same, the whole context seemed to be reaching towards an extreme realism, towards an environment capable of conveying those claustrophobic sensations of entrapment that, as stated in relation to Broomfield's *Ghosts* (Chapter 4.1), are present throughout experiences of new slaveries. Not by chance, before entering the container the audience was ominously warned that anyone could be let out if he or she banged on the door, but no re-admission would be allowed.[41] In David Farrier's words (2011: 183), 'the production sought to achieve an experience of heat, confinement and disorientation that was as close as possible to the real thing'.

According to Oldfield's *Chords of Freedom* (see Chapter 1.1), a similar effect was the aim of some slavery museums in their recreation of the Middle Passage and in their effort to 'capture or simulate this experience – "to make it authentic"' by employing walk-through displays, atmospheric noises and assorted sound recordings. Visitors' feedback ranged from saying that they felt frightened to pointing out 'the risk of trivialising the Transatlantic Slave Trade'. Oldfield's reflections are worth quoting here: 'The presumption here is that we can "know" the past by experiencing or re-experiencing it. Even if these were possible, where are the limits? ... We need to ask ourselves whether, in cases such as these, "absolute empathy" is either possible or desirable' (Oldfield 2007: 123–5). In his analysis of *The Container*, Farrier (2011: 184) raises similar issues, about 'the efficacy of acts of substitution and the potential for affective experiences to convey *response* to a more defined sense of *responsibility*'.

Bayley's play certainly employs space in a highly effective way, constraining its audience in a much more all-encompassing atmosphere than the museums described by Oldfield. The ensuing empathic effect that it produces undoubtedly constitutes the first, necessary step for any artistic work dealing with new slaveries, if one wishes to operate in a direction opposite to the spectralisation that new slaves are subjected to.[42] On the other hand, one might be feeling as doubtful as Oldfield and Farrier, as far as 'absolute empathy' is concerned. In *The Container*, this empathy is sought for through a textually mono-layered simplicity, a lack of significant connotations and suggestiveness, as if dealing with new slaves necessarily implied being limited to a verbal straightforwardness related to their tragic condition. Can this dramatic language run the risk of over-simplifying their 'right to complex personhood' (Gordon 2008: 4), one might wonder. Can it risk reaffirming, in spite of its gut-wrenching reconstruction and declared aim, the infra-human nature (Gunning 2011: passim) that is constantly expected of new slaves?

In the light of these questions, the second play examined in this chapter is to be seen as sharing *The Container*'s dramatic technique while at the same time departing from it. In the opening scene of Bissett and Smith's *Roadkill* (2011: 23–6), the audience is transported by bus to the performance flat where the story takes place. While they are being driven, they witness Nigerian fourteen-year-old Mary's childish enthusiasm for her arrival in Britain. In order to render the scene more credible and empathic, the 'Performance Note' (18) and the stage directions (23, 58) recommend adapting these scenes (and the policeman who later intervenes) to the town where the play is performed.[43] On the bus, one senses that something shady is going on when 'auntie' Martha briskly silences Mary, who is recounting to the audience/passengers how only five days earlier she discovered that she would be travelling to Scotland (25). After that the audience is led into the performance flat by an usher, who will manage their movements among the various rooms to help them follow the story (26, 27, 31, 52–3): the rape of Mary by her 'master' Djall and how she is made to meet a great many punters.

The dramatic conception sustaining *Roadkill*, then, shares *The Container*'s hyper-realism based on a highly credible immersion in a real-life environment, on a vision close to Broomfield's and Winterbottom's mockumentary (see Chapter 4.1). The play's empathic effect, though, is also enriched by non-naturalistic strategies that, on the whole, are to be seen as Brecht-like alienating effects, triggering reflections on some facets of the new slaveries. Mary's rape, for example, is shown on a TV set through an animated cartoon, thus eschewing any prurience towards gruesome events and introducing a medium disquietingly hinting at Mary's young age: '*The TV which was playing Beyoncé fades to an animation; it is MARY, recognisable, the little girl in the white dress; she is breathing heavily, figures loom towards her; men's faces morph into wolves ripping a ragdoll that is MARY apart*' (28–9). Later on, 'field reports' on Mary from 'PunterNet review site' are heard and projected on to walls, ceilings and her silent body (33), which reminds one of Abigail's written body in Abani's novel (Chapter 3.2); besides giving a crowd effect, this is likely to leave room for reflection on the ambiguous facets of that Internet culture everyone is so familiar with. Unlike *The Container*, *Roadkill* is not after a passively emphatic inclusion of the audience into the story, but it tries to instil an ethical feeling of responsibility that harks back to the question posed by Farrier above: when Martha organises a party for the flat's punters, she 'improvises greeting the audience in the hallway. Offers services, drinks, drugs' (52). This scene is particularly apposite to Farrier's reflections on *The Container*, when he makes reference to Julie Salverson's study of drama concerning asylum seekers, which is in turn inspired by Boal's theory of the theatre of the oppressed, 'where both spectator and actor become spect-actors: active agents in the negotiated representation of oppression' (Farrier 2011: 187–8).[44]

In *Roadkill*, the most non-naturalistic moment comes when Martha recounts how she deceived Mary's parents while her victim is sleeping beside her:

> A MAN *appears through the hole in the bed; spreads* MARY's *legs and begins having sex with her aggressively. His thrusts are in time with Martha's laughter, growing in manic-ness ... They both keep going to a climax. Huge video projections of other men's faces in orgasmic frenzy are projected onto the scene and the wall behind the bed; loud, aggressive, pounding rock music screeches over the scene.* MARTHA *and the* MAN *disappear.* MARY *slides through the hole as if escaping from her body ... to under the bed.* (Bissett and Smith 2011: 34)

Such a suggestive, symbolically charged scene may be read from the perspective of nightmare and trauma. The following pages analyse two plays that, like *Roadkill*, explore the centrality of traumas in new slaveries (suggested also by the last sentence of Warsan Shire's epigraph opening this chapter) through a non-naturalistic disruption of stage co-ordinates. The import of trauma and Post Traumatic Stress Disorder on new slaves has already been explored in Chapter 3.1. Here it is worth examining how their consequent peculiar way of narrating and seeing the world can be translated on the stage, in two plays where the traumatic experience of new slaves is performed, rather than through a detailed reconstruction of their ordeal, by way of an expressionist destructuring of stage spaces. This destructuring is designed to hint at the destructured space of the new slaves' traumatised minds; in other words, the performing stage is turned into a non-naturalistic equivalent of the troubled psychological state of these migrants, in a continuous overlapping of temporal and spatial dimensions. In Cathy Caruth's words, the traumatic event refuses 'to be simply located, in its insistent appearance outside the boundaries of any single place or time' (Caruth 1995: 9). As in the case of *Roadkill*, one can also assume

The British concentrationary archipelago 121

that this mode of presentation creates a sort of Brechtian 'alienating effect' which, rather than inspiring self-identification, may be capable of triggering critical distance and reflection.

Abi Morgan's *Fugee* is a text centred on the lives of undocumented minors in Britain, whose institutional detention is liable to leave deep marks on their mental health (see Chapter 3.3). The play is meant for a large cast of (mostly) boys and girls, but it is often specified that this is the story of Kojo – a French-speaking, fourteen-year-old boy from the Ivory Coast. He is being lodged in a children's refuge and later, when he is age-disputed by the authorities, in a refugee hotel. The point is that Kojo is unable to simply narrate his ordeal to his counsellor, as bureaucracy requires:

> COUNSELLOR: Would you like to tell us a bit about your story, Kojo?
> *Silence.*
> Why you came to England?
> *Silence.*
> It says here...
> *The Counsellor reads the Social Worker's report in her hand.*
> You last saw your family on –
> KOJO: My eleventh ...
> TRANSLATOR: His eleventh –
> KOJO: Birthday.
> COUNSELLOR: I see. Would you like to tell me about it, Kojo?
> KOJO: No.
> COUNSELLOR: I can't help you if you don't tell me your story, dear.
> *Kojo stays silent.*
> So you're fourteen now ... It was three years ago.
> KOJO: Yes.
> COUNSELLOR: You must miss them very much.
> *Kojo suddenly scrapes back his chair.*
> TRANSLATOR: He doesn't want to talk about this.
> COUNSELLOR: Tomorrow, Kojo. We'll talk again tomorrow.
> (Morgan 2008: 170–1, original ellipsis)

As Bohmer and Shuman (2008: 141) write, 'Not being able to talk about a traumatic experience is, in fact, one of the hallmarks of PTSD'.[45] There are analogies, here, with what Gupta and Waugh had to struggle with during their research, with their interviewees swinging between the desire to speak and their inability to do so (see Chapter 3.1). How does *Morgan* narrate Kojo's story, then? *Fugee* often returns to its key moment, a street scene when Kojo has just stabbed a passer-by to death. See, for instance, the very beginning of the play:

SCENE ONE
> *An urban street, frozen mid moment like some dark, classical painting.*
> *[… A list of frozen street characters follows.]*
> *The blur of human traffic, frozen mid-step, all around.*
> *Kojo, a young boy, suddenly illuminated.*
>
> KOJO: My name is Kojo. The person playing me is an actor. I don't exist. Except in this story. This is my story. I choose where it starts. It starts now –
> *Suddenly the scene springs into action.*
> TRADER: Fuck fuck fuck –
> *The woman is screaming.*
> GIRL: He's gone, man. Dat man's gone.
> BOYFRIEND: Please can someone please get help?
> CLEANER: Turn him on his side. Turn him on his side. There's stuff coming from his mouth, bro.
> *The scene freezes again.*
> *Kojo points to the body of the Man stabbed on the pavement.*
> KOJO: That man. The man on the ground… I don't know his name. *(Pointing to Woman.)* There's a woman screaming.
> *The Woman starts screaming again and then freezes, silent.*
> She's screaming a lot.
> *The Woman starts screaming again.*
>
> (Morgan 2008: 145–6)

As this quotation shows, Morgan makes use of a series of non-naturalistic devices that tend to interrupt the flow of the story and the ensuing emotional involvement on the part of the audience. Besides its Brechtian implications, this expedient also harks back to Boal's theory of drama, 'halting the action to propose alternative gestures' (Farrier 2011: 188). Morgan's devices include the division into very short scenes (thirty-six of them composing a sum total of fifty-six pages); the employment of frozen scenes, where only some characters are allowed to move and explain or contextualise their role in the play; the recurring statement, by several actors coming out-of-character, that there are differences between themselves as actors and their respective role; and that the play is Kojo's story and not someone else's. Take, for example, Scene Three:

> *An urban street.*
> *The Young Woman with the buggy screams.*
> YOUNG WOMAN *(to audience)*: Hi, I'm the girl with the buggy, the one earlier?
> *The Young Woman screams to demonstrate –*
> It's really hard to do that. You can really damage your voice if you're

not careful. Don't worry. It's not a real baby.
The Young Woman pulls back the blanket in the buggy, holds up a pink plastic doll.
A real baby is much bigger than this. I don't know why they want me to speak. Just that I was there. Not me. Because I'm an actor. But the girl I'm playing. ...
The Young Woman with a buggy starts screaming at Kojo, the bloody knife in his hand.
Because this is his story. The kid. The kid with the knife... The one who's about to kill me.
The Young Woman starts screaming again.
KOJO: It's OK ... It's OK ...
YOUNG WOMAN: Fuck off.
KOJO: I'm not gonna ...
(Morgan 2008: 151–2, original ellipsis)

But the most important alienating device in *Fugee* is the constant, abrupt and uncontrollable intrusions of Kojo's past into the present, of his lost Ivorian life into his present asylum-seeking condition in Britain. This dismantling of spatial and temporal boundaries is effected through the presence of Kojo's family members, now dead. As Cathy Caruth writes when commenting on Freud's studies (1995: 5), 'the returning traumatic dream ... is, purely and inexplicably, the literal return of the event against the will of the one it inhabits'.[46] This is what happens immediately after Kojo proves unable to tell the Counsellor his story:

COUNSELLOR: Tomorrow, Kojo. We'll talk again tomorrow.
Kojo's Brother passes, dribbling a ball. Kojo watching him.
The Counsellor and the Translator follow his gaze, seeing nothing.
Kojo?
Kojo nods, sinking back into his chair.[47]

SCENE TWELVE
Kojo stands alone.
KOJO: *(to audience)* This is part of my story. Just part of my story. The story of my eleventh birthday.
I am walking along the dust track near my home. I am buying Coca-Cola for my mother.
Kojo's Mother passes, singing.
MOTHER: You see your father yet? Run and meet him.
(Morgan 2008: 171)[48]

Kojo's isolation is here indicative of the fact that traumatic memory 'has no social component; it is not addressed to anybody ... it is a solitary activity' (Van der Kolk and Van der Hart 1995:

163). Scene Twelve marks one of the attempts, on Kojo's part, to recount what happened to him on his eleventh birthday, when child soldiers stormed his village. The staging of that tragic day in Kojo's life will not emerge smoothly, but in bits and pieces, until a supposedly complete picture is delivered towards the end of the play, when Kojo narrates how he was turned into a child soldier himself (Morgan 2008: 182). In any case the completeness of Kojo's story remains in doubt: his past is complicated by moments, such as Scene Thirty-Four (196), when Kojo has become a child soldier and is made to kill his own father, who had supposedly been killed on the fateful day mentioned above: is it a real event or a projection of the guilt related to other atrocities he might have committed? Bohmer and Shuman (2008: 138) notice how the institutional approach towards asylum seekers is 'based on the (invalid) assumption that, for a story to be true, it must be told the same way each time. Many people, especially those who have suffered trauma, remember things somewhat differently each time.'[49]

If one agrees that *Fugee*'s mode of representation (based on a constant porosity between past and present, the inside of a sheltering refuge and a menacing outside) might enhance critical distance, what kind of awareness is it likely to stimulate? First, one might infer that the accommodation provided for Kojo by British authorities is very far from being safe, sheltering homes. As stated above, British institutions have not been conspicuous for their care of undocumented minors – the lack of educational facilities is a case in point (Crawley and Lester 2005: 14). Not only is Kojo surrounded by the ghosts of his past, experiencing a condition not far from Abani's Abigail and Cleave's Little Bee (see Chapter 3.2 and 3.3); like many new slaves in Britain, he is treated as a ghost himself, uncared-for as he is by the authorities who are supposed to look after him.[50] 'The history of a trauma', Cathy Caruth writes, 'can only take place through the listening of another' (1995: 11). When the authorities age-dispute him, believing he is eighteen when he is actually fourteen,[51] Kojo is sent away from the refuge home (where he has made some friends, at least) and sent to a distant hotel. His friends would like to see him there, but the ticket collector makes them get off the train because they have no ticket:

> Kojo waves them goodbye. Kojo is now alone on the train.
> He scoops up his black bin bag, staring out blankly.
> A Man suddenly appears, sitting down in front of him. He looks up from over his paper.

KOJO: Papa.
It is Kojo's father.
FATHER: Take your feet off the seat.
Kojo takes his feet off the seat.
The train goes through a tunnel. Blackout.
The train comes out of the tunnel.
Kojo looks, the seat in front of him now empty.

SCENE TWENTY-THREE
The hotel.
The slam of the door.
Distant whooping.
Kojo stares down at his bin bag, sinks down on the seat.
He leans over. Touches a radiator. It is cold.
Kojo's Mother passes, drinking from a bottle of Coca-Cola.
MOTHER: Is this where you're going to sleep?
KOJO: Yes, *maman*.
MOTHER: Tuck your blanket in tight. Ssh ... Go to sleep ... Go to sleep ...
Kojo lies back on the bed. Kojo's Mother pulls the blanket across Kojo.
KOJO: The radiator's broken.
MOTHER: Ssh. Go to sleep.
(Morgan 2008: 186–7, original ellipsis)

Kojo is thus ignored, marginalised, turned into a ghost, made hard to distinguish from the very ghosts from his past. He can find neither solace nor safety after three traumatic years in which his family was massacred and he was turned into a child soldier, forced to commit unspeakable crimes.

Thus spectralised, Kojo becomes vulnerable and liable to further abuse, by the pervert living at his hotel and by the street trader employing him and bossing him around. This represents the second awareness-raising effect of Morgan's mode of presentation: a palpable continuity between the traumas of Kojo's past and his newly enslaved condition in Britain. In the following passage, where past and present abuses overlap, Kojo's insistence-through-repetition on 'I have to remind myself' signals exactly its opposite, i.e. that nothing much has changed:

KOJO: I'm fourteen. A fourteen-year-old kid shouldn't be put in a place alone with weirdos and sickos like this. But there are worse places I have been. I know what the man wants from me. There are worse things I could do to him.
Two Kids pass, carrying guns, waving to Kojo. Kojo turns, trying to ignore them.

And I have to remind myself to forget all of that. I have to remind myself I am safe. I am in the United Kingdom. I have to remind myself I am just a kid.
The two Kids smile, swaggering with their guns, past him.
Go away.
The two Kids with guns exit.
Go away –
The Man [pervert] keeps banging on the door.
– or I will kill you.
The banging stops.

(Morgan 2008: 189)

Morgan's technique brings to the fore the analogies between the protagonist's past and his present, and how fresh wounds can re-awaken old ones;[52] writing about Pierre Janet's studies, Van der Kolk and Van der Hart (1995: 163) state that 'traumatic memory is evoked under particular conditions. It occurs automatically in situations which are reminiscent of the original traumatic situation.' This leads to a third kind of awareness, regarding the reason why Kojo stabs the passer-by – a key scene which is performed many times during the play. The continuous interpenetration of past and present, of the dead and the living, induce Kojo to resort to violence again as a way to reaffirm himself, turning him into a telling embodiment of Michel Foucault's assertion (2003: 45) that 'actual relations of subjugation manufacture subjects'; threatening the pervert who is knocking at his door is only a first symptom.[53] More and more stressed and sleepless, Kojo ends up carrying a knife and feeling angry at his refuge mates. During his underpaid work as a street vendor's help, he is bumped into by hurrying passers-by: 'People like you are invisible to people like him', his boss tells him, emphasising his ghostly state in British society (Morgan 2008: 188). This builds up until, one day, while he is having an argument with his mate Cheung, a man pushes into Cheung and Kojo instinctively stabs him, as a way to affirm his identity:

The Man turns, freezes on seeing the knife in Kojo's hands.
The scene freezes –
KOJO *(to audience)*: My name is Kojo. I am fourteen years old. The person playing me is an actor. I don't exist. Except in this story. This is my story. I was a boy. Then a soldier. Then somehow I got here. I'm a kid ... but to him ...
The Man, frozen, mid-step, his arms raised imploringly –
He fears me ...

(Morgan 2008: 198)

Lucy Kirkwood's *It Felt Empty When the Heart Went at First but It Is Alright Now* is centred, like *Roadkill*, on sexual trafficking. CLEAN BREAK is a women's theatre company focusing on stories of imprisoned women. When writing as its Resident Playwright (2007–9), Kirkwood's concern was with the plight of sexually enslaved women in Britain. Thanks to the help offered by organisations supporting former sex slaves, such as the Poppy Project and the Helen Bamber Foundation, she had the opportunity to meet and talk to some victims. Here again, the marks left by their ordeal are read from the perspective of PTSD:

> They weren't happy women. They were women who couldn't sleep with the lights off, women who told me that if they had a son they would not trust him, women who had had extensive dental surgery to correct the chronic grinding of their teeth (an effect of the Post Traumatic Stress Disorder they were suffering), women who jumped every time a Renault car drove past, women who lost their hair, women who lost their sight. (Kirkwood 2009: 'Author's note')

Some of the features mentioned by Kirkwood in this paragraph return in *It Felt Empty*, which is centred on the story of Dijana from Croatia; she fell in love with Babac, a man who made her pregnant and then turned her into a prostitute, enslaving her in a brothel-flat in Dalston. Most of the play is constructed as her monologue in broken English. Once again, what is most interesting here is the dramatic language and conception chosen by the author to stage Dijana's traumatised life.

On one hand, Kirkwood faithfully reproduces some symptoms of stress originating from Dijana's story. She brushes at her arms, '*sweeping invisible pests away*' (Kirkwood 2009: 13); hyperventilates (14); her right hand shakes uncontrollably (20).[54] She is also terrified by darkness: in Part Two, when she finds herself in a women's refuge, she is offered comfort and friendship by Gloria, a former sex slave from Africa: but after lights out, she panics and bites Gloria who is trying to calm her down (34).[55]

Throughout the first two parts, Dijana speaks to her aborted baby as if she really existed. The baby is the 'you', the addressee of her monologue. In Part One, when Dijana is imprisoned in her brothel-flat, she tells her baby that she has been counting all her sexual intercourses:

> I keep account. I keep account of money I earn very careful because when this number reaches twenty thousand UK pounds then I will

> have earned all the money I owe to Babac and he will give me my passport and I can stop. ...
> When Babac tell me the deal I am like Oh! Yeah! Sure! Like I am gonna fucking trust you! Do I look like some IDIOT?! But I make it proper. We have a contract. I draw it myself and I make him sign it so yeah. It is all on paper. ...
> So the next client he will be my last.
> *Beat.*
> The next is last.
> *Beat. This is a momentous thing to absorb.*
> So tomorrow I come to find you.
> The first thing to do is to buy you chips and a swimming suit.
> We are going to swim in the sea. ... In Brighton.
>
> (Kirkwood 2009: 7–8)

Here naturalism is based on the utterings of a traumatised, deluded mind, which speaks to an aborted child, believes a self-made contract will be respected by a sex-trafficker, and even claims she likes sex (Kirkwood 2009: 13). Her gift for maths also carries other, sometimes disquietingly ironic, connotations: Dijana counts the used condoms and the related money with precision, which leads her to a significant reflection on the image and role of women in our contemporary media culture:

> L'Oréal shampoo. And conditioner too. Because I'm worth it!
> *She pulls her hair out of its ponytail like she's in a shampoo advert and shakes her head in slow motion.*
> See.
> *But she doesn't laugh.*
> This is extra funny because I know exactly how much I am worth. How many people can say this! I am worth, one thousand euros because that is how much Babac pay for me.
>
> (Kirkwood 2009: 9)

Side by side with this detailed, naturalistic approach, Kirkwood makes use of expressionistic language analogous to that employed in *Roadkill* and *Fugee*, here again linked with the tropes of the ghost and the prison. Part One, set in Babac's brothel-flat, connotes this space as a sort of cage which limits freedom, embodied in an animal image:

> *everything goes completely black. ... You hear bird wings flapping. The sound is all around you. It gets more and more frantic.*
> *A scream. A loud, repeated thwacking sound. The flapping cuts out, and the lights come up. ...*

> *Dijana is standing on a bed with a rolled-up newspaper. She is dressed in a miniskirt and a strappy top. She breathes sharply and deeply.*
>
> (Kirkwood 2009: 5)

The text associates the dead bird lying on the floor to Dijana's baby, but also to Dijana herself, as when she is visited by a customer who is not shown on stage:

> *A knock at the door. She quickly sits on the bed. The door swings open.*
> He is here! Twenty-two. The last man.
> *She waits as the client, invisible to us, enters. The door swings shut again. We hear footsteps. ...*
> He does not want to talk.
> *She lies down on the bed. Opens her legs. Turns her head to look at us as she starts to be fucked by the client. Her body jolts with his invisible movements. ...*
> *The fucking gets harder, faster.*
> What do I think about? ...
> *Harder, faster. She looks right at us. The sound of bird wings flapping ...*
> *Her hair has been grabbed, her head is yanked back, her neck stretched.*
> Is better to think about nothing.
> I think about nothing
> and count to twenty-two.
> Harder. Faster. Harder. Faster. Harder –
> *The bird wings suddenly stop. Dijana flops onto her front, her face against the bed, looking at us.*
> Thank you. Have a nice day.
>
> (Kirkwood 2009: 15–17)

This dramatic language might imply that Dijana, whose perspective is the centre of this play, is too traumatised to really take notice of her clients, of the world outside as it is. The scene overturns the usual divide between citizens and new slaves: Dijana is the real person, the paying client (possibly a 'respectable' citizen) is the ghost. Dehumanisation dehumanises those who dehumanise, not only the victims – analogously to Broomfield's reformulation of the Gothic double examined in Chapter 4.1. Or, from another perspective, her being shown alone during the intercourse, like a stringless puppet, conveys a deep sense of how animalised and objectified she is, disconnected from any humane ties.[56]

Dijana narrates in Part Two how the police came to the flat and arrested Babac for a credit card scam; ignoring her completely as if she did not exist (has she become a ghost, after communing too much with her ghostly baby?), they went away leaving the flat door open. But at the end of Part One Dijana's escape is described as entailing another dimension, an expressionist use of space possibly more in tune with her distraught mind and her unreal wish to enjoy the seaside with her baby:

> *Suddenly a vent falls from the wall. Wind whistling through it. The smell of the sea. A dark chasm big enough for a person to disappear into. DIJANA opens her eyes. She goes to the vent. Puts her hand in. Takes it out. Sprinkles a handle of sand to the floor. Smiles.*
> See?
> I told you.
> I told you I was coming. I don't think you believe me.
> But now you see.
> *She picks up her bags. She climbs into the vent. And then she is gone.*
> (Kirkwood 2009: 18).

Part One is closed by another page of unrealistic and suggestive images and sounds, anticipating Dijana's arrest in Brighton for shoplifting. In Part Two she finds herself after the arrest in a refuge centre: as the initial stage direction says, here too this setting (reminiscent of the Robert Wiene's famous expressionist movie *The Cabinet of Dr. Caligari*, 1920) could be interpreted as a projection of her mental state, of how she perceives the place to be:

> *The size of things in here seems all wrong. The walls are lined with doors of all sizes, too-big doors, too-thin doors, too-small doors. Exits all over the place but no feeling they go anywhere. Some things in the room seem larger than they should. Others smaller. It is a sterile, impersonal place. You are not meant to feel at home.*
> (Kirkwood 2009: 20)

As Kirkwood argues in her 'Author's note', many trafficked women are criminalised by institutions, rather than treated for their trauma, and this unhomely stage might be seen as embodying the past–present continuity experienced by Kojo in *Fugee*, too. At the end of Part Two, after wasting her chance to find a friend in Gloria, she reacts through another Alice-in-Wonderland-like escape originating from her physical symptoms:

> DIJANA: I'm not sposed to talk to you no more.
> The doctor says it's not healthy.
> DIJANA *suddenly starts to choke, coughing. Eventually she brings up a tiny golden key. She stares at it. Then looks up. There is a tiny door in the opposite wall, the only one with a keyhole. She runs to*

it, unlocks it, it swings open. DIJANA *kneels, crawls head-first into the space. And disappears.*
(Kirkwood 2009: 35)

Part Two, too, is closed by a page of suggestive, hard-to-stage images and sounds, leading to Part Three, which is set back in time, when Dijana was pregnant, in love with Babac, overjoyed and with a world of possibilities ahead of her. This is represented through a setting composed of a room opening into nature, and described by Kirkwood's lyrical, impressionistic stage directions:

A wide-open corn or wheatfield. The sense that we are in a huge space of freedom and light. Dark green, lush hedgerows, and a clear blue sky. There is a door in the horizon.
There is a standard lamp in one corner of the field. An armchair. A small side table. A TV. A stereo.
...
  DIJANA *is hoovering the field. She is pregnant. Five months gone.* ...
  Music plays from the stereo. She sings along. Dances a little.
  Then: the sound of a plane roaring overhead. ... *She feels her stomach. Then points upward. Excited.*
DIJANA: Did you see that! Shit. Did you hear it? That will be me tomorrow! On a plane NEEEEEEEEEOOOOO – OOOOW flying away! *(She puts her hand to her belly.)* That will be us baby! We are going on holiday tomorrow! Babac and me and you!.
(Kirkwood 2009: 36)

This is the tone of the whole of Part Three, where Dijana has no PTSD symptoms yet. She is a loving and humane human being, made of flesh and blood, talking to a living foetus. Dijana has not yet been turned into a spectral plaything. Though much less realistic than the brothel-flat imprisoning her in Part One, this setting throbs with life: paradoxically, the spaces of this play seem to be most real and least ghostly when least realistic.

Dijana's joy has a bitter taste for the knowing audience, and Part Three is interspersed with clues about what is going to become of her (which she does not grasp). The ending of the play, when Babac comes home, also marks the beginning of Dijana's end:

As she turns away from us, we see now there is a little blood on the back of her dress, where she has been sitting on it. A spreading stain.
  She's about to open the door but stops. Smiles. Turns back.
  You know. He think I not see but
  he put my passport in the safe. With all the monies.

> When I see that it almost make me cry.
> He put it in the safe to keep me safe.
> ...
> *She pushes on the door handle. The door will not open. She is surprised.*
>
> (Kirkwood 2009: 51–2)

According to Cathy Caruth, 'in trauma ... the outside has gone inside without any mediation' (1996: 59). Morgan's and Kirkwood's expressionistic techniques seem to operate along an opposite trajectory, giving an external materiality to their protagonists' traumas. The Greek etymon of the word 'trauma', meaning 'bodily wound',[57] represents another way in which these playwrights externalise their characters' traumas on stage; see, for example, Dijana's stain, and the laceration given by Kojo to another man through the stabbing.

After reading these plays about traumatised new slaves at the mercy of their traumas, the pressing question is: what space is left for recovery and agency? This represents a controversial issue, within trauma studies. Caruth, conceiving of the literal return of the event (1995: 4–5, 6), for instance, has been taken to task for assuming a passive victim 'bereft of any interpretive agency' (Crownshaw 2010: 7). In the plays analysed here, hope certainly represents a starting point to achieve agency. In her 'Author's Note', Kirkwood describes the women she met before writing the play as human beings 'who had their ambition and hopes used against them to the point that they had lost all ability to trust fully in another human being'. By centring the final part of *It Felt Empty* on a hopeful, enthusiastic Dijana, she points to a way to counter that traumatic process whereby the subject 'finds himself to have become a trace of what he was, a cinder marking the passing of disaster' (Boulter 2011: 9). It is a possible strategy to recover the human hope described in these lines from Reza Mohammadi's poem 'Illegal immigrant' (2012: 27):

> it is possible
> the sun has risen
> and over the mountains
> the clouds are there still,
> the winds are driving
> and families arriving
> and there is the sound of a party
> sound of dancing, chanting,
> ...

and happiness and also
me, with my big heart,
in a ship or strapped under
the truck, I am crossing
the border and moment
by moment am entering
with glory England

Fugee, too, places hope in its protagonist's past, when life was as yet untouched by trauma. This past again constitutes a resource pool of possibilities to be tapped, if one wants to attempt a recovery from trauma itself. After the stabbing scene quoted above, the play closes with a birthday party for Kojo in which all the characters, living and dead, past and present, friends and passers-by, participate:

KOJO: Everyone is here. ... I am eleven, It is my eleventh birthday.
Kojo's Mother smiles, holding out the cake for him to blow.
I am safe. I am home.
ALL: Happy birthday, Kojo.
MOTHER: Blow.
Kojo blows out the candles.
Blackout.
The End.

(Morgan 2008: 200–1)

It is a celebratory ending which reflects the mood of the play, where 'fun' is a key word as the author writes in her 'Production notes': the play 'is intentionally not sombre or preachy despite being about issues of immigration and trauma' (203). In such a mood, and through an expressionist use of the stage, both plays' endings confer a sort of recovered agency, at least on a human or psychological level, to Kojo and Dijana. Furthermore, the collective ending of *Fugee* gestures one key issue in the contested relationship between trauma theory and postcolonial studies: if postcolonialists tend to consider social suffering rather than placing excessive reliance on individual psychology as in much trauma theory (Craps and Buelens 2008: 4), but concurrently new slaves in Britain are marked by their debilitating isolation from communal forms of living, can Morgan's ending be regarded as a way out of this impasse?

A similar ending, though by no means tinged with humour and joy, takes place in *Roadkill*. Mary, too, looks back on her family and pre-traumatic situation to find the necessary strength: 'I must remember the warmth of them ... of home ... it comes to me like a soft ash after a raging fire'.[58] Accordingly, she writes her real name (Adeola) on the floor (Bissett and Smith 2011: 51).[59] Her being pregnant helps her make a final decision: the play ends on Adeola simply walking out of the performance or brothel-flat, shown on TV as running through the city 'not sure where she is running to, but not stopping' (64). There is a concretisation of Kojo's and Dijana's hopes here, just as she wishes to make real something akin to the expressionist staging of the final part of *It Felt Empty* (when speaking to her foetus, like Dijana):

> I feel you baby. I do. ... By the time you arrive we can be a proper family, here in Scotland. And we can have our own house, and maybe a dog. And I will *paint the sky on every ceiling* so we never feel trapped and we can plant flowers in the garden ... It's impossible, but we will make it possible. ... We need to get away baby. We will find a way, *we will grow tall and big until the entire house bursts open* ...
> (Bissett and Smith 2011: 55; italics mine)

With regard to the issue of agency, *The Container* sounds excessively heart-on-sleeve:

> JEMAL. Think how strong we have been, just to get here! We've had bad luck in our countries, but we've taken the chance to change our luck. You can't say we just sat there and waited. ... we outwitted them. They tried to stop us, but they couldn't.
> (Bayley 2007: 44–5)

Reading and comparing these four playwrights' gestures towards agency, reference to trauma theory might yet again be of some interest. In what I see as an imaginative stretching of the 'narrative therapy' mentioned in Chapter 3.1, some psychotherapists suggested to their patients

> an alternative, less negative or even positive scenario [concerning the returning traumatic event]. Memory is everything. Once flexibility is introduced, the traumatic memory starts losing its power over current experience. By imagining these alternative scenarios, many patients are able to soften the intrusive power of the original, unmitigated horror. (Van der Kolk and Van der Hart 1995: 178)

This playing with the past risks being seen as a sacrilege for a therapist (179), but it is certainly a sacred prerogative for a creative writer.

Notes

1 Faced with the 'enticements to experience "Edinburgh's haunted past"', Siobhan feels 'more concerned with its haunted present' (Rankin 2004: 81).
2 '[C]rime fiction grows out of the tradition of Gothic fiction, with Poe being the obvious hinge between the Gothic and the modern detective story' (Diemert 2005: 166). On the long and complex transition from the Gothic to crime fiction, see Ascari (2007: 37–90).
3 Lucie Armitt (2000: 305), for instance, writes that 'much contemporary Gothic eschews "pattern" altogether, favouring new direction'. According to David Punter (1998: 211), the Gothic proves to be an extremely hybrid, adaptable mode, which 'does not admit easily to canons, any more than it admits abjection before a monotheism'.
4 An analysis of the hellish conditions of living in contemporary China can be found in Pai (2008: xv–xvii).
5 The smugglers' ever-changing methods are to be seen as a 'response to legal changes and law enforcement activities. Flexibility is the key to their survival' (Gupta 2007: 150).
6 For examples of this, see Pai (2008: 56, 84, 134, 152, 214).
7 This atmosphere is a constant reminder of the 'palpable sense of deportability' which constitutes the lives of the undocumented (De Genova 2002: 439).
8 With regard to this, Paulina's words from Christine Bacon's verbatim play *The Illegals* (2008: n.p.) are remarkable: 'I spend a lot of time thinking about getting caught by immigration, that's my nightmare. I know of a person who was caught in the underground station – Elephant and Castle. Instead of taking the train to see my brother, I go by bus which is two hours longer. Also, most of the time, I'm scared that someone will report me, that has happened to friends. If someone doesn't like you, they might report you. I've been threatened with that.'
9 In the nineteenth century, Fujian also provided the British Caribbean colonies with many indentured labourers meant to replace the liberated African slaves (Gupta 2007: 140, quoting Zai Liang and Wenzhen Ye, 'From Fujian to New York: Understanding the new Chinese immigration', in D. Kyle and R. Koslowkski (eds), *Global Human Smuggling: Comparative Perspectives* (Baltimore: Johns Hopkins University Press, 2001), pp. 187–215).
10 Michael Winterbottom's film *In This World* includes a similar scene.
11 Yosefa Loshitzky (2010: 63) detects a pervasive claustrophobic atmosphere in the London depicted by Stephen Frears's *Dirty Pretty Things* (2002), where 'there are very few scenes ... that take place outdoors'.
12 More symbolically, Ai Qin calls her family in China (this is shown at the beginning) and sings a song to her child.
13 See, for example, Coleridge's *The Rime of the Ancient Mariner* (1798),

Mary Robinson's 'The haunted beach' (1800) and Robert Southey's 'The ballad of Inch-Cape Rock' (1815). In 1800, one vessel a day was estimated to be shipwrecked around British coasts (Bathurst 1999: 35).
14 This latter category may be embodied in the white Englishwoman who observes, from behind her window, a police raid targeting the protagonists.
15 They have been preparing onions for chains like ASDA, Tesco and Sainsbury; when they shop in one of them, their bitter humour is expressed with: 'We wrapped those onions, we can't even afford them'.
16 See, for instance, Hsiao-Hung Pai's observation during her undercover research (2008: 51): 'We wandered the streets of Thetford. I noticed, once again, how close, yet how distant, we were from the locals going about their daily lives with their shopping bags and their dogs on the lead. Such a tranquil life, theirs seemed. The two worlds crossed each other without the locals knowing anything of ours.'
17 Modiano quotes here R. M. Maniquis, 'Holy savagery and wild justice: English Romanticism and terror', *Studies in Romanticism*, 28 (1989), 377.
18 Here Knox-Shaw refers to Rousseau's *The Miscellaneous Works* I, 1767, pp. 180, 230; Hegel's 'Independence and dependence of self-Consciousness: Lordship and bondage', in *The Phenomenology of Mind*, trans. J. Baillit, 1977, pp. 228–40; Montesquieu's *The Spirit of Laws*, trans. T. Nugent, 1949, XV:i, p. 235.
19 Trauma studies have formulated similar arguments, when remarking how perpetrators can also be traumatised by their own violence (Rothberg 2008: 231; here Rothberg refers to Dominick La Capra's *History and Memory after Auschwitz* (Ithaca: Cornell University Press, 1998), p. 41). Frantz Fanon (1968: 60) had translated this concept clinically, writing that 'The Negro enslaved by his inferiority, the white man enslaved by his superiority alike behave in accordance with a neurotic orientation.' Or, to put it more bluntly in Alan Sillitoe's words (1995: 6), 'Maybe as soon as you get the whip-hand over somebody you do go dead.'
20 Or, to put it in Guillermo Del Toro's words, the Gothic 'is the only genre that teaches us to understand otherness' (Nelson 2009: 18).
21 Pai was also the Associate Producer of the film; her book was published one year after the release of *Ghosts*.
22 Accordingly, Broomfield cast non-actors who really had experienced the harrowing life of a migrant in Britain; the lead Ai Qin (whose full name is Ai Qin Lin) is one of them. The gangmaster Mr Lin is played by Zhan Yu, owner of two restaurants in North London; according to Broomfield, his over-confident attitude during casting sessions made him a 'natural actor' for the role: he was 'basically acting himself' (Hoeferlin 2006).
23 On the relationship between *In This World* and documentary genre, see also Farrier (2011: 193–8). Notably, Pawel Pawlikowski, director

The British concentrationary archipelago   137

of *Last Resort* (see beginning of Chapter 3), is also a documentarist; on his fictional aesthetics as akin to documentary realism, see Roberts (2002a: 88 and 2002b: 95, 97).
24 See also Botting (1996: 38–43).
25 The main bulk of Lizabeth Paravisini-Gebert's essay on the Caribbean Gothic (2002: 229–47) similarly emphasises the dreadful supernaturalism of voodoo and zombies, and their recent carnivalisation by contemporary authors, as one of the main topoi of the genre. David Punter proposes an interesting elaboration of Abraham and Torok's concept of cryptonymy, based on 'the notion of a psychic space which contains transgenerational phantoms of which the bearer might be entirely unaware' (2000a: 21); starting from here, Punter discusses the traces left by the historic horrors of colonialism in authors such as Fred D'Aguiar and Arundhati Roy (67–94).
26 Here Baldick and Mighall quote David Punter, *The Literature of Terror: A History of Gothic Fiction from 1765 to the Present Day* (Harlow: Longman, 1996, vol. II), p. 201.
27 Analogous to the 'ethical sublime' represented by slavery within the 'heart of darkness of modernity', according to Bianca Del Villano (2007: 14).
28 Furthermore, one Chinese immigrant interviewed by Waugh (2007: 200) declared that she was repaying her loan to the Snakeheads by putting money in a *British* bank account.
29 www.ghosts.co.uk.
30 I personally visited it at the Photofusion Gallery in Brixton, London, on 28 July 2009.
31 One claustrophobically emblematic image is to be found in the TV drama *Sex Traffic*. Once Elena's ordeal is over (incidentally, she too is Moldovan), she longs for a 'normal', bright and serene house in London. When she visits her younger sister Vara (also a former sex slave) who has apparently made that wish of normality come true, she has to hide in the wardrobe because her former trafficker (now working with her sister) arrives: once again Elena becomes a ghost, a 'skeleton in the closet'.
32 Amongst them, one can include Sonja Linden and Christine Bacon's *Asylum Monologues* (2006) and *Asylum Dialogues* (2008), and Christine Bacon's *The Illegals* (2008).
33 'We want to share with you our stories', is the beginning of *Asylum Monologues*. However, David Farrier (2012: passim) aptly throws light on some aspects of these plays which mitigate their supposedly passive implications.
34 First performed at the Edinburgh Festival Fringe in 2007.
35 For not knowing the country you are in at the moment of arrival in Britain, see Mary's arrival in Edinburgh in *Roadkill* (Bissett and Smith 2011: 24), examined further on in this chapter.

36 Tan quotes the Production Notes to *In This World*, available at www.milestonefilm.com/pdf/InThisWorld.pdf.
37 On the risks of teaching girls in Afghanistan, see Bohmer and Shuman (2008: 206).
38 See also this passage from Sonja Linden's verbatim play *Asylum Dialogues* (2008: n.p.): 'From Glasgow they took us all the way to Yarl's Wood detention centre in Bedford in the back of the van, me and the babies. Eight hours. In the back the van was blacked out so you can't see anything. It was difficult with the kids on such a long journey and I didn't have any food to give them.'
39 The same note specifies that 'it could also be performed in more conventional venues'.
40 On 27 July 2009.
41 For the effect that the play had on the young people before whom it was first performed as part of a school project, see Bayley (2007: ix).
42 See Chapter 1.2 on the role of literature.
43 This also entails some improvisation, if necessary (Bissett and Smith 2011: 23, 25).
44 Here Farrier quotes: Julie Salverson, 'Performing emergency: Witnessing, popular theatre, and the lie of the literal', *Theatre Topics*, 6:2 (1996), 184; Augusto Boal, *Theatre of the Oppressed* (1979), trans. C. A. McBride and M. O. Leal McBride (London: Pluto Press, 1998), pp. 103, 113.
45 This of course is likely to affect negatively the victim's application for asylum or refugee status, even more so because one's case is supposed to be enhanced by the narration of the gruesome details of one's ordeal (Bohmer and Shuman 2008: 10).
46 Moorehead (2006: 220–1) writes about a Rwandan asylum seeker, victim of rape and torture, who said that she saw her children (still living in Rwanda) sitting near her in her London hostel room.
47 In Whittaker Khan's *Bells* (2005: 132, 151, 176, 191), too, the troubled family past of the transvestite Pepsi recurrently returns. In this case, though, it happens when Pepsi is alone, in front of the mirror, and speaks in the voices of his mother or father. The overall effect, then, is of a half-voluntary projection of Pepsi's suffering mind, rather than something unpredictable, external and objectified.
48 Kojo has one moment of clarity about the effects of his trauma on the way his mind organises time and space: 'When I replay the moments in my life, they are like snapshots – ... Held, suspended in time' (Morgan 2008: 180–1). Not by chance, it is after this moment of clarity that he is able to recount fully his traumatic experience, the killing of his family, his being turned into a child soldier (see Scene Twenty, pp. 181–3).
49 Here Bohmer and Shuman make reference to Jane Herlihy, Peter Scragg and Stuart Turner's 'Discrepancies in autobiographical memories: Implication for the assessment of asylum seekers: Repeated interviews studies', *British Medical Journal*, 9 February 2002, 324–7.

50 'KOJO [to Counsellor and Translator]: You don't care. This country doesn't care. We just get under your feet' (Morgan 2008: 193).
51 The final scene of the play (200) opens with some characters reminding the audience that, in 2005, 2965 unaccompanied minors applied for asylum in the UK, and 2425 of them were age-disputed. Crawley and Lester (2005: 5) mention the 'evidence that asylum applicants whose age is disputed are not being independently age-assessed … failure of decision-makers to give age-disputed asylum-seekers the benefit of doubt'. On the issue of minors, see Chapter 3.3.
52 See Moniza Alvi's poem 'Candle', quoted in Chapter 3.3.
53 In his reading of Maurice Blanchot's *The Writing of Disaster* (1995), Boulter (2011: 8–9) states that the fractured subject may have his ethical relation to history ruptured, 'because his interiority, his sense that there is a space for history, … is no longer continuous or stable'. In Danuta Reah's crime novelette *Not Safe*, two members of the police force investigating a murder consider the position of their main suspect, an asylum seeker: if he really has undergone what he claims, one of them says, then he may be mentally disturbed and therefore dangerous; his colleague, an expert in the field, replies: 'Most asylum seekers – they're more likely to hurt themselves than someone else.' Faced with her boss's sceptical expression, she adds: 'It's just – that's the statistics. That's all' (Reah 2011: 30).
54 Cf. the character of Mimi in Anna Jordan's *Chicken Shop* (2010), who is literally driven to madness by her sexual slavery.
55 When commenting on the 'missed encounters' between victims of different persecutions in Caryl Phillips's works, Rothberg (2009: 163, 169) remarks how victimisation erodes the base of relationships.
56 In *Sex Traffic*, too, the camera lingers on Elena's face while her body is being used.
57 See Caruth (1996: 3).
58 Curiously, the image of fire is used here with destructive connotations, whereas Boulter employs it above with vital suggestiveness.
59 On the importance of naming, see Chapter 2.2 and 3.1.

5

Dystopian narratives

> Why bother fictionalizing immigration controls when the novel *Nineteen Eighty-Four* so well describes the world constructed through controls: a world of totalitarianism, of Big Brother, of the Thought Police, of Newspeak, of memory holes, of perpetual war.
> Steve Cohen, *Deportation Is Freedom!* (2006: 14)

Following on from Chapters 2, 3 and 4, and from their analysis of various literary and visual works, some general considerations on the mode of representing British new slaveries are now appropriate. Baldly, is there supposed to be a privileged mode for depicting new slaves in Britain, given the ghostly and imprisoned life that they lead? Could one assume a dominant stylistic approach capable of embracing the postcolonial and Holocaust implications that their condition entails?

In his reading of Caryl Phillips's narrative intertwining of (post)colonial and Holocaust histories of victimisation, Michael Rothberg identifies in Phillips's 'fragmentation[1] and intertextuality' an apposite vehicle 'to develop an aesthetics premised on nonappropriative hospitalities to histories of the other' (2009: 25), and to eschew 'redemptive closure and easy analogy across histories and identities' (162), while highlighting 'both similar structural problems within those histories and missed encounters between them' (137).[2] This reading was (perhaps unconsciously) encouraged by Caryl Phillips himself, who in his essay 'Extravagant strangers' (2001b: 288–97) envisions the formal experimentation of British outsider writers (from Conrad to Rushdie and Ishiguro, to mention but a few) as symptomatic of their dissatisfaction with the supposed continuity and homogeneity of the British sense of self.

Undeniably, some of the works analysed here share this rapport between devastated (and devastating) content and shattered form, possibly when most related to the presence of sexual enslavement and its concurrent traumas: see, for instance, *Becoming Abigail*'s continuous shifts of temporal planes (Chapter 3.2), Popa's decentred photographic subjects (4.2) and the non-naturalistic plays by Bissett, Morgan and Kirkwood examined in Chapter 4.3. However, in the light of the previous pages, it would be reductive to limit oneself to such a facile analogy. If in trauma studies it may be 'axiomatic that traumatic experiences can only be adequately represented through the use of experimental (post)modernist textual strategies',[3] Craps and Buelens (2008: 4–5) contend that some postcolonial novels narrate trauma through realism. Some works studied here show a similar reliance on realism: Chris Cleave's childhood perspective (Chapter 3.3) and Broomfield's documentary-like accuracy (4.1) appear to be inspired by an ethical urgency to expose the daily mechanisms of new slaveries. The rationale behind their stylistic choices has to do with making ghosts real, with countering the asylophobic demonisation of migrants so often bound to the mystery and obscurity inherent both in the new slaves' condition and in deliberate propaganda. Not to mention Rendell's, Lewycka's and Rankin's novels (Chapters 2.2, 3.4 and 3.5), whose realism is inextricably intertwined with their own generic requirements: crime solving and humour need solid reality as a touchstone for comparison.[4]

Hence, rather than focusing on the purportedly prevailing modes or styles for conveying British new slaveries, the formal analysis of this book concentrates on the genres that constitute their most suitable frame – and on how these very genres sometimes undergo adjustment under the pressures of the specifics of new slaveries. Following my examination of crime and humour fiction and the role of the Gothic, this chapter is concerned with dystopian writing and film. According to Alexandra Aldridge (1984: 17), the dystopian author 'instead of recreating some fragments of the actual world, extrapolates from his concept of actuality in order to make a holistic framework, a complete alternative (inevitably futuristic) structure'.[5] I contend that the works examined in this chapter (Cuarón's movie *Children of Men* and Ishiguro's novel *Never Let Me Go*) construct alternative structures that are increasingly close to present reality, in spite of the outlandishness of their narrative premises – humanity's loss of fertility and organ-donating clones. The overall impression is that, on one hand, the accelerated pace of late twentieth and early twenty-first-century globalisation may have contributed to reduce the gap; on the other hand, doesn't dealing with the systematic dehumanisation of whole categories of people inevitably lead to the sensible perception of how dystopian the *present* British condition is? This is probably what makes Steve Cohen read the British world of immigration control through the lens of Orwell's *Nineteen Eighty-Four*, in his singular book *Deportation Is Freedom!* (2006, see epigraph above). And this is perhaps what made the director Alfonso Cuarón tell his cast and crew that he wanted *Children of Men* to create an easily recognisable world, an 'anti *Blade Runner*': 'I would say, "I don't want inventiveness, I want reference. Don't show me the great idea. Show me the reference in real life"' (Cuarón 2006, bonus disk, 'Futuristic Design').[6]

The best example of how, in the context of British new slaveries, ghastly reality has caught up with the wildest imaginings is provided here by a (necessarily cursory) reading of Salman Rushdie's *The Satanic Verses* (1988), and more precisely of its third part 'Ellowen deeowen'. There Rushdie focuses on the 1980s abuses against minorities resulting from Margaret Thatcher's xenophobic policies. The perfectly anglicised Saladin Chamcha finds himself magically metamorphosed into a man-goat: mistakenly taken for an 'illegal', he is arrested, beaten up and made to eat his own excrement by an immigration squad inside a Black Maria van, before being sent to a detention centre where other immigrants possess animal and/or object-like features. Though magical, his physical transformation is presented as intertwined with the colonial-inspired categories by which institutions conceive of him:[7] 'They describe us,' goes the oft-quoted explanation from one of his fellow inmates, '[t]hat's all. They have the power of description and we succumb to the pictures they construct' (Rushdie 1992: 168). This engenders the same vicious circle described in Chapter 2.2 about *Simisola*, whereby dehumanising someone justifies further dehumanisation and oppression: '"Animal," Stein cursed him as he administered a series of kicks, and Bruno joined in: "You're all the same. Can't expect animals to observe civilized standards, eh?"' (159). Significantly, Chamcha's 'metamorphosis into this supernatural imp' is treated by the policemen 'as if it were the most banal and familiar matter they could imagine' (158).

Rushdie's novel may be regarded as contextualising the road to 1990s–2000s British new slaveries, thanks to its unmasking of the hollowness of Thatcherite liberalism (Brennan 1989: 148, 163),[8] and to its magical-realist reshaping of a period that laid the foundations of both the deregulation of the labour market and the construction of an asylophobic cultural climate, the fertile twin terrains for the growth of new forms of enslavement. Read today, *The Satanic Verses* displays its gift for foreseeing (and for magnifying through its magic realism)[9] the following decades' ghastly animalisation of new slaves, whose bodies become (like Chamcha's) political fields of oppression caught in a 'Foucauldian nightmare' (Bassi 1999: 57), as some stories analysed in this volume testify.[10] Or, more simply, the novel shows Rushdie's capacity for perceiving the process of spectralisation developing around that time;[11] Andrew Teverson (2007: 147) aptly writes that Chamcha enters an England 'that is "visible" for those who are prepared to look for it, but remains largely "unseen" by the wilfully blind citizens of the modern metropolis'.[12]

5.1 The camp's liminal centrality: From P. D. James's *The Children of Men* (1992) to Alfonso Cuarón's *Children of Men* (2006)

> Instead of deducing the definition of the camp from the events that took place there, we will ask: What is a camp, what is its juridical-political structure, that such events could take place there? This will lead us to regard the camp not as a historical fact and an anomaly belonging to the past (even if still verifiable) but in some way as the hidden matrix and nomos of the political space in which we are still living.
>
> Giorgio Agamben, *Homo Sacer* (1998: 166)

P. D. James's *The Children of Men* is set in the year 2021, when humankind has mysteriously lost its ability to reproduce. Extinction looming ahead, with a population of thirty-six million and twenty per cent of them over seventy (James 2006: 126), Britain has turned into a bizarre society which, as is often the case with dystopian narratives, could be construed as a projection of our present – in this case, of our present incapability of conceiving our future. In the words of the protagonist, Theo Faron, 'We can experience nothing but the present moment, live in no other seconds of time, and to understand this is as close as we can get to eternal life' (9). This is incarnated in the last children (born in the year 1995) called 'Omegas', who echo the way children are mis-educated in our present society:

incapable of human sympathy. ... a race apart, indulged, propitiated, feared, regarded with a half-superstitious awe. ... Perhaps we have made our Omegas what they are by our own folly; a regime which combines perpetual surveillance with total indulgence is hardly conducive to healthy development. If from infancy you treat children as gods they are liable in adulthood to act as devils. (James 2006: 10–11)

The lack of any hope for the future has worsened citizens' indifference to active participation in politics and decision-making. Parliament meets only once a year; everything is ruled by decree of the Council of England, composed of five members including Xan Lyppiatt, 'Warden of England' and Theo's cousin:

> The system has the merit of simplicity and gives the illusion of democracy to people who no longer have the energy to care how or by whom they are governed as long as they get what the Warden has promised: freedom from fear, freedom from want, freedom from boredom.' (James 2006: 89)

It is not by chance that one of the members of the Council, when reminding Theo of the rise in crime during the 1990s, declares: 'The other freedoms are pointless without freedom from fear' (James 2006: 96).

Note that this is a significant departure from the Preamble to the 1948 Universal Declaration of Human Rights, whose goal was to promote 'freedom of speech and belief and freedom from fear and want'; once state policies are centred on freedom from fear, and freedom from speech is eliminated, monopolising the source of fear for specific interests becomes very rewarding. P. D. James's near future resonates with the emptying out of values and ideals in contemporary politics and social debate. The 'Crime Deal' as the main thrust of contemporary European politics is based on the criminalisation of migrants; as discussed above apropos Rushdie's *Satanic Verses*, since the period of Thatcher's government Britain has been one of the European countries leading this process (see also Chapter 1.1). In the documentary 'The Possibility of Hope', annexed to the DVD version of *Children of Men*, Slavoj Žižek connects fear with the main issue of the novel and movie:

> today, the main mode of politics is fear. ... Political groups today are bands of people who are afraid, who are mobilised by fear, fear of immigrants – even leftists – fear of too-strong state, fear of taxation. This is the definition of infertility: when your mobilising principle is just pleasure and fear. (Cuarón and Elías 2006)

Dystopian narratives

In the same documentary, Tzvetan Todorov points to an important connection with the conditions of new slaves: 'It is because we were so afraid of what will happen that we accepted torture. If you are really frightened, you get accustomed to different transgressions of the rules of normal life between human beings.' In order to justify the system, one of the Council members makes reference to the 1990s, speaking the oft-heard language of asylophobic demagogy and racial superiority that neglects the (neo)colonial mechanisms working behind the scenes:

> People became tired of invading hordes, from countries with just as many natural advantages as this, who had allowed themselves to be misgoverned for decades through their own cowardice, indolence and stupidity and who expected to take over and exploit the benefits which had been won over centuries by intelligence, industry and courage. (James 2006: 97)

James dystopically transfers this dominant political ideology on to her novel: criminals (even petty ones) are given a life sentence in the penal colony on the Isle of Man, where anomie and violence reign.[13] Migrants, here called 'Sojourners' (a curious consonance with the nickname Rendell's Wexford assigns to Simisola, see Chapter 2.2), are employed for menial jobs such as caring for the elderly, road repair and rubbish collecting, and then sent back (sometimes 'forcibly repatriated') when they reach the age of sixty: 'They work for a pittance, they live *in camps*, the women separate from the men. We don't even give them citizenship; it's a form of legalized slavery' (58; italics mine).

In theory, James's 'sojourners' would make this novel, published in the year before Rendell's *Simisola*, the pioneering narration on the issue of new slaveries in Britain. Nevertheless, sojourners are given an extremely marginal role in the novel. They are mentioned only nine times, sometimes as fleeting presences in the background, casually noticed by the protagonist. This might be seen as a way, on James's part, to communicate the ghostliness of new slaves. The second part of the book turns into a fugitive plot (with Nativity echoes) where Theo and a group of radicals protect a miraculously pregnant woman and are chased through the English countryside, which depopulation has turned into an empty, liminal and dangerous no-man's-land gradually consuming civilisation. But in this second half, sojourners disappear altogether, and their ghostliness turns into an utter absence.

In his film *Children of Men* (no article in the title here), Alfonso Cuarón shifts James's perspective on this dystopian world, thanks to a series of radical changes involving plot, characters, liminal spaces – changes which in many cases revolve around a marked centrality assigned to migration issues in British society.[14] In other words, Cuarón takes new slaveries to centre stage; as a consequence, they shed some of the spectrality that the novel conferred on them, whereas the trope of the concentration camp acquires full force. The film's changes are mainly based on three elements: the carefully woven background, the figure of the pregnant woman and the setting of the final part of the movie.

The protagonist Theo is followed against a background teeming with references to migrants. This background presents an accumulation of details that are much more value-laden than James's sparing references: loudspeakers blaring that 'to hire, feed or shelter illegal immigrants is a crime. ... Protect Britain'; groups of people caged along train platforms, lamenting their fate in a Babel of languages and guarded by fully armed soldiers (see Plate 7); coaches with grilled windows taking refugees to detention camps ('our government hunts them down like cockroaches', says Theo's friend Jasper).

Accordingly, the director's camera focuses more and more on the suffering faces of these people: in the DVD extras, Slavoj Žižek calls this procedure 'anamorphosis ... the true focus of the film is there in the background ... This fate of the individual hero remains a kind of a prism through which you see the background even more

7 Migrants caged along railway platforms, while Theo is walking by.

sharply' (Žižek 2006). What emerges very clearly, even more than in the novel, is that citizenship makes the important difference between life and death, human dignity and total denial of rights. 'We're British citizens!' becomes the watchword one must shout to the ever-present soldiers, in the event of trouble. What Cuarón seems to have recreated here is a Foucauldian scenario of permanent conflict, whereby war rages behind all mechanisms of power:

> [W]e have to interpret the war that is going on beneath peace; peace itself is a coded war. We are therefore at war with one another; a battle front runs through the whole society, continuously and permanently, and it is this battle front that puts us all on one side or the other. There is no such thing as a neutral subject. We are all inevitably someone's adversary. (Foucault 2003: 51)

Theo is initially apathetic to the world around him, wishing to remain neutral. Thanks to his meetings with his ex-wife Julian and with his old friend Jasper, his awareness re-awakens, thus embodying Foucault's statement. Together with Julian, who leads a radical group called 'The Fishes', Theo becomes involved in a journey to the southern coast aiming at protecting the pregnant woman Kee, whose miraculous gift runs the risk of being kidnapped or exploited by the oppressive regime. In the novel, the pregnant woman was the white Briton Julian, who thanks to her deformed hand was exempted 'from the six-monthly, time-consuming, humiliating re-examinations to which all healthy females under forty-five were subjected' (James 2006: 39); the child's father, Luke, was

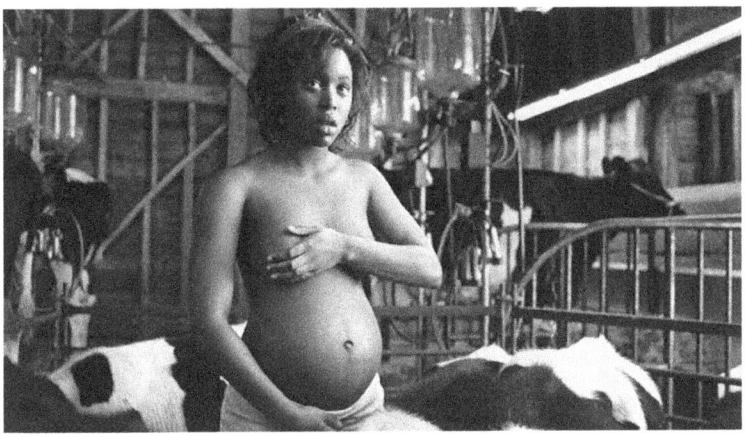

8 The pregnant Kee in a cowshed.

also excluded because he had mild epilepsy as a child; hope, then, resided in those who are, generally speaking, excluded. The film places this hope in a more specific category – Kee is a black and a fugee – thus emphasising the crucial importance of migrants for contemporary British society (see Plate 8).[15]

As I have said, I argue that this is the key to its transposition of the novel: it can be accounted for by the director's personal history, but also by the increasing centrality of migrations in the fourteen-year period between the publication of the book and the release of the film. Incidentally, this 1992–2006 time-span also reflects the trajectory of the present volume: from the early 1990s (see Chapter 2) to the first decade of the twenty-first century.

The same perspective helps to make sense of the setting of the film's final part: though similarly hinting at a Nativity imagery (see Plate 8, where the pregnant Kee is surrounded by cows),[16] it is very different from the novel's abandoned countryside. Situated on the coastline of southern England, the refugee camp of Bexhill[17] is a dilapidated town that is controlled on the outside by ruthless soldiers (provided with all kinds of high-tech equipment) who unleash their brutal violence on migrants, and left to total anarchy inside (see Plate 9).[18]

This place is turned into a battlefield – its dark, frightening entrails are reminiscent of a slave castle on the West African coast. In the movie, before entering, inmates are stripped of their belongings, and Theo of his watch; remarkably, the testimonies by Nazi

9 Military violence at the entrance of Bexhill detention centre.

camp prisoners emphasise how this practice deprived them of their individual integrity, dignity and personality (Giustini 2010: 38). Meanwhile, a recorded voice shouts propaganda slogans (inevitably reminding the spectator of ARBEIT MACHT FREI), such as 'Britain supports you and provides you shelter. Do not support terrorists.' There again, what comes to mind straight away is a sort of recognition of the present, e.g. with the slogan at the entrance to Lindholme Removal Centre: BUILDING A SAFE, JUST AND TOLERANT SOCIETY. Cohen (2006: 97) describes this as a 'doublethink slogan ... in the manner of Big Brother' – but doesn't it perfectly define the Nazi and Cuarón's slogans, too?

Paradoxically, Theo and Kee need to enter this hellish landscape in order to reach the ship that could rescue them, and that could allow Kee's baby to be born and humankind to live on.[19] The detention camp, a liminal site *par excellence*, the place where all rules are suspended or violated, is presented as an unavoidable means of understanding and regenerating our society. Cuarón's interpretation of P. D. James's novel, then, is not dissimilar from what Giorgio Agamben argues in the field of theory. His writings offer a number of possible theoretical paradigms that could be employed to analyse the British concentrationary archipelago shaped by new slaveries. Starting from classical societies, his *Homo Sacer* is centred on the genealogy of the figure of the prisoner in Nazi concentration camps, seen as someone who was deprived of any of the rights usually pertaining to humankind, and thus reduced to 'bare life'. Some of Agamben's definitions are highly appropriate to the new forms of slavery studied here, and its legalised equivalents such as detention centres. The concentration camp, for instance,

> is the space that is opened when the state of exception begins to become the rule. In the camp, the state of exception, which was essentially a temporary suspension of the rule of law on the basis of a factual state of danger, is now given a permanent spatial arrangement, which as such nevertheless remains outside the normal order. (Agamben 1998: 168–9).

According to him, the camp's 'vocation is precisely to realize permanently the exception' (Agamben 2000: 40). These words resonate with the conditions of those undocumented migrants for whom the suspension of human rights has become so common, and with what happens in detention centres, where this same suspension becomes normative – where the liminal, I would add, becomes central, normative, systemic. Agamben himself traces the connection between Nazi camps and their contemporary versions:

> if the essence of the camp consists in the materialization of the state of exception and in the consequent creation of a space for naked life, we will then have to admit to be facing a camp virtually every time that such a structure is created, ... regardless of the denomination and specific topography it might have. The soccer stadium in Bari in which the Italian police temporarily herded Albanian immigrants in 1991 before sending them back, the cycle-racing track in which the Vichy authorities rounded up the Jews before handing them over to the Germans, the refugee camp near the Spanish border where Antonio Machado died in 1939, as well as the *zones d'attente* in French international airports in which foreigners requesting refugee status are detained will all have to be considered camps. In all these cases, an apparently anodyne place (such as the Hotel Arcade near the Paris airport) delimits instead a space in which, for all intents and purposes, the normal rule of law is suspended and in which the fact that atrocities may or may not be committed does not depend on the law but rather on the civility and ethical sense of the police that act temporarily as sovereign. [...] We must learn to recognize it [the concentration camp] in all its metamorphoses [...]. We can expect not only new camps but also always new and more delirious normative definitions of the inscriptions of life in the city. (Agamben 2000: 41–2, 44, 45)

The following section deals with Kazuo Ishiguro's *Never Let Me Go*: to many readers, a shattering novel[20] – for the present volume, also a seminal book (together with its powerful film version) for the early twenty-first century, precisely because of how it conjures one 'more delirious normative definition' of the camp.

5.2 Spectral slavery and the disappearing camp: Kazuo Ishiguro's *Never Let Me Go* (2005)

> Do androids dream? Rick asked himself. Evidently; that's why they occasionally kill their employers and flee here. A better life, without servitude.
> Philip K. Dick, *Do Androids Dream of Electric Sheep?* (2007: 160)

Never Let Me Go begins thus:

> My name is Kathy H. I'm thirty-one years old, and I've been a carer now for over eleven years. That sounds long enough, I know, ... Now I know being a carer so long isn't necessarily because they think I'm

fantastic at what I do. ... So I'm not trying to boast. But then I do know for a fact they've been pleased with my work, and by and large, I have too. My donors have always tended to do much better than expected. (Ishiguro 2010: 3)

Questions inevitably surface: who are carers? Who are donors and what do they donate? Kathy sometimes talks affectionately with her donors about Hailsham, the boarding school where she studied until her majority, which had no contact with the rest of England. The first part of *Never Let Me Go* is composed of Kathy's flashbacks about Hailsham, from the childhood of the protagonists (Kathy, Tommy, Ruth) to their late adolescence. At the beginning of Kathy's recollections they are thirteen, but her memories go as far back as the age of five. But who are they? What is Hailsham, exactly? Why are all these boys and girls without a family?

Little by little, sometimes almost casually as if extracting details from an apparently nondescript background, readers are told facts that gradually form a whole picture: Hailsham students used to have a medical check-up every week; they had a very good relationship with their 'guardians'/teachers/tutors, but they longed for a more affectionate bond with them; they were encouraged to produce works of art (paintings, sculptures, poems), but Tommy was told by Miss Lucy (one of their tutors) that it was not important to be creative (23); a woman called Madame came to collect their best work for her 'Gallery', whose nature and purpose was unknown to the youngsters (30); when Ruth assumed that Madame was 'scared of us', they all contrived a chance group encounter as a sort of game, pretending to run into her to see her reaction, and she actually looked horrified:

> [i]t was like we'd walked from the sun right into chilly shade. Ruth had been right. Madame *was* afraid of us. But she was afraid of us in the same way someone might be afraid of spiders. We hadn't been ready for that. It had never occurred to us to wonder how *we* would feel, being seen like that, being the spiders. (Ishiguro 2010: 35)

The truth is that Hailsham was a college where cloned babies were raised and educated into their adulthood, in order to create a race of organ donors for 'normal' people in need. What is significant here is the ambiguous, half-spoken way in which they came to realise their peculiar nature and purpose, thanks to their guardians' attitude. Their principal Miss Emily is remembered as behaving ambivalently:

Her general drift was clear enough: we were all very special, being Hailsham students, and so it was all the more disappointing when we behaved badly. Beyond that, though, things became a fog. ... Ruth remarked how odd it was they [Miss Emily's speeches] should have been so unfathomable, since Miss Emily, in a classroom, could be as clear as anything. (Ishiguro 2010: 43)

Towards the end of Part One Kathy recollects how Miss Lucy, one of their teachers, decided to go against this pervasive ambiguity and spoke out, telling them what they would have to do because 'You were brought into this world for a purpose'. She could not contain herself any longer in the face of boys and girls who were innocently dreaming of their own future: 'you've been told and not told. You've been told, but none of you really understand, and I dare say, some people are quite happy to leave it like that. But I'm not' (Ishiguro 2010: 81). Later in their lives, the protagonists discuss this and assume that their guardians might have conditioned them by deliberately telling them pieces of information when they were still too young to fully comprehend them (82–3).

Thus, given that the introductory epigraph reads 'England, late 1990s', the end of Part One implicitly states that Ishiguro's dystopia is, more precisely, a sort of alternative history or 'ucronia',[21] a particular take on that kind of novel that sees organ transplants as a form of exploitation (Fiedler 1996: 136–46). This alternative history novel offers itself to a wide range of interpretations linked with actual history. One well-known such example is the inhuman degeneration in the use of medical experiments operated in Nazi concentration camps (Levi 1989: 98–100). Nevertheless, it would be reductive to read Ishiguro's novel as simply fictionalising the degenerations of medicine: Georges Bensoussan (2002: 108–10) argues that Nazi medicine was but an instrument of the purposes of an organised bureaucratic machine. As Giorgio Agamben (1998: 143) similarly claims, 'The Nationalist Socialist Reich marks the point at which the integration of medicine and politics, which is one of the essential characteristics of modern biopolitics, began to assume its final form.' This is why in these pages I consider Foucault's biopolitics and its concept of control over the biological existence of populations as apposite theoretical paradigms for the analysis of Ishiguro's complex book.

Bio-power is closely connected with the emergence of colonial racism, inasmuch as the boundaries between supposed races constitute a justification for the death of some groups being seen as functional to strengthen biologically the health and purity of the purportedly superior ones (Foucault 2003: 254–8). Contemporary examples of this phenomenon are international organ trafficking and the unethical, unsafe and sometimes illegal experiments conducted by pharmaceutical multinationals in developing countries (Shah 2007: passim),[22] something that inevitably springs to mind while reading *Never Let Me Go*.[23] In her trenchant reflections on the forms of bio-politics in contemporary Western society, the political philosopher Simona Forti focuses on the human body as the imaginative object of the last traces of utopia; after the demise of collective religious and political ideologies, this is an individual utopia based on a promise of eternal youth. As often happens, however, utopian imaginary is faced with reality, its dystopian side – with the *abject* bodies who are often unseen, whose toiling is functional to the maintaining of *utopian* bodies unwilling to toil, whose ageing (like Dorian Gray's portrait, I would add) bears the sign of the utopian bodies' refusal to face decay (Forti 2011: 155–61). Forti identifies in the aestheticisation of utopian bodies one of the key developments of contemporary bio-politics. Foucault himself poignantly reflected on the indirectness of death, when he described bio-power as a complement to traditional sovereignty (which took lives and let live), in so far as bio-power exercises its right to 'make live and let die' (Foucault 2003: 241), and this letting die can assume many different forms:

> When I say 'killing', I obviously do not mean simply murder as such, but also every form of indirect murder: the fact of exposing someone to death, increasing the risk of death for some people, or, quite simply, political death, expulsion, rejection and so on. (Foucault 2003: 256).

Never Let Me Go's dystopian vision, based as it is on an utterly depoliticised and deracialised England devoid of any multicultural connotation, points to one key issue of this volume, namely the fact that the abject bodies of new slaveries do not necessarily belong to the traditionally colonial or postcolonial racial faultlines (see Chapter 6.2). In the following pages I consider Foucault's bio-politics and Forti's category of abject bodies as enabling a political reading of *Never Let Me Go* in relation to the two specific tropes characterising British new slaveries: ghostliness and the camp. These, in turn, yet again powerfully highlight the connections of British new slaveries with both postcolonial and Holocaust studies. At the same time, I contend that Ishiguro moves a step beyond the centrality of these two features or tropes, when he effectively fictionalises the spectralisation not only of the victims but also of the camp and of slavery itself.

That the clones' slavery is emptied of their concrete dimension is suggested, first of all, by the above-mentioned ambiguous way in which they were told of their true nature during their Hailsham years, speaking and not speaking about it at the same time. The gradual revealing of some truth, by accumulating thin layers of (sometimes doubtful) data, is on one hand typical of Ishiguro's fiction and of his unreliable, reticent, fractured first-person narrators, 'apparently transparent but often purposely obscuring [... where the] impulses to reveal and to suppress compete for dominance in a disturbing dynamic, ... A compulsion to confess competes, in tone, with a casual but devastating tendency to disguise' (Wormald 2003: 228).[24]

In this case, however, Ishiguro's usual strategy is to be construed as an effect of the educational strategies imposed on Kathy and her fellow students. The protagonists' perception of Hailsham was dominated by the 'terrible stories about the woods' surrounding the place:[25] rumours narrated of a student's ghost haunting the vicinity since, some time earlier, 'she'd climbed over a fence just to see what it was like outside' and had not been allowed back in, and of a boy who had tried to escape and had later been found with his hands and feet chopped off. Besides carrying echoes of escapees' stories in the context of US slavery, these rumours bear a sinister connotation in the way they are ambiguously allowed to circulate:

> The guardians always insisted these stories were nonsense. But then the older students would tell us that was exactly what the guardians had told *them* when they were younger, and that we'd be told the ghastly truth soon enough, just as they were. (Ishiguro 2010: 50)

This represents one instance of how the students were subtly induced, from a very early and vulnerable age, to stay in Hailsham, and of how they were psychologically conditioned, rather than forced, not even to conceive (or want to conceive) of the crossing of its boundaries into the outside world. Far-fetched as it may sound, I deem it appropriate to compare this method of subjugation to that employed by the 1976–83 Argentinian junta, one of the most ruthlessly oppressive dictatorships in the twentieth century.[26] The systematic 'disappearance' of thousands of political opponents was constantly carried out in secret and denied by the authorities. In Avery Gordon's words, 'everyone must know enough to be terrified, but not enough either to have a clear sense of what is going on or to acquire proof that is usually required by legal tribunals'. This policy had the effect of turning disappeared people into ghosts, and of leaving citizens in a state of confused terror, as potential spectres: it was 'designed to destroy not just the organized and overt opposition, but the disposition to opposition, the propensity to resist injury and injustice, and the desire to speak out, or simply to sympathize' (Gordon 2008: 110, 124). Significantly, Amnesty International traces the origins of this 'system of repression known as disappearance' to the 1941 Nazi 'Night and fog' decree (72).[27] Primo Levi (1986: 235), too, emphasises how the maintenance of an 'indefinite terror'[28] was one of the purposes of the Nazi regime.

Hailsham's educational methods work on analogous principles, rooted in the deep-reaching power of ghostliness:[29] its students are left to grow in an atmosphere immersed in ambiguous, spectral fears – and therefore turned into potential ghosts themselves. Brainwashed into not imagining the possibility of leaving Hailsham's boundaries, moreover, they also become ghosts for the rest of the British population.

Unlike brutal dictatorship, though, Hailsham is not based on coercive force – on the contrary, it develops along opposite (but equally conditioning) routes, as testified by the importance of the students' affectionate feelings towards their guardians.[30] Kathy and her fellow students, as she remembers, always approached the most delicate topics concerning their own existence very cautiously, partly because of this profound bond:

> We certainly knew – though not in any deep sense – that we were different from our guardians, and also from the normal people outside; we perhaps even knew that a long way down the line there were donations waiting for us. But we didn't really know what they meant. If we were keen to avoid certain topics, it was probably more because it *embarrassed* us. We hated the way our guardians, usually so on top of everything, became so awkward whenever we came near this territory. It unnerved us to see them change like that. (Ishiguro 2010: 69)

The effectiveness of this educational setting on Hailsham's students is exemplified by the dominating lack of oppositional ideas in their minds throughout most of the novel – something that can be rather frustrating for the reader. Ishiguro also communicates this through his Beckettian gift for using apparently commonplace phrases that, on closer scrutiny, carry important implications:

'the idea of a guardian giving [to a student] a present like that was so *beyond the bounds*' (57; italics mine), Kathy remembers, thus showing how the thought of the impossibility of physically leaving Hailsham is deeply ingrained in their language and thoughts.[31] Ishiguro's linguistic choices are also significant in the case of the word related to the most dangerous consequence of their enslavement – the never-mentioned 'dying', which is replaced by the euphemism 'completing'. Once again readers are reminded of Orwell, specifically of his prophetic words about the political uses of language in hiding unpleasant truths in his 1946 essay 'Politics and the English language' (1986: 153): in order to achieve the 'defence of the indefensible ... political language has to consist largely of euphemism, question-begging and sheer cloudy vagueness' (three features echoing Hailsham pedagogy). More specifically, Foucault identified in this modern habit of seeing death as the most private and shameful event, the most concrete manifestation of the effects of bio-politics (Foucault 2003: 247), for which dying has become a taboo just as it has for Kathy and her friends.

The efficaciousness of this pedagogical policy is embodied exemplarily in the most evident (and shocking)[32] stylistic feature of the novel: Kathy's calm tone of narration. She 'never gets overwrought and distraught' and exudes fondness for her 'halcyon childhood' at Hailsham (Sim 2010: 80, 82) and for the disciplined control characterising the years she spent there.[33] *Never Let Me Go* is constantly focused on her feelings, thoughts and memories, sometimes reporting her conversations with her best friends Tommy and Ruth. Its most overt meaning is dominated by 'workaday' and 'pedestrian' preoccupations (Sim 2010: 82), especially in its first two sections; Part One is a story about growing up, about friendship cherished and sometimes betrayed, about teenagers discovering sex, about the sentimental bond between Kathy and Tommy later disrupted by Ruth's intervention: these are the preoccupations that mostly inform the novel's narrative perspective. Full awareness of their enslaved state (not to mention the absence of forms of rebellion or reaction against it: that is completely beyond the novel's horizon) is conspicuous by its absence. During the whole of Part One, the only moments of friction or frustration are represented by Tommy's tantrums, which take place when he is teased by his fellow students; significantly, they are expressed through a lack of linguistic fullness and meaningfulness: 'he began to scream and shout, a nonsensical jumble of swear words and insults ... just raving, flinging his limbs about at the sky, at the wind' (9–10). Just as significantly, Tommy learnt to control himself with the passing of time.

Ishiguro's clones are representative of today's new slaves in Britain inasmuch as they point to the abject bodies theorised by Simona Forti, whose consuming role sustains the utopian thrust of the bio-politically protected bodies of 'normal' citizens. Nevertheless, the analogy works only up to a point, because for the new slaves exploited in today's Britain coercion constitutes an inescapable fact, as highlighted in the previous chapters. A more direct representation of how the abject bodies of new slaves in Britain are potentially liable to cannibalisation is found in Stephen Frears's movie *Dirty Pretty Things* (2002), where a hospital is set up in a London hotel for illegal organ transplants; as Yosefa Loshitzky writes (2010: 66, 74), Frears's London is 'a cannibalistic city that devours their energy, vitality and innocence [... where the] migrants supply the vital organs to the sick and aging nation which they rejuvenate'.

Rather, I consider Ishiguro's novel a powerful dystopian imagining of how, in our contemporary society, the ghostliness and imprisonment characteristic of new slaveries can deviously seep outside its expected boundaries and into other categories, its victims unaware. When Miss Lucy teaches a lesson about poetry and the Second World War prison camps, Kathy's class start laughing at one student's impersonation of being electrocuted by barbed wire:

> I went on watching Miss Lucy through all this and I could see, just for a second, a *ghostly* expression come over her face as she watched the class in front of her. Then – I kept watching carefully – she pulled herself together, smiled and said: 'It's just as well the fences at Hailsham aren't electrified. You get terrible accidents sometimes.'
>
> She said this quite softly, and because people were still shouting, she was more or less drowned out. But I heard her clearly enough. 'You get terrible accidents sometimes.' What accidents? Where? But *no one picked her up on it*, and we went back to discussing our poem. (Ishiguro 2010: 77; italics mine)

If today's new slaves are to be identified in the novel, then, they might be compared more directly with the clones raised in other institutions, who are brutalised into submission, as readers discover in the following sections of the novel; this is what Miss Lucy was possibly thinking of. The students' attitude on that occasion is further evidence of their lack of awareness of their condition. What the above excerpt signifies, too, is that Hailsham is successful in spectralising not only slavery but also the existence of the camp, since Kathy's classmates do not show any sign of awareness that they live in such a place.

Miss Lucy is expelled from Hailsham for having spoken the truth to her students about their condition (108), and that event marks the end of Part One. As early adults, Kathy's coevals leave Hailsham as required, to be dispersed through various smaller farm communities. Kathy, Tommy and Ruth find themselves at the Cottages, living with other, non-Hailsham clones, all of them supposed to spend two years writing an essay (113) before becoming carers or donors. Although they are far from Hailsham, its conditioning is still profoundly active: 'We certainly didn't think much about our lives beyond the Cottages, or about who ran them, or how they fitted into the larger world. None of us thought like that in those days' (114). As in Hailsham, they live separately from the rest of England, but even less coercive force is needed to detain them: the 'chains that hold them are primarily ideological or mental', writes Wai-chew Sim (2010: 82).[34] As Part Two progresses, readers realise disconcertingly that these mental chains make it impossible for Kathy to conceive of rebellion. As any web search can show, *Never Let Me Go* is often compared with the memorable 1982 movie *Blade Runner* (inspired by Philip K. Dick's 1968 novel *Do Androids Dream of Electric Sheep?*), because they both raise questions about the limits of humanity by focusing on a group of organic replicants. Curiously, both novels are set in the 1990s, the decade when the phenomenon of British new slaveries started.[35] Ishiguro's characters, however, are unable to react as Dick's androids do (see epigraph above). Somehow, Ishiguro's de-industrialised, placid countryside setting, completely different from Dick's post-atomic city, is not only consistent with Kathy's limited narrative perspective but shows analogy with the attitude expressed by Alfonso Cuarón towards *Blade Runner* (see Chapter 5.1) and with his striving for recognition rather than outlandishness. In other words the pastoral, verdant England of Ishiguro's dystopia achieves an effect similar to Cuarón's, thus reinforcing the feeling that new slaveries can involve purportedly normal, everyday lives in a not-so-distant time.

At the Cottages, the three protagonists' lives continue to be dominated by everyday preoccupations, such as making sense of sex and relying on Hailsham bonds (thus providing a hint at the novel's title):[36] 'fearful of the world around us, and – no matter how much we despised ourselves for it – unable quite to let each other go' (Ishiguro 2010: 118). It goes without saying that the deep affective bonds among the clones are simply natural, given their lack of natural families and parents. If contextualised in the phenomenon of new slaveries, as in these pages, this lack may be seen as overcoming the highly debated issue of family dismemberment, which goes back to the late eighteenth-century abolitionist debate (see Chapter 3.3); at the same time, their mutual fondness might be compared to those women imprisoned in Nazi concentration camps who, after having lost their dear ones, reacted by constituting new, putative families with fellow prisoners (Giustini 2007: 55).[37]

At the Cottages, the students do not talk much about those who have recently left (Ishiguro 2010: 129–30). They tend to eschew contacts with the rest of England, in spite of the passing of time and the concomitant weakening of the bounds restraining them from doing so. The prohibitions holding them are shown to be founded less and less on coercive limits, and this is linguistically conveyed by the emphasis placed on the apparently harmless phrase 'to be supposed to' (148, 223). Significantly, the only way in which they project themselves into the outside world is through the elaboration of 'dream futures' (140), the wish for a normal life regardless of their inevitable function. Ruth's dream future in a 'dynamic, go-ahead' office, though, was based in detail on some glossy magazine, as Kathy realises (141–2), just as she notices that all Cottages students' mannerisms are copied from the TV shows that they usually watch (118–19). Coming after the brainwashing that they had been subjected to in Hailsham, this subsequent form of conditioning (more typical and widespread for *our* time) reinforces a reading of *Never Let Me Go* as a fictional rendition of how contemporary generations are potentially liable to be turned, unaware, from subjects into objects of consumption.

In Part Two, the only significant event involving a real outing into the world is described in Chapter Twelve, when the three protagonists drive all the way to the Norfolk seaside town of Cromer because their non-Hailsham mates Chrissy and Rodney believe they saw a 'possible' for Ruth there, that is to say a woman strongly resembling her, from whom Ruth might have been 'cloned'. The possibles are yet another topic that students deal with carefully: 'back at Hailsham, we sensed we weren't supposed to discuss it, and so we hadn't – though for sure, it had both intrigued and disturbed us' (136). Notice the use of 'supposed to' again, besides the linguistic connotation of uncertainty represented by 'possible': the vagueness and doubtfulness of Ishiguro's language are structured on words like these, and like 'somehow', 'perhaps', 'but also'. When the expedition for her possible proved to be a failure, Ruth gives vent to her disappointment very bitterly:

> They don't ever, *ever*, use people like that woman. ... We all know it. We're modelled from *trash*. Junkies, prostitutes, winos, tramps. Convicts, maybe, just so long as they aren't psychos. That's where we come from. We all know it, so why don't we say it? ... If you want to look for possibles, if you want to do it properly, then you look in the gutter. You look in rubbish bins. Look down the toilet, that's where you'll find where we all came from. (164)

Kathy apparently disagrees, but her saying 'sometimes you speak *garbage*, Ruth' (165; italics mine) only confirms that she harbours the same anxiety about their origins. The images employed by Ruth and Kathy to express their fears inevitably remind one of Bauman's vision of the excluded in postmodern society as wasted lives (see Chapter 1.1). In itself, though, their reaction goes further back, to the complex theorised by Frantz Fanon, whereby colonised people develop a feeling of inferiority resulting from an economic assault that is subsequently internalised (Fanon 1968: 11). More particularly, this scene from *Never Let Me Go* recalls Fanon's description (1967: 60) of the Negro who, 'having been made inferior, proceeds from humiliating insecurity through strongly-voiced self-accusation to despair'.[38] The need to overcome this inferiority complex, as formulated by Fanon, will be taken up again below.

The characters' day-trip to Cromer represents a key point of the novel's plot. It is organised by Chrissie and Rodney as an occasion to verify a widespread rumour: could a couple of Hailsham students manage to obtain a deferral of their donations, if they proved they were 'properly in love' (Ishiguro 2010: 151)? Although the three protagonists never heard anything like that, in their remaining time at the Cottages these rumours acquire a sort of real status in their minds: not only as a form of wishful thinking but partly because this can explain the purpose of Madame's gallery during their Hailsham years – in other words, artistic creation as proof of their profundity and sensitivity. From their point of view, this growing belief does make sense, not least as a way to assuage their inferiority complex: what is commonly considered to be the epitome of humanity, its distinguishing traits, more than art and love? Part Two closes with Tommy showing Kathy the animal pictures he had been secretly drawing at the Cottages, to compensate for his artistic inability at Hailsham:

> I was taken aback at how densely detailed each one was. In fact, it took a moment to see they were animals at all. The first impression was like one you'd get if you took the back off a radio set: tiny canals, weaving tendons, miniature screws and wheels were all drawn with obsessive precision, and only when you held the page away could you see it was some kind of armadillo, say, or a bird. ... For all their busy, metallic features, there was something sweet, even vulnerable about each of them. (Ishiguro 2010: 184–5)

Tommy's drawings embed within themselves two of the most common processes of dehumanisation: animalisation and mechanisation (Volpato 2011: 5) – processes from which new slaves in Britain are not excluded.[39]

Before the end of their period at the Cottages, Kathy is disappointed by Ruth's malice in spoiling her friendship with Tommy, and decides to apply for a position as a carer, working to help donors go through the horror and pain of their donations. Much closer to the present time of Kathy's narration, Part Three narrates her period in this role, and her reunion with Tommy and Ruth, who have started to donate their organs. As she mentions at the beginning of the novel, Kathy is doing quite well in her capacity as carer, in spite of its drawbacks:

> Then there's the solitude. You grow up surrounded by crowds of people, that's all you've ever known, and suddenly you're a carer. You spend hour after hour, on your own, driving across the country, centre to centre, hospital to hospital, sleeping in overnights, no one to talk to about your worries, no one to have a laugh with. (Ishiguro 2010: 203)

This description of Kathy's new lifestyle recalls the kind of life that new slaves in Britain are made to live, as seen in the previous chapters: forcibly shifted around the country in a way that, deliberately or not, denies all forms of communal existence, just as Kathy is made to live the gravest period of her life without any social and emotional support.[40] When Ruth expresses her frustration at not being told clearly how often donors 'complete' after their second donation, she imagines a deliberate plan behind this policy: 'I bet it happens much more than they tell us .... That's one reason why they keep moving us between donations' (221). This impediment to a place-based communal identity is later related to wholeness in a more bodily sense, when Kathy compares this kind of life to the suffering experienced by donors, and specifically Ruth after her second donation:

> I took one glance at her in that hospital bed under the dull light and recognized the look on her face, which I'd seen on donors often enough before. It was like she was willing her eyes to see right inside herself, so she could patrol and marshal all the better the separate areas of pain in her body – the way, maybe, an anxious carer might rush between three or four ailing donors in different parts of the country. (Ishiguro 2010: 231)

After a sedentary life, this perennial shifting around may obviously be construed as a way to make it difficult for clones to develop any communal resistance against the destiny planned for them, now that they are adults. Moreover, their utter lack of spatial and social points of reference is exacerbated by the disappearance of Hailsham. The news of its closure clearly unsettles Kathy (and presumably her former schoolmates, too), who is left without the only place she considers 'home': when she sees a clown holding a bunch of balloons, she imagines the closing of Hailsham as 'someone coming along with a pair of shears and snipping the balloon strings just where they entwined above the man's fist' (209). What I deem to be a key point of this novel, especially for its implications for British new slaveries, is the fact that Hailsham students do not know its exact location: 'You still hear stories', Kathy thinks at the end of the novel, 'about some ex-Hailsham student trying to find it, or rather the place where it used to be. And the odd rumour will go round sometimes about what Hailsham's become these days – a hotel, a school, a ruin' (280). This is important for the clones' potential agency: as Georges Bensoussan writes about the attitude towards the remnants of Nazi concentration camps (2002: 11), the survival of a political and collective memory demands that the material traces of such places remain. Ishiguro's dystopia thus constitutes an extreme projection of the concentrationary archipelago of British new slaveries: rather than scattered, the camp here ends up being pulverised, vaporised, spectralised – an important detail that Romanek's film version (otherwise accomplished and close to the book), unfortunately, ignores.[41]

There are moments in Part Three where not all ex-Hailsham students are presented on an equal footing. Kathy's role as a carer, for instance, distinguishes her from her two most important donors, first Ruth and later Tommy. In her suffering frustration, Ruth angrily remarks that Kathy could not possibly know (yet) what it is like to go through donations (222). Kathy's way of presenting her task, too, sometimes cannot help revealing its ambiguities. From the very first page of her composed narration, she declares her pride in her controlled way of dealing with her donors:

> Their recovery times have been impressive, and hardly any of them have been classified as 'agitated', even before fourth donation. ... it means a lot to me, being able to do my work well, especially that bit about my donors staying 'calm'. (Ishiguro 2010: 3)

To put it bluntly, her quiet approach to life infuses in her donors a quiet acceptance of their destiny. The subtle ways in which Hailsham has penetrated into the thoughts and actions of its students calls to mind the pervasiveness of Foucault's conception of the nature of power in *Discipline and Punish*, which sometimes carries resonant connotations for *Never Let Me Go*: Foucault's power's 'disciplinary methods' are described as resting on 'projects of docility' based not on force but on 'the elegance of the discipline'; its 'calculated manipulations' produce 'docile bodies' who are more obedient as they become useful 'and conversely' (Foucault 1995: 136–8), and who are both 'objects and ... instruments of its exercise'.[42] When commenting on the panopticon *dispositif*, Foucault envisages its inmates

> caught up in a power situation of which they are themselves the bearers [... the inmate] becomes the principle of his own subjection. By this very fact, the external power may throw off its physical weight; it tends to the non-corporal; and, the more it approaches this limit, the more constant, profound and permanent are its effects. (Foucault 1995: 201, 203)

True, Kathy's process of remembering Ruth's, Tommy's and her own past might be construed as a form of positive agency, a 'communal re-membering as opposed to physical dismemberment' and to the dehumanising narratives imposed on them (Bressy 2012: 5, 7–10).[43] On the other hand, it is hard not to notice the dark facets of her role, paralleled by her sedate narrative tone: let some clones deal with the dirty job of caring for those bodies undergoing abjection, so that non-clones' bodies may maintain an unscathed, utopian vision of themselves. Much easier, and much less painful, is not seeing what it takes to prop those utopian bodies. In accomplishing the task required of her as she does, Kathy complies with the needs of a social structure that is analogous to the 'indirect rule' of British colonialism[44] (and of much contemporary neo-colonialism): as Edward Said writes (1993: 316), 'continuously native mediation was needed to avert resistance or hold it down'. Concerning Kathy, then, it is worth here repeating Primo Levi's statement: 'love for a job well done is a deeply ambiguous virtue' (1989: 98).

The importance of clones being carers surfaces again in Chapters Twenty-one and Twenty-two (Ishiguro 2010: 241–70), where Tommy and Kathy (now his carer and partner) finally manage to find Madame's house in order to verify the rumour about deferrals. Madame's address comes as a sort of last gift from Ruth, who has 'completed' after her second donation (assisted by Kathy); there is no time to be lost, because Tommy is waiting for his fourth. At Madame's they surprisingly find Miss Emily in a wheelchair, and are able to have a revealing talk with both women. The truth is that the artworks produced by Hailsham students were not gathered to display their souls and therefore to see whether they could really be in love, deserving of a deferral – there have never been such things as deferrals. The purpose, Miss Emily explains to the bewildered couple, was *'to prove you had souls at all'* (255); Hailsham's educators, then, were involved in a controversy reminiscent of the late eighteenth-century debate about the humanity of Africans (Kitson 1998: 18–23).[45] In a world that had found the cure for terrible diseases thanks to clones, the reaction of 'normal' people was to consider cannibalisable clones as abject, to employ Simona Forti's categories. In Miss Emily's words:

> However uncomfortable people were about your existence, their overwhelming concern was that their own children, their spouses, their parents, their friends, did not die from cancer, motor neurone disease, heart disease. So for a long time you were kept *in the shadows*, and people did their best not to think about you. And if they did, they tried to convince themselves you weren't really like us. That you were less human, so it didn't matter. And that was how things stood until our little movement came along. (Ishiguro 2010: 258; italics mine)

On a first level, what is described here is a trope on which this volume's analysis of new slaveries rests: the spectralising procedure that negates the existence of a category in order to dispose with the uneasy thought of their existence; in his study on the Holocaust, Zygmunt Bauman (1989: 26) considers the invisibility of victims to be a key factor for the exterminating machinery to develop; not by chance, when scandals later spoilt the progressive movement embodied in Hailsham, Miss Emily says that public opinion 'wanted you back in the shadows' (Ishiguro 2010: 259). Second, when spectralised clones could not but be faced, dehumanising them was another well-known procedure in order to make their function more acceptable (Volpato 2011: passim). Sara Wasson (2011: 79) describes *Never Let Me Go* as imaginatively engaging with a process equivalent to the effects of cyclosporines: precisely as this substance prevents physical rejection in the bodies of organ recipients, so spectralisation and dehumanisation are functional to prevent *emotional* rejection.

When Kathy asks what was the point of it all, given the inevitability of donations, Miss Emily reminds her of how brutally clones were (and still are) reared in other institutions, and she is adamant in defending the educational policy on which Hailsham was founded, including its hiding of the truth:

> Hailsham was considered a shining beacon, an example of how we might move to a more humane and better way of doing things. [...] I can see ... that it might look as if you were simply pawns in a game. It can certainly be looked at like that. But think of it. You were lucky pawns. [...] You see, we were able to give you something, something which even now no one will ever take from you, and we were able to do that principally by *sheltering* you. Hailsham would not have been Hailsham if we hadn't. Very well, sometimes that meant we kept things from you, lied to you. Yes, in many ways we *fooled* you. ... Look at you both now! I'm so proud to see you both. You built your lives on what we gave you. You wouldn't be who you are today if we'd not protected you. You wouldn't have become absorbed in your lessons, you wouldn't have lost yourselves in your art and your writing. (Ishiguro 2010: 253, 261, 263)

While acknowledging the political message of the novel,[46] Wai-chew Sim seems to espouse Miss Emily's principles, and concludes his chapter on this novel by positing Hailsham as a place of hope: thanks to the importance it confers on art outside any market logic (here Sim places emphasis on Hailsham's Exchanges over its Sales), Hailsham might be seen as creating room for an alternative social worldview 'where corporate profit-making doesn't trump all considerations' (Sim 2010: 88). Therefore, it assumes a 'proto-utopian weight' (89) and 'provides a space to ponder and imagine the radical transformation of society' (78).

Sim seems to be underrating the complexity of the novel's critique.[47] In the above excerpt, by employing terms like 'pawns', 'fooled' and (maybe less deliberately) 'lost yourselves' and 'absorbed', even Miss Emily shows that she is aware of the ambiguities implicit in her position. Another intriguing detail consists in Miss Emily's appearing in a wheelchair: has she faced (or will she face) the choice of having a transplant from a clone to be cured, one is likely to wonder.

Before, during and after Miss Emily's explanation, as a counterpoint to her firm educational beliefs, the novel presents Madame's attitude, tinged with tearful regret and bitter sarcasm about Hailsham's results: 'Why Hailsham at all? ... It's a good question for you to ask. [...] Because I have to say, it's a question I ask myself all the time. [...] Poor creatures. What did we do to you? With all our schemes and plans?' (254, 248, 249) What this chapter contends is quite close to Madame's views. Stifling the students' possibility of a full awareness of their condition, Hailsham denies their chances to develop a full personhood, an issue that has repeatedly entered this volume's reflections on new slaveries in Britain. They are raised to consider love, emotional bonds and artistic creativity as the highest values in life (and to relate their art to their emotional bonds with their guardians and with each other),[48] as liberal humanism tends to think, only to be thrust into the jaws of neo-liberal, pervasive commodification (isn't this reminiscent of teachers or educators in the humanities, of their feeling of impotence about the destiny of their students after their studies?). In the devouring gap between these two poles, their art cannot but be seen as sterile, an end in itself – sensitive and enriching as it may seem. Or, more pessimistically, as a sedating activity functional to their organ-donating task;[49] when Kathy and Tommy try to explain to Madame the reason for their visit, she interrupts them: '"Because of course" – Madame cut in suddenly – "your art will reveal your inner selves! That's it, isn't it? Because your art will display your *souls*!"' (248). Together with the indignation pervading her tone, what should be noticed is the gruesome ambivalence embedded in an apparently innocuous phrase like 'inner selves': certainly it must be taken as their depth of character, but only within Hailsham's bounds. Outside, 'inner selves' inevitably suggests their organs, ready for cannibalisation.[50] What role, then, can be envisioned in their art? What real changes from the perception of the Holocaust as a symptom of the failure of Enlightenment's reason and education (Bensoussan 2002: viii), or from Adorno's memorable dictum 'To write poetry after Auschwitz is barbaric' (Adorno 1981: 34)? *Never Let Me Go* conveys this diminished importance of the students' creative work at the beginning of Part Two, too, when Kathy describes the essays they are supposed to write (yet again carrying disquieting tones, for any teacher in the humanities, about the relative importance of final dissertations): they were meant to be a topic that would absorb us properly for anything up to two years. But somehow – maybe we could see something in the guardians' manner – no one really believed the essays were that important, and among ourselves we hardly discussed the matter. I remember when I went in to tell Miss Emily my chosen topic was Victorian novels, I hadn't really thought about it much and I could see she knew it. But she just gave me one of her searching stares and said nothing more. (Ishiguro 2010: 113)

Given the surprisingly relative value attached to the essays, the keyword of the above passage (which significantly involves Miss Emily) may again be identified in 'absorb' – in the sense of distracting them from their inevitable sacrifice.

Shameem Black's essay is equally critical of art as envisaged by Hailsham's educational vision. Nevertheless, despite noticing the resonance of these clones for 'the fate of postcolonial and migrant laborers who sustain the privileges of First World economies', asking us 'to recognize how many people in our own world are not considered fully human' (Black 2009: 796, 803), Black inexplicably takes at face value their supposedly inhuman identity: Hailsham's final defeat stands for the failure of liberal humanist art *tout court* (and of its founding concept of empathy) in so far as it reveals its own exploitative nature, whereas the inhuman character of the clones is best represented by Tommy's drawings, which prove that the 'absence of a soul does not signal the absence of pro-social imperatives' (790–803). I contend here that Black's reading is not only contradictory (if the clones symbolise exploited migrants, how can we negate their humanity?) but also misleading: empathy is precisely what Kathy's neglected humanity is likely to inspire in readers: as John Mullan writes (2009: 113), her 'inadequate attempts to make a story of herself and others who might be like her takes us to the elementary principles of human sympathy. Experimentally, but movingly.' *Never Let Me Go* incarnates, in my view, the general definition of dystopia as critique of that scientific outlook and 'its adherence to instrumental values, its elevation of functional and collective ends over the humanistic and individual' (Aldridge 1984: 17).

What is at stake here is analogous to the issue debated in Chapter 1.2: *what kind of* humanist art is deemed more effective for them? When eschewing facile calls for humanity, charity and equality, Frantz Fanon (1968: 30) set for himself the primary task 'to help the black man to free himself of the arsenal of complexes that has been developed by the colonial environment'. But if the creativity of Ishiguro's clones is so disconnected from their condition, how could they possibly employ it to overcome their consuming inferiority complex, which is bluntly evident in Ruth's reference to trash? Tommy's drawings are something else not because they are inhuman or posthuman, but precisely because they point to the clones' neglected humanity, to their condition as inheritors of a long history of dehumanisation based on objectification and animalisation (as expressed in this chapter by Salman Rushdie's metamorphoses).

It is apposite here to return to the statement by Adorno quoted above, contained in his 1955 essay 'Cultural criticism and society'. Those pages point to the sterility of criticism whenever it idealises culture and does not root it in its postwar material reality. The closing of that essay (where the famous sentence on Auschwitz is contained) throws light on the ineffectual import of Ishiguro's clones' art:

> Cultural criticism finds itself faced with the final stage of the dialectic of culture and barbarism. To write poetry after Auschwitz is barbaric. And this corrodes even the knowledge of why it has become impossible to write poetry today. Absolute reification, which presupposed intellectual progress as one of its elements, is now preparing to absorb the mind entirely. Critical intelligence cannot be equal to this challenge as long as it confines itself to self-satisfied contemplation. (Adorno 1981: 34)

In the same perspective, another non-clone character whose importance should not be underrated is Miss Lucy, given the principles behind her attempt to make her students face the reality of their lives, at the end of Part One (when Miss Emily recalls this episode with Kathy and Tommy, she dismisses Miss Lucy as 'theoretical' and 'idealistic', Ishiguro 2010: 262). Miss Lucy's anger and frustration at Hailsham's pedagogy are embodied in what she says to the students during her revelation: 'If you're to have decent lives, you have to know who you are and what lies ahead of you, every one of you' (80). She considers awareness, then, a necessary step towards a 'decent' role in the world, against any form of delusion and self-delusion, not so differently from the role envisaged by Frantz Fanon (1968: 100) for himself as a doctor: 'my objective, once his [patient's] motivations have been brought into consciousness, will be to put him in a position to choose action (or passivity) with respect to the real source of the conflict – that is, toward the social structures.' This is what makes Tommy say, after their visit to Madame and Miss Emily, 'I think Miss Lucy was right. Not Miss Emily' (Ishiguro 2010: 268),[51] before getting out of Kathy's car and giving vent to his rage, as he used to do at Hailsham, in an emotional moment of the novel which recalls the above image of the balloons cut loose:

> I caught a glimpse of his face in the moonlight, caked in mud and distorted with fury, then I reached for his flailing arms and held on tight. He tried to shake me off, but I kept holding on, until he stopped shouting and I felt the *fight* go out of him. Then I realized he too had his arms around me. And so we stood together like that, at the top of that field, for what seemed like ages, not saying anything, just holding each other, while the wind kept blowing and blowing at us, tugging our clothes, and for a moment, it seemed like we were holding onto each other because that was the only way to stop us being swept away into the night. (Ishiguro 2010: 269; italics mine)

Kathy later tells him that perhaps he used to behave like that at Hailsham because 'at some level you always *knew*' (270). Tommy's 'fight' bursts out of his frustration at not having been given a chance to know fully what he already perceived – at having wasted his chance to 'fight' consciously. In spite of the undoubtedly good intentions of Hailsham's educators, they keep students hidden like ghosts, just as society prefers them to be. Consequently, the students become ghosts to themselves, stifled in their self-awareness, in their possibility to see their exploitation for what it is, to conceive a beyond, if only imaginatively.[52] In order to avoid a real concentration camp (and to confer some precarious serenity), the students' self-vision is narrowed with mental barbed wire.[53]

Significantly, barbed wire reappears in the final moment of the novel, after Tommy's death. Her first donation looming ahead, Kathy is still driving around the country as a carer, sometimes thinking she has spotted where Hailsham really was, but always keeping her composure in spite of everything. '*The only indulgent thing* I did, just once',[54] she recalls, is getting lost among fields, and stopping before

> a fence keeping me from stepping into the field, with two lines of barbed wire ... All along the fence, ... all sorts of rubbish had caught and tangled. It was like the debris you get on a seashore: the wind must have carried some of it for miles and miles before finally coming up against these trees and these two lines of wire. ... I half-closed my eyes and imagined this was the spot where everything I'd ever lost since childhood had washed up [she imagines seeing Tommy

approaching from a distance]. The fantasy never got beyond that – *I didn't let it* – and though the tears rolled down my face, *I wasn't* sobbing or *out of control*. I just waited a bit, then turned back to the car, to drive off to wherever it was *I was supposed* to be. (Ishiguro 2010: 281–2; italics mine)

Alongside the political reading of *Never Let Me Go* expressed in these pages, the novel offers itself to more abstract, universal interpretations, too, such as a meditation on the quality of life, encouraging 'our own assessment whether in our dreams and plans we are pursuing what really matters or what is important', hinting at 'what we wish or need to do before we die' (Sim 2010: 82, 83). In Romanek's movie version, Alex Garland's script closes on a reflection which is not included in the novel: 'What I'm not sure about is if our lives have been so different from the people we save. We all complete. Maybe none of us really understand what we've lived through, or feel we've had enough time.'[55]

One might wonder at the fact that such a reading totally obliterates the distinction between cannibalised clones and those who profit from their dismemberment. Nevertheless, I do not mean to assert that the protagonists' story can only be referred to exclusive readings. What I hope that these pages demonstrate is the urgency of the novel's political concerns, in so far as it gestures at the condition of the newly enslaved individuals in today's Britain and, at the same time, at a long history of (neo-)colonial subordination.[56] The strength of *Never Let Me Go* also lies in its emphasising the potential pervasiveness of this terrain, which again carries Foucauldian echoes. Ishiguro's visionary England is an allegory of the vampirish nature of contemporary society and its exploitative structures. More generally, it resonates with the contemporary nature of dystopia; according to Darko Suvin, in today's dystopia the Leviathan is represented no longer by the state but by multinational corporations, which operate through both psycho-physical alienation (especially for the upper and middle classes) and the militarised violence of their police states for those who are excluded (Suvin 2004: 150): a process of spectralisation of reality and one of forced seclusion go hand in hand, similarly to the gap between Hailsham's 'enlightened' pedagogy and the other brutal institutions for clones in the novel.

The feeling of how anyone can be potentially enslaved is also embedded in the very narrative structure of *Never Let Me Go*. At the beginning, Kathy starts describing Hailsham to a suffering donor who was raised in another, less 'illuminated' institution

(Ishiguro 2010: 5). In the course of her remembering, readers are sometimes reminded of the presence of this particular narratee through expressions like 'I don't know how it was where you were' (67). At other times, however, Kathy acknowledges the presence of her listener(s) with more neutral, colloquial expressions, such as 'Mind you' (280).[57] Thanks to this, Kathy's cannibalised donor, who grew up in a very harsh institution, merges disquietingly with the novel's readers.

Ishiguro powerfully conveys how the menace of new slaveries extends well beyond new slaves themselves – something that is further discussed in Chapter 6.2. But he also captures another important aspect of this phenomenon, in showing how the concentration camp is moving closer and closer to the spectral nature of the ghost, since the novel's students did not perceive it as the camp that it was and later they cannot locate it any longer: the two key tropes of this volume, then, the ghost and the concentration camp, are shown as two faces of the same coin – an issue examined in Chapter 6.1.

Notes

1 Eckstein (2007: 154) rightly describes Phillips's *A Distant Shore* as a 'broken mirror which provides little sense of unity' and which leaves readers the task of recomposing it.
2 Rothberg (2009: 169) is also eager to specify that Phillips's technique reaches well beyond the nature of postmodern pastiche, and is to be seen as related to the traumatic nature of these histories.
3 Luckhurst (2008: 88–9) even detects a tendency to consider other forms of representation as unethical.
4 Incidentally, this feature may be explainable by the fact that the authors analysed in this book are not (ex-)slaves, and therefore they are less likely to have lived through traumatic experiences; Chapter 6 will return to the issue of the authors' background.
5 The 'inevitably futuristic' part, of course, does not apply to Ishiguro's alternative history, set in the 1990s.
6 This was certainly enhanced by the movie's 'documentary, handy-cam style' (Korte 2008: 321), which constitutes an analogy with Broomfield's *Ghosts* (see Chapter 4.1).
7 Reading the novel alongside a previous essay by Rushdie, Brennan (1989: 149) aptly traces the colonial roots of Thatcher's anti-immigration practices in the author's worldview, which is pervaded by a marked anti-institutional anger (147).
8 On the novel's engagement with the cultural climate of Thatcher's England, see also Dawson (2007: 126–34) and Teverson (2007: 145).

9 For the novel's magic realism in relation to immigration issues, see Eckstein (2007: 143–7).
10 Concerning the echoes of this part of the novel with new slaveries, it is worth noticing that the police are called for fear that 'illegals' are disembarking on British shores (Rushdie 1992: 139); that Chamcha is described as being plunged into a 'universe of fear' (159); that his wife, the community relations officer Pamela, is faced with Kafkaesque cases of deported immigrants (183). And it is hardly happenstance that the third section of the novel is studded with references to ghosts.
11 Brennan (1989: 148) describes *The Satanic Verses* as the book, among Rushdie's first novels, which is most based on his direct experiences, where 'the characters are for the first time people living in the world'.
12 Here Teverson refers to another section of the novel set in London, entitled 'A city visible but unseen'.
13 See James (2006: 61–4; 95–6). The Isle of Man actually hosted internment camps for 'civilian enemy aliens' during both the First World War and the Second World War. Confinement to an island anticipates the issue of deterritorialisation of sovereign power that will be touched upon in Chapter 6.1.
14 See also Korte (2008: 322).
15 See also Korte (2008: 322, 324).
16 On the recurrence of Biblical themes in images and artistic representations of refugees, see Farrier (2011: 82).
17 Just like the East Sussex town Bexhill-on-Sea.
18 Possibly a development of the penal colony on the Isle of Man, or to the camp for 'sojourners', mentioned in the novel.
19 The ship's name is *Tomorrow*: a sort of utopia is envisaged at the end of this dystopian movie (Korte 2008: 317). Though biased by a Western-centric perspective which reads the movie through the lens of a state of crisis bringing conflict from the periphery to the centre, Peter P. Paik observes how Theo and Kee receive decisive help from Marichka, an apparently shady woman of unspecified (possibly Gipsy) origins who trafficks in Bexhill: her 'devotion and grace', Paik writes (2012: 67–8), underscore the rapacious approach of both the institutions and the Fishes towards Kee's pregnancy, while institutional brutality against migrants 'cuts the state off from the source of its salvation'.
20 Wai-chew Sim (2010: 8, 119) rightly asserts that *Never Let Me Go* 'is starting to attract innovative readings addressing a number of pressing issues and challenges. ... With the passage of time, it could conceivably become Ishiguro's most culturally and intellectually important book'; its 'depth and fecundity ... will have a sustained cultural and intellectual impact'.
21 Matthew Beedham (2010: 137) defines it as 'parallel Britain', while Shameem Black (2009: 785) opts for 'counterfactual ... England'. Incidentally, this is something that the Italian edition unfortunately distorts:

the translation 'Inghilterra, tardi anni Novanta' could leave the doubt that it refers to the Nineties of another century (*Non lasciarmi*, trans. Paola Novarese, Turin: Einaudi, 2006).
22 The most appalling cases include the two hundred Nigerian children who were given an experimental antibiotic against meningitis by Pfizer, killing 11 and maiming 189 of them (Smith 2011: passim), and the 2011 experimentation with an Italian anti-AIDS vaccine in South Africa (Agnoletto and Gnetti 2012: 99–108). For such practices operated by contemporary states, see the Israeli scandal concerning the contested administering of contraceptives to Falasha women, which reduced the fertility rate in the community of Ethiopian-origin Jews (Dawber 2013: passim). For other examples of medical (and military) experiments on the 'global periphery', see Brennan 2005: 114.
23 See Sim (2010: 87); strangely, Sim never mentions *Never Let Me Go* when dedicating a chapter to 'Ishiguro, Multicultural Britain and Postcolonial Studies' (124–32).
24 See also Shaffer (1998: 7). For a critical survey of this facet of Ishiguro's fiction before *Never Let Me Go*, see Sim (2010: 105–12).
25 Romanek's film version of the novel significantly places this in one of its very early scenes.
26 It is estimated that thirty-thousand people disappeared during those years (Gordon 2008: 72).
27 Gordon quotes Amnesty's 1981 *Disappearances: A workbook* (New York: Amnesty International Publications, p. 2).
28 Translation mine.
29 Coincidentally, if Kathy's memories begin in the 'Late 1990s' when she is thirty-one (3), her Hailsham period is contemporaneous with the late 1970s crimes in Argentina (in *our* alternative history, of course). In Romanek's film version, the caption at the beginning of Part I is 'Hailsham, 1978'.
30 Kathy recalls: 'Didn't we all dream from time to time about one guardian or other bending the rules and doing something special for us?' (Ishiguro 2010: 60)
31 On a similar note, letting someone down is described as treating him 'like a spare part' (Ishiguro 2010: 122), and at the beginning of the novel Kathy says that 'carers aren't machines' (4).
32 See Sim (2010: 79).
33 Romanek's film is very effective in depicting, amongst other things from the novel, the unruffled and smooth disciplinary system characterising life in Hailsham.
34 In his overly narratological examination of the novel, Mark Currie (2009: 101–3) neglects the political implications of these places for the clones, and reads them simply as 'total institutions' (like colleges) with the social control they imply.
35 And curiously, Dick's novel is set on 3 and 4 January, 1992 – only

one year earlier than the publication of the first works on British new slaveries examined in Chapter 2.

36 Even though the most explicit reference to the title is represented by a song of the same title that Kathy is extremely fond of, which again points to affective bonds (Ishiguro 2010: 69–70).

37 Giustini makes reference to S. L. Kremer, 'Memorie di donne', in R. Ascarelli (ed.), *Oltre la persecuzione: Donne, ebraismo, memoria* (Rome: Carocci, 2004).

38 See also Fanon (1968: 7–8, 25).

39 Incidentally, his animals are made of the same materials (and provoke in Kathy a similar empathy) as the artificial animals in Dick's *Do Androids Dream of Electric Sheep?*: obsessively loved by the humans, or at least by those who cannot afford live animals, which nuclear fallout has made rarer and rarer.

40 At the beginning of Romanek's film the first scene set at Hailsham sees the students in their morning assembly, singing a school hymn which, though joyous, anticipates their unhappy future: 'When we are scattered afar and asunder / Parted are those who are singing today / When we look back and forgetfully wonder / What we were like in our learning and play / ... / Echoes of dreamland, Hailsham lives on.'

41 On their way to see the stranded boat, Tommy says something about the closure of Hailsham (and about the fact that the clones' institutions left are like 'battery farms'), but the issue is left undeveloped.

42 Curiously, Foucault (1995: 158–62) takes the school as one of the significant examples of his theory.

43 I am grateful to my former student Bianca Bressy for making this point (and relating it to narrative therapy) in her postgraduate paper 'Re-membering the Cyborg: Narrated Identities and Lost Communities in Ishiguro's *Never Let Me Go*' (July 2012).

44 I am grateful to my former student Giulia Marcassoli for exploring this issue in her postgraduate paper 'Being a Carer: From Kazuo Ishiguro's *Never Let Me Go* to a Postcolonial Perspective' (July 2012). John Mullan (2009: 108) states that the carer 'is an accomplice, we eventually understand'.

45 'By now the rules are in place and the situation is taken for granted – as slavery was once – by beneficiaries and victims alike', wrote Margaret Atwood in her review of the novel ('Brave New World', in *Slate*, 1 April 2005, quoted in Beedham 2010: 138).

46 Ishiguro 'relates the commodification of human beings to a culture where the demands of corporate profit-making penetrate all aspects of social life and trump all consideration' (Sim 2010: 87).

47 Furthermore, Sim appears to overstretch his reading of this facet of the novel even further, when considering the lack of rebellion from the protagonists as a rejection of expected directionality in the novel's plot, mirroring a radical eschewal of social theories about growth as a way

of solving problems (2010: 89).
48 As Kathy says: 'I can see now, too, how the [art] Exchanges had a more subtle effect on us all. If you think about it, being dependent on each other to produce the stuff that might become your private treasures – that's bound to do things to your relationships' (Ishiguro 2010: 16)
49 In Dick's *Do Androids Dream of Electric Sheep?*, there is a chapter set in a museum hosting an exhibition of Edvard Munch. Two hunters of androids find themselves facing the famous *The Scream* (1893), the description of which echoes the self-contained, isolating effects of Hailsham's students' art: 'The painting showed a hairless, oppressed creature with a head like an inverted pear, its hands clapped in horror to its ears, its mouth open in a vast, soundless scream. Twisted ripples of the creature's torment, echoes of its cry, flooded out into the air surrounding it; the man or woman, whichever it was, had become contained by its own howl. It had *covered its ears* against its own sound. The creature stood on a bridge and no one else was present; the creature screamed in isolation. *Cut off by – or despite – its outcry*. ... "I think," Phil Resch said, "that this is how an andy [android] must feel."' (Dick 2007: 113; italics mine).
50 See also Black (2009: 794).
51 The same vindication of awareness closes Dick's *Do Androids Dream of Electric Sheep?*, when Deckard's enthusiasm for having found a live toad is damped by the discovery that it is an electric one: '"I'm glad to know. Or rather" – he became silent. "I'd prefer to know"' (Dick 2007: 211).
52 Is there an intended word-play on Ishiguro's part, in 'Hail, sham!'? In her review, Margaret Atwood recalls *Great Expectations*' Miss Havisham, 'exploiter of uncomprehending children' (Beedham 2010: 140).
53 Shameem Black (2009: 793) writes that Hailsham built 'a virtual electric fence through an emphasis on artistic production'.
54 This 'purported moment of immoderation shows ... the limited range and closed horizons of the clones' (Sim 2010: 80).
55 On the other hand, the film version includes some details that Ishiguro totally omitted, regarding the technological forms of control of this dystopia: once in each of the three parts, the protagonists undergo a scanning of their wrists when they enter or return to their places of residence. In a 104–minute-long translation of such a complex novel (an apparently impossible task), it is not surprising that some contextual details were made more explicit.
56 For the sake of completion, it must be added that in some interviews Ishiguro conceives of this novel from the more universalist perspective that these pages do not favour. He sees *Never Let Me Go* as a novel on mortality and the value of life (Freeman 2008: 197; Wong and Crummett 2008: 214–15); Hailsham as representing the fact that we tend to keep our children in a bubble to preserve their innocence (Grigsby

Bates 2008: 199), and therefore Miss Emily as the one who knows best for the students (Wong and Crummett 2008: 218–19). It goes without saying that this should not hinder a different reading of an elaborately articulated novel which offers itself to many interpretations – and which, as literature often does, goes well beyond authorial intentions.
57 For further occurrences of the first kind of narratee, see also 13, 36, 38, 94, 274; for the second, 140 and 280.

6
Conclusion

> The colonial, or postcolonial, model has collapsed. In its place we have a new world order in which there will be soon one global conversation with limited participation open to all, and full participation available to none. In this new world order nobody will feel fully at home. ... we are all being dealt an ambiguous hand, one which may eventually help us to accept the dignity which inform the limited participation of the migrant, the asylum-seeker, or the refugee.
> Caryl Phillips, *A New World Order* (2001b: 5–6)

> The tradition of the oppressed teaches us that the 'state of emergency' in which we live is not the exception but the rule. We must attain a conception of history that is in keeping with this insight.
> Walter Benjamin, 'Theses on the Philosophy of History' (1968: 257)

6.1 Spectralising the camp

> when language is seriously interfered with, when it is disjoined from truth, be it from mere incompetence or worse, from malice, horrors can descend again on mankind.
> Chinua Achebe, 'Language and the destiny of men' (1975: 37)

Never Let Me Go operates a fusion between the two key tropes through which this book examines new slaveries in Britain: the ghost (postcolonial studies) and the concentration camp (Holocaust studies). This chapter contends that such a process, rather than a fruit of Ishiguro's dystopian imagination, is to be seen as a fictional translation of a well-established pattern rooted in the contemporary managing of new slaveries which, in turn, has identifiable historical antecedents. In the light of what the following pages show, the need to tackle representations of new slaveries through a 'multidirectional' approach, to employ Rothberg's paradigm, is even more pressing.

The phenomenon of British new slaveries distinguishes itself by its removal of imprisoned migrants from public view, whereby new forms of concentration camp are increasingly spectralised, reduced to a haunting trace rather than an evident reality; it should not be forgotten that negation has always been a constitutive facet of atrocities (Volpato 2011: 36). Not only does this happen to those migrants who are illicitly enslaved, given the criminal nature of their ordeal; the spectralisation of the camp also concerns institutional forms of detention. Before discussing this through references to politics, media and cultural theory, however, this chapter offers an analysis of two French films on new slaveries, because they both show another symbolic conflation of spectral and imprisoning tropes.

Philippe Lioret's feature film *Welcome* (2009) and Sylvain George's arthouse documentary *Qu'ils reposent en révolte* (May They Rest in Revolt, 2010) both focus on the undocumented migrants notoriously amassing in the so-called 'jungle' of Calais, waiting for an opportunity to cross the Channel.[1] 'The significance of Calais is its status as the main ferry port to Britain, so comprising the main transit route for many migrants', state Howarth and Ibrahim; they emphasise the amphibious identity of Calais,[2] where migrants are caught between French laws and the British press campaign delegitimising migrants and construing them as a threat.[3] The ensuing tensions between the two countries' authorities (Howarth and Ibrahim 2012: 205, 210), and above all the French/British negotiations for the constitution of a British zone in Calais including a detention centre for the filtering of migrants (Sciurba 2009: 263),[4] turned Calais into a key place for issues of immigration in Britain. David Farrier (2011: 30–3) aptly states that this British deterritorialising policy for expanding borders has involved a great number of immigration officers on foreign soil, who are given substantial powers but no mandatory consideration of potential asylum rights.

Both Lioret and George convey the erasure of the humanity of these people whose bodies and hopes, though the individual is very often free to roam without being technically detained, are nevertheless blocked in Calais for months: symbolically, Sylvain George's camera often lingers on detritus soaked in foamy water, analogously to the 'debris you get on a seashore' closing Ishiguro's *Never Let Me Go* (2010: 282).[5] For these migrants in Calais, an illegal crossing seems to represent the only way out, with the high levels of risk that it implies[6] – even though remaining there did not prove a safer option:

Conclusion

By 2009 reportedly 700–800 refugees were camped in scrubland near the port and that September the French authorities demolished their 'Jungle' encampment in a dawn raid with bulldozers, vans and up to 500 riot police armed with flame throwers, stun guns and tear gas. (Howarth and Ibrahim 2012: 200)[7]

In *Welcome*, the migrants constitute an example of Rothberg's 'multidirectional memory', in so far as they immediately remind viewers of anti-Jewish persecutions (when they are not allowed entry into public supermarkets (see Plate 10) and swimming-pools)[8] and of the transatlantic slave trade (when the protagonist Bilal drowns while attempting to swim over to the English coast).

But, once again, how do these movies translate the specificities of new slaveries into the symbolic realm?

Sylvain George's *Qu'ils reposent en révolte* follows – all the way to the razing of the 'Jungle' – the everyday existence of these migrants without any voyeuristic or sentimental complacency (Piccino 2010: 20). For instance, George's camera hides with a migrant who is waiting for an appropriate truck to stop by, in order to sneak underneath its chassis; when that actually happens, the director's view dwells on the void left by the departed vehicle.[9] His documentary begins with the image of a barbed-wire noose and ends on a migrant's body lying on a bed, completely covered by a white sheet. In addition to this symbolic frame opening and closing the documentary, the ghost and the camp tropes are most fused together when George takes a long, static and silent close-up of a migrant's head enveloped by the collar and the hood of his sweater (see Plate 11).

Significantly, Lioret's *Welcome* articulates a very similar image through the story of Bilal, a young Kurd who attempts to cross the

10 From *Welcome*: Migrants are denied entry into a Calais supermarket.

11 From *Qu'ils reposent en révolte*: A migrant with his head covered by a hood and sweater.

Channel hidden in the back of a truck. He is caught by the new sophisticated systems of control because he cannot bear to keep his head inside a plastic bag (see Plate 12).

Later, he explains to his angry fellow stowaways that he had been traumatised by the Turkish police who had kept him in that condition for eight days, almost suffocating him to death. He then astonishes Simon, his only French friend, when he resorts to training himself to endure this ordeal, with the prospect of trying to cross over to England again. Even the friendly Simon will force Bilal's head into a plastic bag, in a sudden burst of helpless rage (see Plate 13).

Once again, what straightaway comes to mind is Foucault's notion of peace as a coded war (2003: 51). The impressive recurrence of the hooded head image, in different contexts throughout the movie, conveys a sense of continuity and questions the purported dichotomy between the neglect of human rights in states like Turkey and 'civilised' Europe.[10]

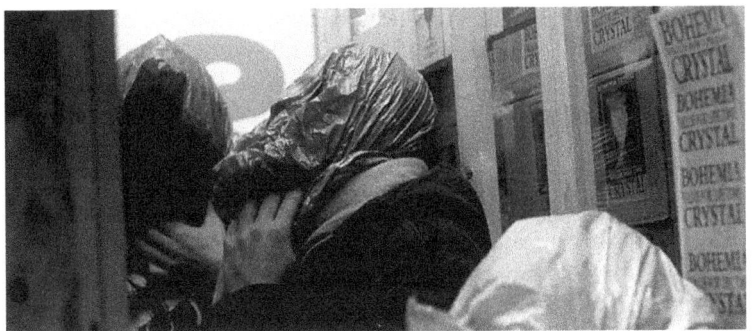

12 From *Welcome*: Bilal's head in a plastic bag, in the back of the smuggling truck.

I see the hooded head as symbolic of the way in which these migrants are at once spectralised, through an effacement of their most individual and human traits, and imprisoned, in a process that negates any form of collective agency, cutting them off from one another. In other words, the hooded head powerfully embodies the contiguity of the ghost and the camp – and the fragmented, dispersed nature of the concentrationary archipelago of British new slaveries,[11] a specificity which is also strikingly evident in Bilal's immense loneliness when he tries to break into Britain by swimming across the Channel.

In his 1995 essay entitled 'The face', Giorgio Agamben sees the face as the repository at once of human communicability and of the very impossibility of communicating truth: 'only when I find a face', he writes, 'do I encounter an exteriority and does an *outside* happen to me' (Agamben 2000: 100). In the light of this sentence, it is easy

13 From *Welcome*: Simon forcing Bilal's head into a plastic bag.

to read the image of the hooded head as symptomatic of new slaveries, inasmuch as it represents today's refusal to really 'encounter an exteriority'. At the same time, the hooded head employed by Lioret and George calls for a rethinking of Agamben's view of contemporary state power as 'no longer founded on the monopoly of the legitimate use of violence ... rather, it is founded above all on the control of appearance'; when it comes to new slaveries, actual violence still very much constitutes an issue, rather than being superseded by simulacra of media culture. For the same reason, the hooded head shows that the distinction that Agamben traces between the process of 'falsification and consumption' of the face (in 'advanced industrialized countries') and the outright 'exclusion of any impropriety' dominating in the 'so-called totalitarian states' (Agamben 2000: 95) needs readjustment, if seen from the perspective of the new slaveries produced by globalisation.

The symbolic conflation of the ghost and the camp operated by Ishiguro, George and Lioret trenchantly resonate with both the history and the contemporaneity of concentration camps. Different political systems in different ages have spectralised the camp in different ways, following a tradition analogous to that remarked by Benjamin in the second epigraph to Chapter 6. It is hard to forget, for example, how the Nazi Final Solution was effected through

> the suppression of facts and the disavowal and destruction of pieces of evidence that were an integral part of the murder action and its implementation.[12] The German bureaucracy ... used a variety of euphemistic terms to cover up the mass killings. (Gutman 1990: 682)[13]

The link between the camp and ghostliness was not always so straightforward. Its ambiguity was emphasised, for instance, by Hannah Arendt in an essay which deeply influenced Agamben's vision of refugees, when she observed how institutions insisted on forgetting, when dealing with the Second World War Jewish refugees who had escaped from Germany:

> We were told to forget; and we forgot quicker than anybody could ever imagine. ... In order to forget more efficiently we rather avoid any allusion to concentration or internment camps we experienced in nearly all European countries – it might be interpreted as pessimism or lack of confidence in the new homeland. Besides, how often have we been told that nobody likes to listen to all that; hell is no longer a religious belief or a fantasy, but something as real as houses and stones and trees. Apparently nobody wants to know that contemporary history has created a new kind of human beings – *the*

kind that are put in concentration camps by their foes and in internment camps by their friends. (Arendt 1996: 110–11; italics mine)

Arendt's bitter, subtle irony on the despair of Jewish refugees at what they had lost, and on the cold hostility of the bureaucrats of their new nations, pervades her essay. The closing of this excerpt, with its structural repetition reinforced by alliteration, subtly blurs any substantial difference between the foe's and the friend's camp; it thus resonates with the institutional internment of new slaves in contemporary Britain, and with the continuity between Turkey and Europe conveyed by Lioret's film *Welcome* through the image of the hooded head (not to mention that these interning 'friends' may be identified with Hailsham's educators in Ishiguro's novel).

Theorising the spectralisation of the camp sounds most suited to the context of British new slaveries, in the face of the removal of imprisoned migrants from public view. New forms of concentration camps are increasingly spectralised, reduced to a haunting trace rather than an evident reality. The new shapes assumed by the concentration camp are made insubstantial in many fields and in manifold ways; the following pages take into consideration the language of the propaganda in favour of immigration restrictions and one example from cultural theory.

As regards the peculiarities of the contemporary language of propaganda, Steve Cohen analyses the political and journalistic jargon of immigration controls through the lens of Orwellian Newspeak, thereby showing how crucial the role of dystopian imaginaries is in the analysis of new slaveries. The premise to the whole apparatus is that being a non-person, a ghost, leads very easily to being imprisoned (and vice versa): 'With the proliferation of detention and removal centres ... an increasing number of those subject to immigration controls (including children) exist only as prisoners. Lack of immigration status and absence of freedom are becoming synonymous.' And, it might be added, both conditions are conveyed by the implications of the widely used term 'illegals' (Cohen 2006: 20, 24), rather than fairer definitions such as 'undocumented'.[14] Tracing constant analogies with *Nineteen Eighty-Four*, Cohen lays bare the many strategies employed to spectralise the reality of contemporary detention centres:[15] first of all, making detention arbitrary and irrational, so that 'people (or their lawyers) are usually not told why they have been detained or when they will be released' (Bohmer and Shuman 2008: 75–6). The 'not knowing *if* or *why* or *where* or *how* or *when* or *for how long* detention may occur' sometimes drives undocumented migrants to madness (Cohen 2006: 89), as conveyed by this excerpt from Sonja Linden's *Asylum Monologues* (2006):

> This waiting for the Home Office to decide – me, I always say that it is a diplomatic form of torture. They are not raping us, they are not burning us with cigarettes, they are not hitting us with guns, but they are torturing us mentally, and that's the worst. Because – my scars – they heal – it was painful, but if I touch them now, I feel no pain. But the torture that is mental – this is constant.[16]

Secondly, new slaves' imprisonment is spectralised by distorting detention through ameliorative or euphemistic language, similarly to the Doublethink logic of Orwell's Newspeak (and echoing the centrality of euphemisms in Ishiguro's *Never Let Me Go*), such as the slogan of the Immigration and Nationality Directorate: 'Building a Safe, Just and Tolerant Society', ominously recalling ARBEIT MACHT FREI (Cohen 2006: 97).[17] Thirdly, by making detention a 'compulsory choice':

> Mohammed Ashraf Mughal, a Pakistani citizen, was denied an order of habeas corpus against his wrongful detention on the grounds that he could always agree to be removed to Pakistan and therefore escape the detention. Such are the *doublethink* non-choices given to the undocumented. (Cohen 2006: 49)

The fourth method consists in limiting the evidence of those who are deported ('vaporized' as in *Nineteen Eighty-Four*, according to Cohen) and in detaining and deporting, whenever possible, far 'from the public eye' (Cohen 2006: 57–8, 79).[18] Just as the Nazi 'Night and Fog' decree prescribed prisoners' transportations under 'cover of night' (Gordon 2008: 72),[19] in twenty-first-century Britain the undocumented are usually deported in the dead of night or around dawn, as described by Little Bee in *The Other Hand* (see Chapter 3.3):

> They came for me at four o'clock in the morning. ... They put me in the back of a van. ... All along the streets the windows of the apartment were silent and blind, with their curtains closed. I disappeared without anyone to see me go. (Cleave 2008: 343–4)[20]

The fifth method mentioned by Cohen is, ostensibly, the opposite of the previous one: the spectacularising of immigration controls, which paradoxically produces an effect of spectralisation. When quoting at length from the BBC gameshow *You the Judge* (2003), where viewers were asked to judge real asylum cases, Cohen aptly defines it as:

> a classic example of a mode of thought which in *Nineteen Eighty-Four* is described as doublethink – as thinking two opposites simultaneously (in this case actuality and fantasy) – a mode of thought that will be seen as central to the enforcement of immigration controls in that it leads to the loss of all critical, reflective faculties. (Cohen 2006: 36)[21]

Alongside the propaganda of immigration control, unfortunately, some cultural theory, too, eludes the specificities of new slaveries, thus obliterating the inhuman exploitation they entail. I am thinking here mainly of Marc Augé's mention of refugee camps as one of the many 'non-places' (airports, stations etc.), regardless of their specific material context (Augé 1995: 34). The porous relationship that Augé identifies between places and non-places (78–9, 107) can certainly be applied to the concentrationary archipelago of new slaveries; the same is true of his definition of non-places: non-identitarian, non-relational, non-historical (77–8), because new slaves are devoid of an acknowledged identity and are generally cut off from both fellow new slaves and citizens' society, as this volume shows.

On the other hand, I find Augé's assimilation of refugee camps to non-places where circulation is accelerated extremely perplexing: in my view, the new forms of concentration camps are integral to non-places, and sustain them from their spectral positioning. They ensure the smooth, accelerated functioning of non-places. Augé seems to deploy his study in a reality vacuum, eschewing important discriminations among the socio-political functions of different kinds of locations.

According to him, non-places imply 'the passive joys of identity-loss' once you have proved your identity (103), but in the refugee camp the opposite is certainly true: 'the passive joys of identity-loss' sounds bitterly inappropriate to new slaves, as shown by the two movies examined above.[22] It is evident in Lioret's *Welcome*, for example, in the already mentioned scenes when Bilal and his fellow migrants are not allowed free entry to supermarkets and to the showers at swimming pools, and thus are denied an opportunity to purchase their basic human rights to food and hygiene. Calais teems with migrants, while at the same time not acknowledging their presence: by isolating them through the denial of any form of welfare, power and visibility, Calais exacerbates the ghostliness of these migrants, further exposing them to traffickers, exploitative employers (implying potential slavery) and institutional assaults; in David Farrier's words on asylum seekers (2012: 431–2), 'living without the right to work, and for some with the daily threat of removal, makes it near impossible to experience the everydayness of the everyday' and makes them 'the citizen's dark other'. This is also communicated by the quick trial on Bilal's attempted illegal entry: he is a minor coming from a country at war, but to be taken care of, according to the arrogant judge, is the last thing that Bilal wishes.

In George's *Qu'ils reposent en révolte*, faced with bio-political institutions that aim at cataloguing their identity through the technological control of their bodies, some migrants resort to erasing their own physical existence: the documentary shows a long close-up of their hands using a red-hot screw to burn off their own fingerprints. Significantly, George's shot is never enlarged to include their faces during this process of self-spectralisation: thanks to his visual choice, he poignantly conveys how completely these people's identities are effaced (see Plate 14).[23]

14 From Sylvain George's *Qu'ils reposent en révolte*:
Burnt fingertips, erasing one's identity.

It seems to me that this resorting to such a process of self-spectralisation and self-abjection[24] represents the very opposite of Augé's 'passive joys of identity-loss'; a book like Bohmer and Shuman's *Political Asylum* (2008: 84–108) makes it very clear that identity is likely to be a crucial issue, if not *the* crucial issue, for asylum seekers.

Augé's *Non-Places* was almost contemporaneous with Derrida's and Agamben's theorisations mentioned in this volume, and with the first fictional works on British new slaveries. One must concede that the first half of the 1990s was a time when the full effects of post-Soviet globalisation and neo-liberalism were only beginning to emerge. Nevertheless, I find it highly problematic that not even Augé's introduction to the second edition of *Non-Places* (2008) mentions a change of perspective with regard to the complex relationship between non-places and refugees (Augé 2008: passim).[25] Contemporary theory should strive to expose, rather than validate, the pervasive procedures of spectralisation and detention discussed in these pages, and thus to go beyond the discrimination-free pictures that those very procedures offer for mainstream cultural consumption.

6.2 Postcolonialism, new slaveries and borders

If there is one particular stance I take with respect to the current state of postcolonial studies, it is that we are still considering, slowly, perhaps, and unmethodically, ... with a continuing sense of excitement, the dimensions of the field.
Peter Hulme, 'Beyond the straits' (2005: 42)

In conclusion, then, I choose my own version of the beyond of postcolonial discourse: the question of subaltern consciousness.
Gayatri Chakravorty Spivak, 'The new subaltern' (2007: 235)

The subalternists ... seem now engaged in excellent postcolonial exercises away from the subaltern classes.
Gayatri Chakravorty Spivak, 'Scattered speculations on the subaltern and the popular' (2005: 477)

Given the wide spectrum of the texts analysed in this volume, this final chapter is designed to discuss the theoretical categories around new slaveries: can we still use such umbrella terms as postcolonial or Black British? What are the continuities with and discontinuities from them? To what extent can the art on new slaveries in Britain fall under these critical categories? And if it does, how will it be modified by the study of new slaveries?

At this point, it should be evident that I consider new slaves the 'beyond' of postcolonial studies, following Spivak's remark in the second epigraph to this chapter (and hoping to avoid the flaws mentioned by Spivak in the third epigraph). Even though this book started with clearly Black British or postcolonial critical references – see Oldfield's study of commemorations of the slave trade (Chapter 1.1) or the reading of Rendell's *Simisola* in the perspective of Stuart Hall's essay 'New Ethnicities' (2.2) – 'Black British' and 'postcolonial' do not apply easily, if only for strictly geographical reasons. First, some of the authors analysed here are not from former British colonies (like Lewycka and Popa) or they are white Britons (such as Cleave and Broomfield, to mention two); in the case of crime fiction, this book makes use of precious insights by bestselling, mainstream, non-postcolonial writers such as Rendell, Rankin and P. D. James (arguably the top names in the field).

Secondly, the victims they write of have, in some cases, very tenuous links with the history of British colonialism; see for example, the migrants from Eastern Europe.[26] Narrated by Broomfield and investigated by Pai in Chapter 4.1, Chinese immigrants constitute another case in point, even though they come from the same region that provided indentured labourers for the Caribbean in the nineteenth century. The Chinese case is also significant in so far as a good number of these migrants are, to say the least, far from fluent in English, and these language barriers are a decisive factor in making them third-class citizens (Craig et al. 2007: 17).[27] Thirdly, some of these works are not even set within British borders. In Bayley's *The Container* (Chapter 4.3), Britain is evoked only as an object of desire; Chapter 6.1 deals with two films set in Calais, while staking a claim for considering the French coastal town as a coruscating case of the *British* phenomenon of new slaveries.

Bearing all these provisos in mind, a more apposite term for the study of new slaveries may be 'multi-ethnic', in the light of a collection of essays, *Multi-Ethnic Britain 2000+* (2008), which proposes to go beyond the centrality of ethnic factors in order to investigate artistic representations of immigration and asylum by, amongst others, white (including canonical) authors (Eckstein et al. 2008: 14). In the British context, as Barbara Korte writes in the same book (2008: 321) with regard to *Children of Men*, migration 'is no

Conclusion 189

longer associated with the so-called developing countries only but has become a global and multi-ethnic phenomenon'.

The critical perspective proposed by *Multi-Ethnic Britain* is bound to offer a fruitful contribution to the theoretical work on new slaveries. Korte's above statement, for example, points to an apparent paradox lying behind the chapters of the present book, namely the attempt to maintain rigid geographical boundaries for its research (Britain) for what is ultimately a phenomenon with globalised origins and bearings. This reflection, though, does not apply only to the issues related to new slaveries: in the critical debate about the present state and future developments of postcolonial studies, globalisation (and the theoretical domain usually termed 'globalisation studies') has often been perceived as one of the main driving forces showing the urgency of a redefinition, sometimes even an abandonment, of the field (Loomba et al. 2005: 2).

This chapter takes into consideration two key collections of essays focusing on the topic of reshaping postcolonial studies: Ania Loomba, Suvir Kaul, Matti Bunzl, Antoinette Burton and Jed Esty's *Postcolonial Studies and Beyond* (2005) and Janet Wilson, Cristina Sandru and Sarah Lawson Welsh's *Rerouting the Postcolonial* (2010). One general trend shared by their contributors – and one point that this book strongly underscores – is the role conceived of for postcolonial studies 'as a critical strain posed within and against, as well as antecedent to, dominant notions of globalization' (Loomba et al. 2005: 8). This orientation is obviously dictated by the acknowledgement of the incipient problem represented by the 'underprivileged agencies' produced by globalisation: in this regard, Patrick Williams (2010: 88) explicitly argues for the 'new discourses of resistance' generated by the postcolonial field. See for instance, Simon Gikandi's critical take on cosmopolitanism from the perspectives of the refugee and the coerced migrant (2010: passim), which might well constitute an answer to Marc Augé's notion of non-places (contested here at the end of Chapter 6.1).[28] What is at stake here, then, is the political drive of postcolonial criticism, 'the reassertion of a certain historical urgency that may have been leached from postcolonial studies during its period of theoretical refinement and institutional consolidation' (Loomba et al. 2005: 5) and the reconnection of 'the ethical and the political with the aesthetic' (Wilson et al. 2010: 2) in the context of globalisation.[29] In order to achieve this, some critics bring to the fore the importance of 'the continuities – and indeed the innovations – between today's neo-imperialism and older systems of colonial capitalism', to the point of claiming that, by virtue of this, postcolonial studies is probably finding 'its real critical vocation' (Loomba et al. 2005: 9). Such an approach might account for the constant references made in this book to the linkage between new slaveries on the one hand, and the Atlantic slave trade or postcolonial or Black British issues on the other.

But, to return to the globalised/national question, for the scholar working on new slaveries the greatest challenge consists, I believe, in focusing on specificities, and unravelling the common strands while delving into such a fragmented and diverse universe. Baldly stated, what is at stake for both the future of postcolonial studies and the analysis of British new slaveries is precisely how to maintain this double focus, a close and due attention towards both the systemic and the local, 'residual forms of national sovereignty within globalized institutions' (Loomba et al. 2005: 16). It need hardly be repeated that the study of British new slaveries necessarily implies going beyond a British-based focus, just as the renewal of postcolonial studies must often assume a field of investigation wider than national borders;[30] this book starts from this assumption from Chapter 2.1, which underscores the similarly double focus of Bridget Anderson's study of migrant domestic workers. At the same time, many works analysed in the previous chapters demonstrate the relevance of the *British* specificities of new slaveries. The dissolution of national borders is already at risk of becoming a stale platitude, if only because the tightening of British borders is the root of much suffering, sometimes death, for migrants. What Ania Loomba and her fellow editors note (2005: 21–2) is that

> reports of the death (or atrophy) of the nation-state as a vital organizing force in the contemporary world have been greatly exaggerated. Several contributors fear that such reports advance a facile or premature model of nationlessness that, however unwittingly, answers to the neoliberal fantasy of a borderless planet. To them, postcolonial studies appear especially well situated not just to resist that fantasy but to offer in its place a more detailed, more patient, more accurate representation of the reciprocal flow of power (economic, social, and cultural) between nation-states and globalized capitalism ... to look afresh at the relation between national and transnational forms of government, economy, society, and culture.[31]

Rather than the demise of the nation, then, the crucial issue for this book has been how the nation itself is changed by the currents of globalisation. The phenomenon of British new slaveries has overtaken Hardt and Negri's much-quoted statement (2000: 253–4) according to which 'Third World ... enters into First, establishes itself as the heart of the ghetto, shanty town, favela, always again produced and reproduced'. Britain's concentrationary archipelago is continuously 'produced and reproduced', but it does not originate only from the Third World, and is not simply locatable in any ghetto, or nation's heart. It is more varied in its origins – and it is ubiquitous in its dispersal, by virtue of the proliferation of borders transversal to the nation rather than at its margins, as theorised by Étienne Balibar (2004:1).[32]

This dissemination of borders is necessarily to be tackled with an opening up of critical confines, as premised in Chapter 1.4. This book submits that the twin perspective of postcolonial and Holocaust studies for delving into new slaveries is not a critical ruse: rather, it is dictated by the very primary texts analysed in the previous chapters. In the spirit of Edward Said's concept of 'Traveling Theory' (see Chapter 1.5), these works call for a readjustment of theoretical paradigms, and represent the strongest evidence of the need, for both postcolonial studies and cultural criticism in general, to face the changing conditions of its referent. The same could be said of the chapters which measure their investigation against other critical precincts, such as genre studies (2.2, 3.4, 3.5, 4.1) and trauma theory (3.1, 4.3).

One should not think, though, that this flaunting of the boundedness of categories represents a novelty – on the contrary, it is meant to follow an established and valued theoretical strain. Loomba's and Wilson's collections of essays both underscore the inherent and long-standing characteristic of postcolonial studies as 'a porous entity rather than a discrete field' (Loomba et al. 2005: 3).[33] This tendency manifested itself with particular intensity in the first half of the 1990s – the period when, according to this book, the transformations induced by neo-liberal globalisation laid the foundations and showed the first effects of the widespread new slaveries to come. Those years, which saw the publication of the earliest texts on new slaveries (see Chapter 2) and of some key theory for the present volume (Derrida's *Specters of Marx*, Agamben's first works on the camp), were also marked by a landmark development of postcolonial studies: the publication of Paul Gilroy's *The Black Atlantic* (1993), a significant enlargement of critical confines[34] by virtue of an emphasis on diasporic scenarios that have created a new area within postcolonial studies. Gilroy's work obviously lies behind this volume, given its transnational, transhistorical reflections on the continuities between the Atlantic slave trade and contemporary marginalised communities, but also its attention to how marginalis*ing* and dominated groups have mutually influenced one another. Historically speaking, this questioning may be seen as a continuation of the late eighteenth and early nineteenth-century debate on abolitionism, involving the effects of slavery on traders and on the Christian principles of British society. Gilroy returns to this debate towards the ending of *The Black Atlantic* (1993: 221), where he recalls an interview with Toni Morrison, who told him:

> Slavery broke the world in half, it broke it in every way. It broke Europe. It made them into something else, it made them slave masters, it made them crazy. You can't do that for hundreds of years and it not take a toll. They had to dehumanise, not just the slaves but themselves. ... It made everything in world war two possible. It made world war one necessary. Racism is the word that we use to encompass all this.[35]

Incidentally, this hint at the Second World War is not fortuitous, since in the same section of the sixth chapter of *The Black Atlantic* ('Black culture and ineffable terror') Gilroy discusses the potential cross-fertilisation of Holocaust and Black Atlantic studies, acknowledges his debt to the former and takes to task thinkers such as Bauman and Levinas for their excessively exclusivist approach (1993: 213).[36] Gilroy's approach is not far from Rothberg's concept of 'multidirectional memory' (see Chapter 1.4); besides, he quotes Levi's *The Drowned and the Saved* to trace a parallelism between the journey to the camp and the literature on racial slavery (1993: 215), analogously to the connection suggested by this book in Chapter 4.3 when dealing with Bayley's *The Container*. This pattern of analysis, too, was further elaborated by Gilroy in *Between Camps*, inspired by Arendt's tracing of Nazi worldviews back to the centrality of race in colonial modernity, and by Levi's warning against their survival in modified forms (see Chapter 1.4). In order to counter this racially based ideology that he calls 'raciology', and 'camp-thinking', he theorises a diasporic 'between-camps' thinking capable of connecting colonial people in Europe, Jews and other 'vulnerable minorities' (Gilroy 2004b: 76–7), and exhorts his readers to be 'alive to the camps out there now and the camps around the corner, that are being prepared' (87). Nevertheless, I sense some limitations in his vagueness around specific material experiences (harking back to the above-mentioned call for political urgency in postcolonial studies) and in the centrality he assigns to the concept of race (88, 93) – that, as explained at the beginning of this chapter, requires qualifications if applied to British new slaveries. Perhaps I feel closer to his interest in the 'mixture of ethnicity and identity' that Gilroy, in his *After Empire* (2004a: 155, 156, 159), sees as the basis of the culturalist racism that followed the previous biological hierarchies: he calls them 'wider dimensions of cultural and, thanks to Huntington and company, civilizational difference' that 'have also been attractive to the aspirations of the social-democratic Left'.[37]

To return to the interconnected involvement of the exploiter and the exploited, Gilroy (2004a: 155) rightly underscores the importance of 'the changing cultural and ethical contours of Europe, where the notion of public good and the practice of politics seem to be in irreversible decline, undone by a combination of consumer culture, privatization, and the neoliberal ideology'. My wager is that this further example of how porous categories are in postcolonial studies is a crucial facet for the study of British new slaveries, as already shown by my reflections on the 'double' in Chapter 4.1. This is precisely the issue that the concluding part of this chapter (and of this volume) intends to explore. In his seminal essay 'Beyond human rights', Giorgio Agamben focuses on the pivotal role played by the figure of the refugee as a contemporary development of the concentration camp prisoner; in the wake of Hannah Arendt's essay 'We refugees' (1943, see Chapter 6.1), which called refugees 'the vanguard of their people', Agamben writes:

> the figure that should have embodied human rights more than any other ... marked instead the radical crisis of the concept. [...] If the refugee represents such a disquieting element in the order of the nation-state, this is so primarily because, by breaking the identity between the human and the citizen and that between nativity and nationality, it brings the ordinary fiction of sovereignty to crisis. Single exceptions to such a principle, of course, have always existed. What is new in our time is that growing sections of humankind are no longer representable inside the nation-state – and this novelty threatens the very foundations of the latter. Inasmuch as the refugee, an apparently marginal figure, unhinges the old trinity of state-nation-territory, it deserves instead to be regarded as the central figure of our political history. ... [the refugee is a] limit-concept that at once brings a radical crisis to the principles of the nation-state and clears the way for a renewal of categories that can no longer be delayed.

Only when this renewal is effected, he concludes, 'only in such a world is the political survival of humankind today thinkable' (Agamben 2000: 19, 21–2, 23, 26). Another scholar of the Holocaust, George Bensoussan, identifies in the refugee the embodiment of the weakening of human rights, and describes the concept of citizenship based on nationality as the embryo of state crimes (Bensoussan 2002: 57, 96).[38]

One of the conclusions offered by this book is that such a renewal of categories can no longer be delayed, particularly when it comes to spectralised migrants and the so-called citizens of the nations in which they are enslaved. This renewal is not needed simply for ethical and political reasons, though I firmly believe that 'there can be no freedom unless there is freedom for all' (Farhi 2002: 365).[39] It is inescapable also because new slaves are *not* an exceptional category, or an isolated, restricted case, without any significance for a wider socio-cultural analysis of our contemporaneity, in accordance with Walter Benjamin's conception of history expressed in the epigraph introducing Chapter 6.[40] The case-studies examined in this book demonstrate that the dispersal of new slaveries in Britain is at once liminal and systemic.[41]

It is a *systemic* exceptionality, first of all, because it can be found anywhere, including institutional, legal places, and is enforced by British laws (Rankin's *Fleshmarket Close* offers an effective translation of this phenomenon; see Chapter 3.5). Secondly, new slaves' liminality has a systemic nature in so far as it forms a pillar of the British economy, as Hsiao-Hung Pai asserts in her book (2008: 246):

> Every British person benefits from the existence of these nameless people living and working around us. Undocumented migrant workers are not an anomaly in the system in which we live, but very much part of it. The British economy thrives on this army of workers .... Every time we pick up a pack of skinless chicken breasts or a bag of washed lettuce, we may be unknowingly colluding with the system that exploits them. Doing jobs no locals want to do, for wages and working hours no locals would accept, they are producing social wealth for a country that permanently excludes them.

Considering that a society is defined a 'slave society' not only on the basis of its number of slaves, can contemporary Britain be called a 'slave society'?[42] Historians and economists are certainly more qualified to answer this question than the present book, where economic analysis is to be found only in a very unscientific form.[43] What mostly concerns me in this chapter is that the UK labour market, characterised by extreme flexibility and deregulation,[44] is conducive to the easy exploitation of both undocumented and documented migrants. In addition, repressive policies and policing over immigration (which in many cases make legal sojourn virtually impossible) ensure the reproduction of enslaveable labour without basic rights, whereby a constant state of deportability turns the undocumented into an available commodity (De Genova 2002: 438). This is especially evident in Nick Broomfield's film *Ghosts* (see Chapter 4.1) in the scene of police raids on the Chinese migrants.[45] In this regard, one could also mention the infamous 2009 case of the SOAS cleaners where the close connection between repressive policing or policies and economic demands was shown in all its brutality; in agreement with immigration authorities, contractors set up a fake dawn meeting with campaigning workers: the meeting was raided, leading to the deportation of some cleaners. (Toscano 2009: passim).

In this climate, migrants have become not only scapegoats who can be blamed for the fears, insecurity and economic straits produced by globalisation (Palidda 2011: 6–7) but also labour fodder; as said before, their deportability leads to a state of disposable commodity (De Genova 2002: 438). Most importantly for this chapter, they can be seen a vanguard of the times to come, an extreme exemplification of the erosion of workers' rights that is characterising world labour.[46] Balibar (2004: 41) rightly speaks of Europe's 'recolonization of social relations', when he notices that migrants incarnate 'a regression of citizenship toward a purely formal framework (which amounts not only to an exclusion from all or part of social rights on the basis of nationality but, little by little, to an increased vulnerability of all workers)'. In the case of the UK, another significant example is provided by the infamous legislation known as 'workfare', whereby claimants to unemployment benefits must take up unpaid jobs for up to two years.[47] Far from constituting an exception, then, the condition of new slaves is likely to envelop larger and larger portions of British society[48] – Chapter 5.2 reads Ishiguro's *Never Let Me Go* precisely as a vision of how new slaves can represent and prefigure society as a whole. New slaveries and their forms of imprisoning camps perform one of the functions that Foucault envisioned for his concept of heterotopia (1986: 27): 'to create a space of illusion that exposes every real place, all the sites inside of which human life is partitioned, as still more illusory' – where the object of illusion is democracy and its implied respect of human rights.[49]

As has become obvious from the above, then, the renewal of categories called for by Agamben cannot simply involve new slaves, but involves society at large. In the same 1993 essay ('Beyond human rights') where he saw the refugee as the figure questioning human rights and 'the inscription of nativity as well as the trinity of state-nation-territory that is founded on that principle', he also expressed a warning about incipient atrocities,[50] and attempted to point a way out of this crisis, again based on the opening up of frontiers, inspired by the idea of Jerusalem becoming

> simultaneously and without any territorial partition – the capital of two different states. ... communities that would articulate each other via a series of reciprocal extraterritorialities in which the guiding concept would no longer be the *ius* (right) of the citizen but rather the *refugium* (refuge) of the singular. In an analogous way, we could conceive of Europe not as an impossible 'Europe of the nations', whose catastrophe one can already foresee in the short run, but rather as an aterritorial or extraterritorial space in which all the (citizen and noncitizen) residents of the European space would be in a position of exodus or refuge; the status of the European would then mean the being-in-exodus of the citizen .... European space would thus mark an irreducible difference between birth [*nascita*] and nation in which the old concept of people ... could again find a political meaning, thus decidedly opposing itself to the concept of nation (which has so far unduly usurped it). ... In this new space, European cities would rediscover their ancient vocation of cities of the world by entering into a relation of reciprocal extraterritoriality. (Agamben 2000: 24–5)

In the densely suggestive language that characterises his writings (at times edging towards excessive convolution), Agamben envisions a renewal of society that is very difficult to put into practice, close to utopia.[51] The 'Europe of the nations' is certainly 'impossible' as a value-judgement, but a monolithically formidable entity to be tackled. Utopian thinking, though, seems to be part and parcel of the potential developments of postcolonial studies.[52] Avery Gordon, too, encouragingly sees the utopian as a constitutive function of criticism (2008: 195): according to her, the very figure of the ghost inherently carries both the violence that made it and the utopian, both the degraded reality 'in which we are inextricably and historically entangled and the longing for the arrival of a future, entangled certainly but ripe in the plenitude of nonsacrificial freedoms and exuberant unforeseen pleasures' (207).

Let us move on, then, to the specifics of British new slaveries, and see what hints, what gestures are offered towards the fulfilment of such utopian longings, in the primary and secondary texts analysed in this volume. To start with, it is worth repeating that the scenario of British new slaveries, as it emerges from the said texts, is marked by an exacerbated divisiveness which results, I argue, from the extreme conditions to which new slaves are subjected (in both criminal and institutionalised contexts);[53] to mention just one example, see the lacerating tensions among the protagonists of the plays examined in Chapter 4.3. In some cases, the intervention of British organisations such as Kalayaan for migrant domestic workers (see Chapter 2.1) and the POPPY Project for former sex slaves[54] aims at creating a sort of group solidarity in order to contrast that compartimentalisation of lives. A similar initiative is highlighted by David Farrier (2012: 437) in his study of *Asylum Monologues* and *Asylum Dialogues* (see Chapter 4.3): the self-organisation of the residents of Glasgow's Kingsway estate (2006–8) who set up dawn-time patrols to deter immigration raids and forced removals.[55] In a field such as postcolonial studies, where the agency of the oppressed is rightly given prominence, this may sound paternalistic. But the literary critic cannot neglect the significance offered by the texts at hand. The one exception might be represented by David Belbin's novel *Secret Gardens* (2011), an intriguing story of the bond between two adolescent, undocumented runaways in distress: the Kurdish Aazim and the Ivorian Nadimah. In the midst of a series of persecutions, they seem to find a welcoming home in one of Nottingham's public allotments, albeit temporarily. This public site might be seen as exemplifying Agamben's distinction between nation and people – the dominant metaphor related to popular forms of agriculture as a hope for the future.[56] This reliance on British almost-extinct-but-virtuous popular traditions could again be seen as nostalgically patronising. On the other hand, a survey of the literary products included in this volume shows very little presence of these new slaves' home culture as a source of reliance.[57] This inevitably sidelines a key issue of much postcolonial studies (cultural hybridity), and inevitably constitutes a stumbling block to the recovery of the new slaves' full personhood, so often called for in the previous chapters.[58] Are we facing here the (again patronising) consequence of the citizen (and sometimes white British) perspective of many of the authors, or of the devastated backgrounds many of those slaves originate from?

In any case, what emerges most often in the texts analysed here does not entail group solidarity of whatever origin but, rather, a development of individual awareness in some characters, especially citizens who decide to commit themselves practically against the enslavement they come across. In spite of his proverbial radicality, Frantz Fanon, too, envisioned this kind of contribution (1967: 84):

> This huge task which consists of reintroducing mankind into the world, the whole of mankind, will be carried out with the indispensable help of the European peoples …. To achieve this, the European peoples must first decide to wake up and shake themselves, use their brains, and stop playing the stupid game of the Sleeping Beauty.

This role of citizens may (again) be considered paternalistic, but Balibar, too, sees it as indispensable: according to him (2004: 76–7), change must be the product of the 'common operation … the "shared" act of … those "with" and those "without" … in such a way as to democratize citizenship beginning from its borders'. This volume present cases like this: sleuths like Rendell's Wexford (Chapter 2.2) or Rankin's Rebus (3.5); Theo Faron (5.1) and *Welcome*'s protagonist Simon (6.1), all calling into question their sedated and complacent lives; or even marginal figures like the white Britons sympathising with Ai Qin (4.1), and the clerk at the detention centre *anonymously* calling the police in Rankin's *Fleshmarket Close* (3.5): small but risky gestures of solidarity that break the amoral 'grey zone', the 'banality of evil' which makes us accept the worst forms of atrocities – sometimes turning us into 'desk killers', to continue using Arendt's categories:

> That the model of the citizen in modernity is increasingly seen as having its foundation in obedience to the law (whatever its content), that duty is more and more construed in terms of obedience, is the end result of a long process of debasement of the very concept of the citizen in our civilisation. (Milchman and Rosenberg 1992: 220)

Contrary to this attitude, Balibar (2004: 49) notes how the 1996 struggle of the 'sans-papier' in Paris led to 'reactivate the idea of civil disobedience', which 'forms an essential component of citizenship and contributes to its refoundation in moments of crisis'. In both fiction and history, such rebellious gestures might be seen as replicating (albeit in differing degrees) the righteous reaction against the status quo implicit in all migrants who decide to abandon their suffering, risk their lives and/or break the law in their search for a better existence. Furthermore, these encounters with spectralised slaves produce an effect fittingly described by Avery Gordon's words (2008: 8): 'Being haunted draws us affectively, sometimes against our will and often a bit magically, into the structure of feeling of a reality we come to experience, not as cold knowledge, but as a transformative recognition.' Gordon refers here to the effect produced on the researcher into ghosts[59] (and having worked for a few years on this issue, I can see her point vividly), but I think her 'transformative recognition' could also be applied to the above-mentioned characters. A case in point is represented by Gabriel Lightfoot, protagonist of Monica Ali's *In the Kitchen* (2009), a chef whose life is slowly but inexorably thrown into turmoil after a member of his staff is found dead in the kitchen basement. Gabriel is haunted by nightmares of that corpse, often associated to rotten food and suggesting (see Bauman's and Frears's imagery) the waste implications of both his work as a chef and the new slaves it employs: 'London was all belly, its looping, intestinal streets constantly at work, digesting, absorbing, excreting, fuelling and refuelling, shaping the contours of the land' (Ali 2009: 309). While trying to find out the truth on some human trafficking run by some colleagues, Gabriel starts an ambiguous (and for him, disquieting) sexual relationship with former sex slave Lena, a mistake that will drive him to panic attacks and a final nervous breakdown. I find this story extremely significant in so far as it conveys the sense of how difficult it is, for a single individual, to approach a formidable phenomenon such as the concentrationary archipelago of British new slaveries without being utterly, sometimes sweepingly, overwhelmed by it. Provided one aims at making a change, however small; in the discouraging words of Gabriel's business partner, the politician Fairweather, 'It's endemic, it's a structural problem. You get the odd media's story but that's only the tip of the iceberg ... I'd drop it if I were you' (420–1). Contrary to this piece of advice, Gabriel's rash, self-destroying behaviour will lead the police to arrest his trafficking colleagues – another rebellious gesture against accepted norms of conduct.

Through such socially aware fictional characters, a similar effect may be envisaged at work in the readers of these texts, taking us back to the power of literature and critical humanism discussed in Chapter 1.2. As Robert Spencer writes (2010: 43), the utopian thrust of postcolonial studies, and the alternatives to the status quo it entails, 'take shape either in certain relationships depicted by the work themselves or, more commonly and without doubt more effectively, in the relationship engineered between the characters and events portrayed and the works' readers'.[60]

By way of conclusion, I wish to return to Chris Cleave's *The Other Hand* (Chapter 3.3) and discuss its attempts at exemplifying Agamben's concept of 'reciprocal extraterritoriality'[61] through the relationship between Little Bee and the white Briton Sarah. When the sixteen-year-old Nigerian and her fellow migrants are given shelter by a kind farmer on the day the leave the detention centre, his wife welcomes them with a paean of country life as humane: '*You don't want to go to the suburbs, dear*, she said. *Neither fish nor flesh, the suburbs. Unnatural places, full of unnatural people.* I laughed. I told her, *Maybe I will fit right in*' (Cleave 2008: 110). Little Bee's reply shows that *The Other Hand*'s hopes work along different lines from Belbin's *Secret Gardens*. She manages to reach the suburbs of Kingston-upon-Thames to find Sarah, who saved her life by amputating one of her fingers back in Nigeria two years earlier,[62] and who is living through her own kind of stupefied uprootedness: 'We were exiles from reality, that summer', she says. 'We were refugee from ourselves' (31).[63] Sarah's sense of alienation leads her to perceive the suburbs as a 'purgatory' (124), and she feels like a trapped fly, incapable of making a humane gesture:[64] 'there was no longer one single reason for me to be here – far from the centre of my heart, cast away here in the suburbs' (125). Similarly, at work, she cannot dedicate an issue of their magazine to refugees because, as her colleague says, 'I really don't think you understand how quickly people's eyes will glaze over. It isn't an issue that affects anyone's own life, that's the problem' (291). In other words, her involvement with the traumatic events of Little Bee's tragedy makes her aware of her own (and her society's)[65] traumatic detachment from humane issues, exemplifying the intercultural potentialities that Kathy Caruth detects in trauma:

> In a catastrophic age ... trauma itself may provide the very link between cultures: not a simple understanding of the pasts of others but rather, within the traumas of contemporary history, as our ability to listen through the departures we have all taken from ourselves. (Caruth 1995: 11)

This is why Sarah realises, after Little Bee has overcome all odds and entered her life, that something has changed for good and that she cannot continue simply to survive: 'Little Bee has changed me .... I can't look at her without thinking how shallow my life is' (Cleave 2008: 296). Sarah tells her Nigerian friend that they should start 'helping each other. ... maybe it is time to be serious. Maybe these are serious times.' (213) In the short time they spend together before Little Bee is deported, she seems to find a new perspective, to be ready to change her life completely while helping Little Bee change hers. And vice versa.[66]

Once again, we are faced with a case of going beyond established borders. Both characters, after all, have been driven to cross the boundaries set for their existences (albeit in very different ways). For all the novel's shortcomings (see Chapter 3.3), could this represent a literary exemplification of Agamben's 'reciprocal extraterritoriality'? Sarah's new awareness and consequent actions can with some justification be regarded as following in the wake of Albert Camus's masterpiece *The Rebel: An Essay on Man in Revolt* (1951). The first chapter of Camus's work traces an individual-centred concept of 'revolt' as based on a decision to say 'No', a refusal to accept an imposed condition, but that 'does not imply a renunciation. He [the rebel] is also a man who says yes, from the moment he makes his first gesture of rebellion' (Camus 1991: 13). This apparent paradox is explained by the fact that the rebel's No is at once the defence of a value-laden border – the frontier of one's humaneness (13–16) – and the crossing of this individual frontier to reach towards an Other. In her or his revolt, which can also originate from the oppression that this Other is subjected to (16), the rebel 'identifies himself with other men and so surpasses himself, and from this point of view human solidarity is metaphysical' (17). The affirmation of what he considers the sacred limits of his being human, then, intensifies, rather than veiling, a sense of solidarity, taking us back to the role of critical humanism discussed in Chapter 1.2. The assertive statement concluding Camus's chapter, 'I rebel, therefore we exist' (22) points at a need to transform this individual revolt into a collective project of change.[67] In Cleave's *The Other Hand* there is a hint at this key step when Sarah measures her new decisions against Lawrence's cynicism:

> 'Look at her [Little Bee]', I said. 'I'm so scared. Do you really think I can save her?'
> Lawrence shrugged. 'Maybe you can. And don't take this the wrong way, but so what? Save her and there's a whole world of them behind her. A whole swarm of Little Bees, coming here to feed.'
> 'Or to *pollinate*,' I said.
> 'I think that's naïve,' said Lawrence. (Cleave 2008: 295–6; italics mine)

The possibility of collective projects bridging categories – and of Sarah's supposed naivety – is one of the many questions left unanswered in this book's reading of British new slaveries. Needless to say, these chapters do not pretend to exhaustiveness or finality. The scenario of the British concentrationary archipelago is so diverse, and so rapidly changing, that all that I have been able to do is simply to suggest some directions for further, more detailed, study.

Notes

1 A presence which has raised controversy since 1992 (Sciurba 2009: 188): once again the early 1990s surface as a turning point. The 'jungle' can be considered the unauthorised offshoot of its former version, the Sangatte Red Cross Centre at the mouth of the Channel Tunnel, closed by the French authorities in 2002. For a description of Sangatte, see Isin and Rygiel (2007: 197). For Caryl Phillips's poignant description of his visit to Sangatte (paid in 2001, to write an article for the *Guardian*), see Phillips (2011a: 281–8). See also the scenes set in Sangatte in Michael Winterbottom's film *In This World* (2002).
2 'A liminal no-man's land in the midst of civilized suburbia' (Howarth and Ibrahim 2012: 203).
3 For a detailed description of the xenophobic attitude of British tabloid newspapers, see Moorehead (2006: 142–3).
4 The externalisation of immigration controls has become a worldwide phenomenon: Isin and Rygiel (2007: 176–86) examine some of these 'frontiers', as they call them, and emphasise their function to hinder 'the process of citizenship and rights making' (182). See also Farrier (2011: 28–9); Mezzadra and Neilson (2011: 43).
5 The recurrent image is present in Sylvain George's *Les éclats* (2011), which is also shot in Calais in similarly bleak and uncompromising black and white photography.
6 On the borders of 'First World nations' as places of danger and death, see Mezzadra and Neilson (2011: 35).
7 Sciurba (2009: 187–94) emphasises the informal camps which sprouted in Paris after the closure of Sangatte, again inhabited by migrants waiting to cross the Channel; surprisingly, her analysis does not include Calais's 'jungle'.
8 Lioret's declarations, comparing this with 1940s France, started a controversial national debate (Sciurba 2009: 263).
9 The same stratagem to enter Britain is employed by the protagonist of Michael Winterbottom's *In This World* (2002).
10 On this imprisoning continuity, see Sokol Syla's poem entitled 'I hate Wednesdays' (2005: 22): 'And why an Ipswich cell I don't know, / I've become a prisoner again!'

11 Not to mention the Guantánamo, new-world-order resonance that the hooded head carries.
12 The need to destroy any evidence of the Holocaust became more pressing with the approach of Nazi defeat; see Bensoussan (2002: 135).
13 For more details on these 'language rules' (*Sprachregelung*), see Arendt (1964: 85–6, 108–9).
14 Not surprisingly, the British debate around Calais's 'Jungle' constitutes a classic example of an ideological process of depersonalisation of migrants (Howarth and Ibrahim 2012: 200, 205, 207).
15 Cohen (2006: 18) rightly quotes *Nineteen Eighty-Four*, saying 'you could prove nothing. There was never any evidence' (Orwell 1990: 39).
16 See also Cleave (2008: 316) and Zephaniah (2001: 54). On the issue of indefinite detention as a specifically British phenomenon, see Farrier (2011: 34). Similarly to *Asylum Monologues*, Moorehead (2006: 132–3) describes this state of 'limbo' among Newcastle's refugees as nerve-consuming and mind-disabling, and consequently exacerbating forms of Post Traumatic Stress Disorder (217); she also focuses on the peculiar situation of Kurds around 2004, who were rejected, 'disbenefited', but not liable to deportation because of the war in Iraq (139).
17 With regard to this second strategy of spectralisation of the camp, it could be said that some things never change. When, during the First World War, tens of thousands of 'enemy aliens' were interned in Britain, the German anarchist Rudolf Rocker (detained in Alexandra Palace, London) wrote about his long, harrowing experience at length. He could not help noticing that the most xenophobic British newspapers described life in these camps as a sort of Eldorado, where good wages and healthy diets were the order of the day. He also quoted a long article from the *Daily Mail* (22 November 1918), full of precise details about the easy life of 'our happy huns' (Rocker 2006: 84, 118–19). In a similar spirit, unscathed by the passing of time, in August 1998 the same newspaper 'published the address of an asylum-seeking family it described as "bogus", and their house was subsequently attacked and trashed' (Cohen 2006: 55). This is what leads Cohen (99–100) to play the '*Daily Mail* guessing game', which consists in quoting excerpts from this newspaper dated 2001 (against immigrants from Calais), 1938 (anti-Semitic) and 1900 (ditto), and challenging readers to guess the period they come from. Not surprisingly, in 2003 the Anglo-Indian writer Hari Kunzru refused an award because it was sponsored by this newspaper.
18 This policy is exposed by Melanie Friend's 2007 exhibition *Border County*, where photos of interiors of detention centres do not show any human presence; see Farrier (2011: 68–72). According to Farrier (2011: 66), the camp *dispositif* of the UK asylum system is to be 'understood as *keno-optic*, an emptiness of sight'.
19 Gordon quotes here the 1981 report '*Disappearances*': *A Workbook* (New York: Amnesty International Publications, p. 2).

20 As reported in Linden's *Asylum Dialogues*, the Glasgow Campaign to Welcome Refugees and Asylum Seekers had to start a rota for counteracting dawn raids.
21 As a way to expose this kind of attitude, in 2000 the German film and theatre director Christoph Schlingensief installed a container with twelve asylum seekers in central Vienna. This installation-event-play envisaged the vote of citizens to exclude participants and, Big-Brother-like, a final winner (Farrier 2011: 73–7). At the time of writing (autumn 2013), a controversy is going on in Italy about *The Mission*, a reality show set in refugee camps in Africa, broadcast by the most important state-run channel.
22 To borrow Simon Gikandi's words on his dissatisfaction with cosmopolitanism, 'global cultural flows are still dominated by those coerced migrants rather than the free-willing cosmopolitan subjects' (2010: 28).
23 George shows this practice in detail in his other documentary on Calais, *Les éclats* (2011). This kind of self-effacement as a means of survival, in a system which treats victims as non-persons, resembles what some women declared about their experience in Nazi extermination camps, namely their constant attempt to be 'transparent' (Giustini 2010: 30).
24 In one of her childish imaginative twists, in *The Other Hand* Little Bee makes an unusual agreement with her readers or listeners: 'We must see all scars as beauty. Okay? This will be our secret. Because take it from me, a scar does not form on the dying. A scar means, "I survived"' (Cleave 2008: 13–14).
25 The same could be said of his chapter on the concept of non-place in his later volume *La vie en double: Ethnologie, voyage, écriture* (2011: 152–73).
26 On how Eastern and Central Europe pose questions for the redefinition of postcolonial studies, see Kolodziejczyk (2010: passim).
27 In his essay on the place of China in the reshaping of postcolonial studies, Jeffrey Mather (2010: passim) omits mention of Chinese migrants in Britain.
28 On postcolonial studies as a 'historical corrective to the celebratory theories of globalization', see also Behdad (2005: 77).
29 Commensurate with this, see Benita Parry's criticism of the lack 'of a sufficiently rigorous engagement with the material experiences of "economically enforced dispersal"' in postcolonial studies; Farrier (2011: 3), quoting Parry's 'The institutionalisation of postcolonial studies', in Neil Lazarus (ed.), *The Cambridge Companion to Postcolonial Literary Studies* (Cambridge: Cambridge University Press, 2004), p. 73.
30 See Loomba et al. (2005: 15).
31 See, for instance, Robert Spencer's view of nation states as 'the engines of globalization' (2010: 39), or Erin Goheen Glanville's examination of Canadian refugee fiction (2010: 129). In his study of asylum seekers, Farrier (2011: 4–7) aptly notes that the nation ambiguously represents

32 De Genova (2002: 439) comes to analogous conclusions: 'the spatialized condition of "illegality" reproduces the physical borders of nation-states in the everyday life of innumerable places throughout the interiors of the migrant-receiving states'.
33 These are Tim Brennan's words. See also Wilson et al. (2010: 7, 11).
34 In passing, I should also mention here another epoch-making volume published in 1993, Said's *Culture and Imperialism*, which rejected the 'tendency for fields and specializations to subdivide and proliferate' because they are 'contrary to an understanding of the whole' (Said 1993: 13).
35 Gilroy returned to this idea in his later *Between Camps* (2004b: 67).
36 Gilroy re-expressed this reservation about Bauman's work in his *Between Camps* (2004b: 87).
37 This new, cultural racism is mentioned in Chapter 3.3 in relation to Cleave's *The Other Hand*.
38 Since the early 1990s, the debate on the need to rethink European concepts of citizenship has never ceased. While I am writing this chapter, for instance, an article by Étienne Balibar on the issue in *Libération* (3 May 2013) has fuelled a discussion on the website www.opendemocracy.net.
39 Incidentally, this quotation is from Moris Farhi's unforgettable *Children of the Rainbow* (1999), an epic novel on Romani culture and history, whose Prologue is set in Auschwitz-Birkenau.
40 Giorgio Agamben significantly remarks (2000: 6) that this diagnosis 'has lost none of its relevance'.
41 This is why my essay on the liminal nature of new slaveries was entitled 'Dispersed liminality' (see Deandrea 2012b). In the same year, David Farrier's essay on plays concerning asylum was significantly called 'Everyday exceptions' (Farrier 2012).
42 The debate on what factors contribute to making a society a 'slave society' is still quite open. Alessandro Stella (2000: 40–2) questions the quantitative criteria employed by M. I. Finley (1983: 9, 80), one of the world experts on the subject, and proposes that we might conceive of a 'slave society' as one where slaves are present everywhere, in cities as in villages, in agriculture as in industry, in big as in small houses (I am indebted to my colleague Patrizia Delpiano for indicating this debate to me).
43 It is hard not to agree with Timothy Brennan's call (2005: passim) for a specifically postcolonial theory of economy: 'postcolonial theory should now be ready to move beyond the ethical apprehension of othered subjectivity to a more sophisticated engagement with the public and professional discourses of an ongoing colonial system on which capitalism has feasted and continues to feast' (113).

44 See Anderson and Rogaly (2005: passim). This is what makes Jabez Lam, a social worker for the Chinese community, say: 'The British Government and industry have created this situation between them. Their obsession with deregulated labour and profit margins has led to this underclass of exploited undocumented migrants. These migrants have no value in this country apart from being cheap labour, and they're regarded as disposable and replaceable. The Morecambe Bay cocklepickers were replaced immediately, because there are plenty of other Chinese still desperate enough to go out on to those sands.' Evidence of this is provided by the fact that just 'one week after the Morecambe Bay tragedy, forty migrant workers were once again stranded on the bay's sands, caught by the tides' (Waugh 2007: 189–90, 192).

45 See also the attitude of immigration officers in Frears's film *Dirty Pretty Things* (2002).

46 Contrary to what Jean and John Comaroff argue (2011: 15, 17), then, the most evident effects of neo-liberalism are not necessarily anticipated in the global South.

47 Workfare schemes were introduced by the Labour government, and extended by the Conservatives. Free labour can thus be exploited by companies, including the G4S, which manages prisons and detention centres (see Chapter 1.1; O'Reilly and Clark 2011: passim).

48 In such a police climate deportability, too, may be felt as a threat by growing sectors of society, starting from citizens of immigrant background. In his poem 'The death of Joy Gardner' (on a woman suffocated to death by immigration officers in 1993), Benjamin Zephaniah (1996: 11) writes: 'Here lies the extradition squad / And we should all now pray to God / That as they go about their job / They make not one mistake / For I fear as I walk the streets / That one day I just may meet / Officials who may tie my feet / And how would I escape.' Another omen of the widening of enslaved population is shown by the 2012 unprecedented sentence given to a couple who had forced homeless Britons into servitude (*Reporter*, 18:2: 5).

49 I have explained in Chapter 3.1 the spatial reasons why I consider Foucault's heterotopia only partially applicable in reading new slaveries.

50 'Before extermination camps are reopened in Europe (something that is already starting to happen)' (Agamben 2000: 24).

51 He himself concedes that '[I]t is not easy to indicate right now the ways in which all this may concretely happen' (2000: 24).

52 See Wilson et al. (2010: 5–6), Spencer (2010: 42–3).

53 Significantly, the one notable exception is constituted by the multifarious group of characters of the *humour* novel examined here, Lewycka's *Two Caravans* (Chapter 3.4).

54 Set up in 2001, it accommodates women who have been sexual slaves, or victims of forced labour or organ harvesting – provided they are willing to co-operate with the authorities. Even though it offers an unequalled

range of services (much better than the social services that institutions usually refer to), its supply has never managed to meet the increasingly higher demand of spaces, also because its Home Office funding have never been increased (Waugh 2007: 129–31, 141, 238–39; Gupta 2007: 99–100, 251–2). As further evidence of the neglect of British institutions on the issue, in April 2011 the Home Office planned to stop funding the POPPY Project and to divert the money to the Salvation Army (Townsend 2011: passim).

55 Farrier (2012: 437) sees this initiative as an example of Gilroy's 'demotic or disloyal cosmopolitanism', a form of 'active engagement with the irreducible value of diversity within sameness' (Gilroy 2004a: 74–5). It could also be read as an example of how citizens, according to Agamben's 'Beyond human rights', desert 'codified instances of political participation' to turn into 'denizens, noncitizen permanent residents' (a category he borrows from Tomas Hammar), 'so that citizens and denizens – at least in certain social strata – are entering an area of potential indistinction' (Agamben 2000: 23). In his *Postcolonial Asylum* (2011: 63), Farrier describes another such initiative, the 2007 Gatwick 'No border camp'. And see also the description of community groups in Newcastle in Moorehead (2006: 150–1).

56 It is hardly happenstance that the novel ends with the sentence 'Tomorrow, if I am still here, I'll plant some seeds' (Belbin 2011: 109).

57 This is not valid for Manzu Islam's *Burrow* (2004), a poignant novel where the protagonist, Tapan Ali from Bangladesh, is an undocumented migrant in London constantly described through animal imagery, either as mole (having to hide from authorities) or as bird (mirroring his longing for freedom). Never exploited or enslaved, he is only tangential to the categories studied in this volume (despite showing awareness of the presence of numerous sweatshops around him). Tapan is tangential to the present book also in so far as he is a university student and writer who manages to connect his situation to the invisible condition of the anti-colonial guerrilla back in Bangladesh. In addition, he finds himself surrounded by a supportive multiethnic community in London. It seems to me that *Burrow* includes elements of British new slaveries with issues more typical of Islam's generation.

58 In 2004 Alex Rotas lamented that refugee artists' only chance of escaping invisibility was to show how ethnic they are, if they wanted funding from the Arts Council. (Rotas 2004: 53–60).

59 See also Gordon (2008: 86, 96, 134–5).

60 The literature on new slaveries being often linked to traumatic experiences, this issue relates to the contested topic of the transmissibility of trauma; see on this Visser (2011: 272, 275–6).

61 On a macro-political level, I can see why David Farrier (2011: 63) associates Agamben's concept with the oppressive phenomenon of 'those

states who engage extra-territorial strategies as means of exclusion' (see also Chapter 6.1).

62 Little Bee first appears before Sarah's husband Andrew, whose depression dates back from that day in Nigeria because he could not summon the courage to cut his finger off, and thus condemned Little Bee's sister to death: on seeing her, he believes that he is hallucinating, and significantly takes the Nigerian girl for a ghost (Cleave 2008: 273).

63 Benjamin Zephaniah (2001: 6) closes his preface to *Refugee Boy* on a similar note: 'The Celts, the Angles, the Saxons, the Jamaicans are all refugees of one sort or another. What kind of refugee are you? And what are you scared of?'

64 See Cleave (2008: 43–5).

65 When Sarah tells her lover Lawrence (working for the Home Office) about Little Bee, he replies 'Two *years* in detention? She must have done something' (Cleave 2008: 172).

66 The relationship between these two characters, then, may be taken as an example of what Spivak means by learning 'to learn from below' (2007: 239). While not eschewing the limits and inequality involved in this vision of the subaltern, Cherniavsky (2011: 156, 159) proposes 'a radical openness' based on reciprocity, 'in which a left elite not only teaches democratic subjectivity to the oppressed, but also learns from subaltern interlocutors'.

67 The first chapter of *The Rebel* is a development of a previous essay – 'Remarque sur la révolte', dated 1945, where Camus's notion of revolt is still limited to an individual sphere. Another modification between the previous essay and the later book's first chapter is to be found in its main subject, which changes from the clerk who is used to obeying orders (close to Arendt's desk killer) to the 'slave' (Camus 1991: 13). As seen above, the literature on British new slaveries presents a scenario where the rebellion of both figures may be seen as conducive to change. Another analogy with the context of British new slaveries emerges from Camus's statement that the 'spirit of rebellion can exist only in a society where a theoretical equality conceals great factual inequalities' (20).

References

Abani, C., 2006, *Becoming Abigail: A Novella* (New York: Akashic).
Abani, C., 2007 (2000), *Kalakuta Republic* (London: Saqi).
Achebe, C., 1975, *Morning Yet on Creation Day* (London: Heinemann).
Adorno, T. W., 1981 (1955), 'Cultural criticism and society', in *Prisms*, trans. S. Weber and S. Weber (Cambridge, MA: MIT Press), pp. 17–34.
Adshead, K., 2001, *The Bogus Woman* (London: Oberon).
Afolabi, S. A., 2004, 'Monday morning', *Wasafiri*, 41 (Spring), 46–9; reprinted in Afolabi, *A Life Elsewhere* (London: Jonathan Cape, 2006), pp. 1–15.
Agamben, G., 1998 (1995), *Homo Sacer: Sovereign Power and Bare Life*, trans. D. Heller-Roazen (Stanford: Stanford University Press).
Agamben, G., 1999 (1998), *Remnants of Auschwitz: The Witness and the Archive*, trans. D. Heller-Roazen (New York: Zone).
Agamben, G., 2000 (1996), *Means without End: Notes on Politics*, trans. V. Binetti and C. Casarino (Minneapolis, London: University of Minnesota Press).
Agbaje, B., 2009, *Detaining Justice*, in R. Williams, K. Kwei-Armah and B. Agbaje, *Not Black & White* (London: Methuen), pp. 185–269.
Agnoletto, V., and Gnetti, C., 2012, *AIDS: Lo scandalo del vaccino italiano* (Milan: Feltrinelli).
Ahmad, A., 1994, 'Reconciling Derrida: *Spectres of Marx* and deconstructive politics', *New Left Review*, 208 (November and December), 88–106.
Albrecht, H.-J., 2011, 'Criminalization and victimization of immigrants in Germany', in S. Palidda (ed.), *Racial Criminalization of Migrants in the 21st Century* (Farnham and Burlington: Ashgate), pp. 177–96.
Aldridge, A., 1984 (1978), *The Scientific World View in Dystopia* (Ann Arbor: UMI Research Press).
Ali, M., 2010 (2009), *In the Kitchen* (London: Black Swan).
Alvi, M., 2008, *Europa* (Highgreen: Bloodaxe).
Anderson, B., 1993, *Britain's Secret Slaves: An Investigation into the Plight of Overseas Domestic Workers* (London: Anti-Slavery International and Kalayaan).
Anderson, B., 2004, 'Migrant domestic workers and slavery', in C. Van

den Anker (ed.), *The Political Economy of New Slavery* (Houndmills: Palgrave/Macmillan), pp. 107–17.
Anderson, B., and Rogaly, B., 2005, *Forced Labour and Migration in the UK*, London: TUC/COMPAS, www.compas.ac.uk/Publications/Forced%20Labour%20Report.html (accessed 15 October 2012).
Andrews, H., and Roberts, L., 2012, 'Introduction: Re-mapping liminality', in Andrews and Roberts (eds), *Liminal Landscapes: Travel, Experience and Spaces In-between* (London and New York: Routledge), pp. 1–17.
Arendt, H., 1958 (1951), *The Origins of Totalitarianism* (London: George Allen & Unwin).
Arendt, H., 1964 (1963), *Eichmann in Jerusalem: A Report on the Banality of Evil* (New York: The Viking Press).
Arendt, H., 1996 (1943), 'We refugees', in M. Robinson (ed.) *Altogether Elsewhere: Writers on Exile* (Houghton Mifflin: Harcourt), pp. 110–19, www.leland.stanford.edu/dept/DLCL/files/pdf/hannah_arendt_we_refugees.pdf (accessed 6 November 2010).
Armitt, L., 2000, 'The magical realism of the contemporary Gothic', in D. Punter (ed.), *A Companion to the Gothic* (Malden: Blackwell), pp. 305–16.
Ascari, M., 2007, *A Counter-History of Crime Fiction: Supernatural, Gothic, Sensational* (Houndmills: Palgrave Macmillan).
Ashcroft, B., Griffiths, G. and Tiffin, H., 1995, 'The body and the performance: Introduction', in Ashcroft, Griffiths and Tiffin (eds), *The Post-Colonial Studies Reader* (London: Routledge), pp. 321–2.
Augé, M., 1995 (1992), *Non-Places: Introduction to an Anthropology of Supermodernity*, trans. J. Howe (London: Verso).
Augé, M., 2008, 'Introduction to the second edition', in *Non-Places: An Introduction to Supermodernity*, trans. J. Howe (London and New York: Verso), pp. vii–xxii.
Bacon, C., 2008, *The Illegals*, iceandfire theatre company, unpublished manuscript (October).
Baldick, C., and Mighall, R., 2000, 'Gothic criticism', in D. Punter (ed.), *A Companion to the Gothic* (Malden: Blackwell), pp. 209–28.
Bales, K., 1999, *Disposable People: New Slavery in the Global Economy* (Berkeley, Los Angeles and London: University of California Press).
Bales, K., 2005, *Understanding Global Slavery: A Reader* (Berkeley, Los Angeles and London: University of California Press).
Balibar, É., 2004 (2001), *We, the People of Europe? Reflections on Transnational Citizenship*, trans. J. Swenson (Princeton and Oxford: Princeton University Press).
Bassi, S., 1999, 'Salman Rushdie's special effects', in E. Linguanti, F. Casotti and C. Concilio (eds), *Coterminous Worlds: Magical Realism and Contemporary Post-colonial Literature in English* (Amsterdam and Atlanta: Rodopi), pp. 47–60.
Bathurst, B., 1999, *The Lighthouse Stevensons* (London: HarperCollins).

Baucom, I., 2005, *Specters of the Atlantic: Finance Capital, Slavery, and the Philosophy of History* (Durham, NC, and London: Duke University Press).
Bauman, Z., 1989, *Modernity and the Holocaust* (Cambridge: Polity).
Bauman, Z., 2004, *Wasted Lives: Modernity and Its Outcasts* (Cambridge: Polity).
Bayley, C., 2007, *The Container* (London: Nick Hern).
Beccaria Rolfi, M., and Bruzzone, A. M., 2003, *Le donne di Ravensbrück: Testimonianze di deportate politiche italiane* (Turin: Einaudi).
Beedham, M., 2010, *The Novels of Kazuo Ishiguro* (Basingstoke and New York: Palgrave Macmillan).
Behdad, A., 2005, 'On globalization, again!', in A. Loomba, S. Kaul, M. Bunzl, A. Burton and J. Esty (eds), *Postcolonial Studies and Beyond* (Durham, NC, and London: Duke University Press), pp. 62–79.
Belbin, D., 2011, *Secret Gardens* (Nottingham: Five Leaves).
Benjamin, W., 1968 (1942), 'Theses on the philosophy of history', in *Illuminations*, trans. H. Zohn (New York: Knopf Doubleday), pp. 253–64.
Bensoussan, G., 2002 (1998), *L'eredità di Auschwitz: Come ricordare?* (Turin: Einaudi).
Bissett, C. (conceiver and director), and Smith, S. (writer), 2011, *Roadkill* (London: Oberon).
Black, S., 2009, 'Ishiguro's inhuman aesthetics', *Modern Fiction Studies*, 55:4 (Winter), 785–807.
Bohmer, C., and Shuman, A., 2008, *Rejecting Refugees: Political Asylum in the 21st Century* (London and New York: Routledge).
Bonini, T., 2010, *Così lontano, così vicino: Tattiche mediali per abitare lo spazio* (Verona: Ombre corte).
Bosworth, M., 2007, 'Immigration detention in Britain', in M. Lee (ed.), *Human Trafficking* (Cullompton, Devon: Willan), pp. 159–77.
Bosworth, M., and Guild, M., 2008, 'Governing through migration control: Security and citizenship in Britain', *British Journal of Criminology*, 48, 703–19, http://bjc.oxfordjournal.org (accessed 25 October 2012).
Botting, F., 1996, *Gothic* (London and New York: Routledge).
Boulter, J., 2011, *Melancholy and the Archive: Trauma, Memory, and History in the Contemporary Novel* (London and New York: Continuum).
Boyle, D. (script), 2005, *Fleshmarket Close*, dir. by M. Evans (Scottish TV and SMG TV productions for ITV).
Bradman, T. (ed.), 2007, *Give Me Shelter: Stories about Children Who Seek Asylum* (London: Frances Lincoln Children's Books).
Brennan, T., 1989, *Salman Rushdie and the Third World: Myths of the Nation* (Houndmills: Macmillan).
Brennan, T., 2005, 'The economic image-function of the periphery', in A. Loomba, S. Kaul, M. Bunzl, A. Burton and J. Esty (eds), *Postcolonial Studies and Beyond* (Durham, NC, and London: Duke University Press), pp. 101–22.

Bressy, B., 2012, 'Re-membering the Cyborg: Narrated Identities and Lost Communities in Ishiguro's *Never Let Me Go*' (postgraduate paper, University of Turin, Facoltà di Lingue e Letterature Straniere).
Brock, J. (writer), 2010, *I Am Slave*, dir. by G. Range (an Altered Image/Borough Picture Company/Potboiler/Slate Films production).
Broomfield, N. (writer, producer and director), 2006, *Ghosts* (Tartan Films and Channel Four), www.ghosts.uk.com.
Brydon, D., 2010, 'Cracking imaginaries: Studying the global from Canadian space', in J. Wilson, C. Sandru and S. Lawson Welsh (eds), *Rerouting the Postcolonial: New Directions for the New Millennium* (London and New York: Routledge), pp. 105–17.
Camus, A., 1945, 'Remarque sur la révolte', http://classiques.uqac.ca/classiques/camus_albert/remarque_sur_la_revolte/html (accessed 2 May 2013).
Camus, A., 1991 (1951), *The Rebel: An Essay on Man in Revolt*, trans. A. Bower (New York: Vintage International).
Caruth, C., 1995, 'Introduction', in Caruth (ed.), *Trauma: Explorations in Memory*, (Baltimore: Johns Hopkins University Press), pp. 3–12.
Caruth, C., 1996, *Unclaimed Experience: Trauma, Narrative and History* (Baltimore: Johns Hopkins University Press).
Casciani, D., 2011, 'G4S immigration removal centre complaints revealed', BBC News, 17 June, www.bbc.co.uk/news/uk-13802163 (accessed 15 October 2012).
Cherniavsky, E., 2011, 'The canny subaltern', in J. Elliott and D. Attridge (eds), *Theory after 'Theory'* (London and New York: Routledge), pp. 149–62.
Chikwava, B., 2010 (2009), *Harare North* (London: Vintage).
Christian, E., 2001, 'Introducing the post-Colonial detective: Putting marginality to work', in Christian (ed.) *The Post-Colonial Detective* (Houndmills and New York: Palgrave), pp. 1–16.
Churchill, C., 2008 (2000), *Far Away*, in *Plays: Four* (London: Nick Hern), pp. 129–59.
Cimitile, A. M., 2005, *Emergenze: Il fantasma della schiavitù da Coleridge a D'Aguiar* (Naples: Liguori).
Cleave, C., 2008, *The Other Hand* (London: Sceptre).
Cohen, S., 2006, *Deportation Is Freedom! The Orwellian World of Immigration Controls* (London and Philadelphia: Jessica Kingsley).
Comaroff, J., and Comaroff, J. L., 2011, *Theory from the South: Or, How Euro-America Is Evolving toward Africa* (Boulder, CO: Paradigm).
Conrad, J., 1987 (1902), *Heart of Darkness – Cuore di tenebre*, trans. U. Mursia (Milan: Ugo Mursia).
Cowper, W., 1911 (1785), *The Task*, in H. S. Milford (ed.), *The Poetical Works of William Cowper* (London: Henry Frowde and Oxford University Press), pp. 127–241.
Craig, G., Gaus, A., Wilkinson, M., Skrivankova, K. and McQuade, A.,

2007, *Contemporary Slavery in the UK: Overview and Key Issues* (York: Joseph Rowntree Foundation), www.jrf.org.uk (accessed 14 April 2008).

Craps, S., 2008, 'Linking legacies of loss: Traumatic histories and cross-cultural empathy in Caryl Phillips's *Higher Ground* and *The Nature of Blood*', *Studies in the Novel*, 40:1 and 2 (Spring and Summer), 191–202.

Craps, S., and Buelens, G., 2008, 'Introduction: Postcolonial trauma novels', *Studies in the Novel*, 40:1 and 2 (Spring and Summer), 1–12.

Crawley, H., and Lester, T., 2005, *No Place for a Child: Children in UK Immigration Detention: Impacts, Alternatives, Safeguards* (London: Save the Children).

Cresswell, T., 2004, *Place: A Short Introduction* (Malden, MA, Oxford and Victoria, Australia: Blackwell).

Crownshaw, R., 2010, *The Afterlife of Holocaust Memory in Contemporary Culture* (Houndmills: Palgrave).

Cuarón, A. (writer and director), 2006, *Children of Men*, written with T. J. Sexton, D. Arata, M. Fergus, H. Ostby (Universal).

Cuarón, A., and Elías, J., 2006, *The Possibility of Hope*, an Esperanto Filmoj production, documentary included in the DVD special edition of Cuarón's *Children of Men* (Universal).

Currie, M., 2009, 'Controlling time: *Never Let Me Go*', in S. Matthews and S. Groes (eds), *Kazuo Ishiguro* (London and New York: Continuum), pp. 91–103.

Davies, N., 2009, 'Prostitution and trafficking – the anatomy of a moral panic', *The Guardian* (20 October), www.guardian.co.uk/uk/2009/oct/20/trafficking-numbers-women-exaggerated (accessed 1 July 2013).

Dawber, A., 2013, 'Israel gave birth control to Ethiopian Jews without their consent', *The Independent* (27 January), www.independent.co.uk/news/world/middle-east/israel-gave-birth-control-to-ethiopian-jews-without-their-consent-8468800.html (accessed 23 April 2013).

Dawson, A., 2007, *Mongrel Nation: Diasporic Culture and the Making of Postcolonial Britain* (Ann Arbor, MI: University of Michigan Press).

Deandrea, P., 2009a, 'Human bondage in contemporary UK and its generic transformations: From Bridget Anderson's *Britain's Secret Slaves* to Ruth Rendell's *Simisola* and Kazuo Ishiguro's *Never Let Me Go*', in V. Cavone, C. Corti and M.Trulli (eds), *Forms of Migration, Migration of Forms: Literature* (Bari: Progedit), pp. 402–17.

Deandrea, P., 2009b, 'Unravelling unpersons: Inscribing the voices of contemporary slavery in the UK', *Textus*, XXII:3 (*Marginal Textualities*, ed. by C. Dente and S. Orgel), 665–80.

Deandrea, P., 2012a, 'Contemporary slavery in the UK and its categories', in A. Oboe and F. Giommi (eds), *Black Arts in Contemporary Britain: Literary, Visual, Performative* (Rome: Aracne), pp. 175–93.

Deandrea, P., 2012b, 'Shards in the landscape: The dispersed liminality of contemporary slavery in the UK', in H. Andrews and L. Roberts (eds), *Liminal Landscapes: Travel, Experience and Spaces In-between*

(London and New York: Routledge), pp. 216–33.

Deandrea, P., forthcoming, 'Foreign devils: Visualising the spectres of contemporary British slavery in Nick Broomfield's *Ghosts*', in C. Spooner and F. Botting (eds), *Gothic Bastards: Genre, Innovation and Contemporary Fictions* (Manchester: Manchester University Press).

Deandrea, P., forthcoming in 2015, 'The spectralized camp: Cultural representations of British new slaveries', *Interventions: International Journal of Postcolonial Studies*.

De Genova, N. P., 2002, 'Migrant "illegality" and deportability in everyday life', *Annual Review of Anthropology*, 31, 419–47.

Delpiano, P., 2009, *La schiavitù in età moderna* (Bari: Laterza).

Del Villano, B., 2007, *Ghostly Alterities: Spectrality and Contemporary Literatures in English* (Stuttgart: Ibidem-Verlag).

De Michelis, L., 2011, '"Tutta la vita in un foglio": Il dramma dell'asilo in *The Other Hand* di Chris Cleave', *Mondi Migranti*, 3, 271–96.

Derrida, J., 2000 (1997), *Of Hospitality: Anne Dufourmantelle Invites Jacques Derrida to Respond*, trans. R. Bowlby (Stanford: Stanford University Press).

Derrida, J., 2006 (1993), *Specters of Marx: The State of the Debt, the Work of Mourning and the New International*, trans. P. Kamuf (New York and London: Routledge).

Dick, P. K., 2007 (1968), *Do Androids Dream of Electric Sheep?* (London: Gollancz).

Diemert, B., 2005, 'Ian Rankin and the God of the Scots', in J. H. Kim (ed.), *Race and Religion in the Postcolonial British Detective Story: Ten Essays* (Jefferson, NC, and London: McFarland), pp. 164–88.

Di Nicola, A., 2007, 'Researching into human trafficking: Issues and problems', in M. Lee (ed.), *Human Trafficking* (Cullompton, Devon: Willan), pp. 49–72.

Di Paola, P., 2006, 'Introduzione', in R. Rocker, *Sindrome da filo spinato: Rapporto di un tedesco internato a Londra* (Santa Maria Capua a Vetere: Spartaco), pp. 7–31.

Donovan, P., 2013, 'When a job becomes a jail', *The Tablet* (8 June), p. 10.

Dottridge, M., 2007 (2002), 'Trafficking in children in West and Central Africa', in R. Masika (ed.), *Gender, Trafficking, and Slavery* (Oxford: Oxfam), pp. 38–41.

Dugan, E., 2010, 'Think slavery is a thing of the past? Think again', *Independent on Sunday* (17 October), www.independent.co.uk/news/uk/home-news/think-slavery-is-a-thing-of-the-past-think-again-2108981.html (accessed 11 March 2011).

Durrant, S., 2004, *Postcolonial Narrative and the Work of Mourning: J. M. Coetzee, Wilson Harris and Toni Morrison* (Albany: State University of New York).

Eaglestone, R., 2008a, '"You would not add to my suffering if you knew what I have seen": Holocaust testimony and contemporary African

trauma literature', *Studies in the Novel*, 10:1 and 2 (Spring and Summer), 72–85.
Eaglestone, R., 2008b, 'Holocaust theory?', in R. Eaglestone and B. Langford (eds), *Teaching Holocaust Literature and Film* (New York: Palgrave), pp. 28–36.
Eckstein, L., 2007, 'Three ways of looking at illegal immigration: Clandestine existence in novels by Salman Rushdie, Christopher Hope and Caryl Phillips', in G. Stilz (ed.), *Territorial Terrors: Contested Spaces in Colonial and Postcolonial Writing* (Würzburg: Königshausen and Neumann), pp. 141–57.
Eckstein, L., Korte, B., Pirker, E. U. and Reinfandt, C., 2008, 'A divided kingdom? Reflections on multi-ethnic Britain in the new millennium', in Eckstein, Korte, Pirker and Reinfandt (eds), *Multi-Ethnic Britain 2000+: New Perspectives in Literature, Film and the Arts* (Amsterdam and New York: Rodopi), pp. 9–21.
ECPAT International and ECPAT UK, 2011, *[United Kingdom of Great Britain and Northern Ireland] Country Progress Card*, www.ecpat.net (accessed 15 May 2013).
Eliot, T. S., 1982 (1922), *The Waste Land / La terra desolata*, trans. and ed. A. Serpieri (Milan: Rizzoli).
Equiano, O., 2001 (1789), *The Interesting Narrative of the Life of Olaudah Equiano, or Gustavus Vassa, the African, Written by Himself*, ed. by W. Sollors (New York and London: Norton).
Fanon, F., 1967 (1961), *The Wretched of the Earth*, trans. C. Farrington, pref. by J. P. Sartre (Harmondsworth: Penguin).
Fanon, F., 1968 (1952), *Black Skin, White Masks*, trans. C. Lam Markmann (New York: Grove Press).
Farhi, M., 2002 (1999), *Children of the Rainbow* (London: Saqi).
Farrier, D., 2011, *Postcolonial Asylum: Seeking Sanctuary before the Law* (Liverpool: Liverpool University Press).
Farrier, D., 2012, 'Everyday exceptions: The politics of the quotidian in *Asylum Monologues* and *Asylum Dialogues*', *Interventions: International Journal of Postcolonial Studies*, 14:3, 429–42.
Fekete, L., 2009, *A Suitable Enemy: Racism, Migration and Islamophobia in Europe* (London and New York: Pluto).
Felman, S., 1995, 'Education and crisis, or the vicissitudes of teaching', in C. Caruth (ed.), *Trauma: Explorations in Memory* (Baltimore: Johns Hopkins University Press), pp. 13–60.
Fiedler, L., 1996, *Tyranny of the Normal: Essays on Bioethics, Theology and Myth* (Boston, MA: David R. Godine).
Finley, M. I., 1983 (1980), *Ancient Slavery and Modern Ideology* (Harmondsworth: Penguin).
Forti, S., 2011, 'Corpi democratici, politicamente corretti', in P. P. Portinaro (ed.), *L'interesse dei pochi, le ragioni dei molti: Le letture di Biennale Democrazia* (Turin: Einaudi), pp. 147–61.

Foucault, M., 1986 (1984), 'Of other spaces', trans. J. Miskowiec, *Diacritics*, 16:1, pp. 22–7.

Foucault, M., 1995 (1975), *Discipline and Punish: The Birth of the Prison*, trans. A. Sheridan (New York: Vintage).

Foucault, M., 2003 (1997), *Society Must Be Defended: Lectures at the Collège de France 1975–76*, trans. D. Macey, ed. by M. Bertani and A. Fontana (New York: Picador).

Frassinelli, P. P., 2014, 'Reading contrapuntally now', *Le Simplegadi (International on-line refereed journal of modern languages and literatures) / Special issue: Cultures and Imperialisms*, xii:12 (April), 27–40, http://all.uniud.it/simplegadi.

Frears, S., 2002, *Dirty Pretty Things* (UK: BBC).

Freeman, J., 2008 (2005), '*Never Let Me Go*: A profile of Kazuo Ishiguro', in B. W. Shaffer and C. F. Wong (eds), *Conversations with Kazuo Ishiguro* (Jackson: University of Mississippi Press), pp. 194–8.

Galli, G., 1990 (1989), 'La politica dietro il Giallo', in E. Mandel, *Delitti per diletto: Storia sociale del romanzo poliziesco*, trans. B. Arpaia (Milan: Interno giallo), pp. v–xxv.

George, S. (director), 2010, *Qu'ils reposent en révolte: Des figures de guerre*, dvcam documentary (France: Noir Production).

George, S. (director), 2011, *Les éclats (Ma gueule, ma révolte, mon nom)* (France: Noir Production).

Gikandi, S., 2010, 'Between roots and routes: Cosmopolitanism and the claims of locality', in J. Wilson, C. Sandru and S. Lawson Welsh (eds), *Rerouting the Postcolonial: New Directions for the New Millennium* (London and New York: Routledge), pp. 22–35.

Gilroy, P., 1993, *The Black Atlantic: Modernity and Double Consciousness* (London and New York: Verso).

Gilroy, P., 2004a, *After Empire: Melancholia or Convivial Culture?* (Abingdon: Routledge).

Gilroy, P., 2004b (2000), *Between Camps: Nations, Cultures and the Allures of Race* (London and New York: Routledge).

Giommi, F., 2010, *Narrare la Black Britain: Migrazioni, riscritture e ibridazioni nella letteratura inglese contemporanea* (Florence: Le Lettere).

Giommi, F., 2011, 'Negotiating freedom on scarred bodies: Chris Abani's novellas', in A. Oboe and S. Bassi (eds), *Experiences of Freedom in Postcolonial Literatures and Cultures* (London and New York: Routledge), pp. 176–84.

Giustini, A., 2010, *La corporeità femminile nel sistema concentrazionario nazista* (Naples: ScriptaWeb).

Godwin, W., 2005 (1794), *Caleb Williams (Things As They Are; Or, the Adventures of Caleb Williams)*, ed. M. Hindle (London: Penguin).

Goheen Glanville, E., 2010, 'Rerouting diaspora theory with Canadian refugee fiction', in J. Wilson, C. Sandru and S. Lawson Welsh (eds),

Rerouting the Postcolonial: New Directions for the New Millennium (London and New York: Routledge), pp. 128–38.

Gordon, A. F., 2008 (1997), *Ghostly Matters: Haunting and the Sociological Imagination* (Minneapolis and London: University of Minnesota Press).

Greppi, C., 2012, *L'ultimo treno: racconti del viaggio verso il lager* (Rome: Donzelli).

Gretton, D., forthcoming in 2015, *I You We Them: Thirty-three Journeys into the Mind of the Desk Killer* (London: Granta/Portobello).

Grigsby Bates, K., 2008 (2005), 'Interview with Kazuo Ishiguro', in B. W. Shaffer and C. F. Wong (eds), *Conversations with Kazuo Ishiguro* (Jackson: University of Mississippi Press), pp. 199–203.

Guha, R., and Spivak, G. C. (eds), 1988, *Selected Subaltern Studies* (New York and Oxford: Oxford University Press).

Gunning, D., 2011, 'Infrahuman rights, silence, and the possibility of communication in recent narratives of illegality in Britain', in A. Oboe and S. Bassi (eds), *Experiences of Freedom in Postcolonial Literatures and Cultures* (London and New York: Routledge), pp. 141–50.

Gupta, R., 2007, *Enslaved: The New British Slavery* (London: Portobello).

Gurnah, A., 2001, *By the Sea* (London: Bloomsbury).

Gutman, I., 1990, 'Holocaust, Denial of', in I. Gutman (ed. in chief), *Encyclopedia of the Holocaust*, vol. 2 (New York: Macmillan, and London: Collier Macmillan), pp. 681–7.

Haidari, K., 2005, 'The journey', in J. Langer (ed.), *The Silver Throat of the Moon: Writing in Exile* (Nottingham: Five Leaves), pp. 100–3.

Hall, S., 1988, 'New ethnicities', in K. Mercer (ed.), *ICA Documents 7: Black Film, British Cinema* (London: Institute of Contemporary Arts), pp. 27–31.

Hardt, M., and Negri, A., 2000, *Empire* (Cambridge, MA, and London: Harvard University Press).

Harris, N., 2002, *Thinking the Unthinkable: The Immigration Myth Exposed* (London: Tauris).

Helff, S., 2008, 'Scapes of refuge in multicultural Britain: Representing refugees in digital docudrama and mockumentary', in L. Eckstein, B. Korte, E. U. Pirker and C. Reinfandt (eds), *Multi-Ethnic Britain 2000+: New Perspectives in Literature, Film and the Arts* (Amsterdam and New York: Rodopi), pp. 283–99.

Hoeferlin, M., 2006. 'Shooting ghosts: The making of *Ghosts*', featurette included in N. Broomfield's *Ghosts*'s DVD (Tartan Films and Channel Four), www.ghosts.uk.com.

Hogle, J. E. (ed.), 2002, *The Cambridge Companion to Gothic Fiction* (Cambridge: Cambridge University Press).

Hope, C., 1997 (1996), *Darkest England* (London and Basingstoke: Picador).

Howarth, A., and Ibrahim, Y., 2012, 'Threat and suffering: The liminal space of "The Jungle" ', in H. Andrews and L. Roberts (eds), *Liminal*

Landscapes: Travel, Experience and Spaces In-between (London and New York: Routledge), pp. 200–16.

Huggan, G., 1995 (1989), 'Decolonizing the map: Post-colonialism, post-structuralism and the cartographic connection', in B. Ashcroft, G. Griffiths and H. Tiffin (eds), *The Post-Colonial Studies Reader* (London: Routledge), pp. 407–11.

Hughes, D., 2011, 'UK to join fight against human trafficking', *The Independent* (23 March), www.independent.co.uk/news/uk/crime/uk-to-join-fight-against-human-trafficking-2250047.html (accessed 11 July 2011).

Hulme, P., 2005, 'Beyond the straits: Postcolonial allegories of the globe', in A. Loomba, S. Kaul, M. Bunzl, A. Burton and J. Esty (eds), *Postcolonial Studies and Beyond* (Durham, NC, and London: Duke University Press), pp. 41–61.

Ishiguro, K., 2010 (2005), *Never Let Me Go* (London: Faber and Faber).

Isin, E. F., and Rygiel, K., 2007, 'Of other global cities: Frontiers, zones, camps', in B. Drieskens, F. Mermier and H. Wimmen (eds), *Cities of the South: Citizenship and Exclusion in the Twenty-first Century* (Beirut: SAQI, in association with Heinrich Böll Foundation and Institut Français du Proche-Orient), pp. 177–209.

Islam, M., 2004, *Burrow* (Leeds: Peepal Tree).

James, P. D., 2006 (1992), *The Children of Men* (New York: Vintage).

Jordan, A., 2010, *Chicken Shop* (Without a Paddle theatre company: unpublished manuscript).

Joseph-Vilain, M., and Misrahi-Barak, J. (eds), 2010, *Postcolonial Ghosts / Fantômes postcoloniaux* (Montpellier: Presses Universitaires de la Méditerranée).

Kavka, M., 2002, 'The Gothic on screen', in J. E. Hogle (ed.), *The Cambridge Companion to Gothic Fiction* (Cambridge: Cambridge University Press), pp. 209–28.

Kaye, H., 2000, 'Gothic film', in D. Punter (ed.), *A Companion to the Gothic* (Malden: Blackwell), pp. 180–92.

Kaye, M., 2008, *Arrested Development: Discrimination and Slavery in the 21st Century* (London: Anti-Slavery International).

Kelman, H. C., 1973, 'Violence without moral restraint: Reflection on the dehumanization of victims and victimizers', *Journal of Social Issues*, 29, 25–61.

Kim, J. H. (ed.), 2005, *Race and Religion in the Postcolonial British Detective Story: Ten Essays* (Jefferson, NC, and London: McFarland).

Kirkwood, L., 2009, *It Felt Empty When the Heart Went at First but It Is Alright Now* (London: Nick Hern).

Kirmayer, L. J., 1996, 'Landscapes of memory: Trauma, narrative, and dissociation', in P. Antze and M. Lambek (eds), *Tense Past: Essays in Trauma and Memory* (New York and London: Routledge), pp. 173–98.

Kitson, P. J., 1998, 'Romanticism and colonialism: Races, places, peoples, 1785–1800', in T. Fulford and P. J. Kitson (eds), *Romanticism and*

Colonialism: Writing and Empire, 1780–1830 (Cambridge: Cambridge University Press), pp. 13–34.

Knox-Shaw, P. H., 1993, 'The West Indian *Vathek*', *Essays in Criticism*, 43:4 (October), 284–307.

Kolodziejczyk, D., 2010, 'Cosmopolitan provincialism in a comparative perspective', in J. Wilson, C. Sandru and S. Lawson Welsh (eds), *Rerouting the Postcolonial: New Directions for the New Millennium* (London and New York: Routledge), pp. 151–62.

Korte, B., 2008, 'Envisioning a black tomorrow? Black mother figures and the issue of representation in *28 Days Later* (2003) and *Children of Men* (2006)', in L. Eckstein, B. Korte, E. U. Pirker and C. Reinfandt (eds), *Multi-Ethnic Britain 2000+: New Perspectives in Literature, Film and the Arts* (Amsterdam and New York: Rodopi), pp. 315–25.

Kosofsky Sedgwick, E., 1986, *The Coherence of Gothic Conventions* (New York and London: Methuen).

Lachs, J. 1981, *Responsibility of the Individual in Modern Society* (Brighton: Harvester).

La Guma, A., 1986 (1962), *A Walk in the Night and Other Stories* (London: Heinemann).

Lal, V., 2005, 'The concentration camp and development: The pasts and future of genocide', *Patterns of Prejudice*, 39:2, 220–43.

Langer, J. (ed.), 2005, *The Silver Throat of the Moon: Writing in Exile* (Nottingham: Five Leaves).

Lee, M. (ed.), 2007, *Human Trafficking* (Cullompton, Devon: Willan).

Left, S., 2005, 'Hundreds of African boys go missing in London', *The Guardian* (13 May), www.theguardian.com/society/2005/may/13/children (accessed 20 October 2009).

Levi, P., 1986 (1947), *Se questo è un uomo [If This Is a Man]: Presentazione e note a cura dell'autore*, ed. C. Minoia and F. Cereda (Turin: Einaudi).

Levi, P., 1989 (1986), *The Drowned and the Saved*, trans. R. Rosenthal, intr. P. Bailey (London: Abacus).

Levi, P., 1996 (1947), *If This Is a Man* and *The Truce*, trans. S. Woolf, intr. P. Bailey (London: Vintage).

Lewycka, M., 2006 (2005), *A Short History of Tractors in Ukrainian* (London: Penguin).

Lewycka, M., 2008 (2007), *Two Caravans* (London: Penguin).

Linden, S., 2006, *Asylum Monologues*, iceandfire theatre company, unpublished manuscript.

Linden, S. (script) and Bacon, C. (conception and research), 2008, *Asylum Dialogues*, iceandfire theatre company, unpublished manuscript (June).

Lioret, P. (director and co-writer), 2009, *Welcome* (France: Nord-ouest Films, Studio 37, France 3 Cinema, Mars Films, Fin Août Productions).

Loach, K., 2007, *It's a Free World ...* (BIM).

Loomba, A., 1998, *Colonialism/Postcolonialism* (London and New York: Routledge).

Loomba, A., Kaul, S., Bunzl, M., Burton, A. and Esty, J., 2005, 'Beyond what? An introduction', in Loomba, Kaul, Bunzl, Burton and Esty (eds), *Postcolonial Studies and Beyond* (Durham, NC, and London: Duke University Press), pp. 1–38.

Loshitzky, Y., 2010, *Screening Strangers: Migration and Diaspora in Contemporary European Cinema* (Bloomington and Indianapolis: Indiana University Press).

Luckhurst, R., 2008, *The Trauma Question* (Abingdon and New York: Routledge).

Makenga, D.-M., 2002, 'A tale', in J. Langer (ed.), *Crossing the Border: Voices of Refugee and Exiled Women* (Nottingham: Five Leaves), pp. 120–2.

Mandel, E., 1990 (1989), *Delitti per diletto: Storia sociale del romanzo poliziesco*, trans. B. Arpaia (Milan: Interno Giallo).

Marcassoli, G., 2012, 'Being a Carer: From Kazuo Ishiguro's *Never Let Me Go* to a Postcolonial Perspective' (postgraduate paper, University of Turin, Facoltà di Lingue e Letterature Straniere).

Masika, R., 2002, *Gender, Trafficking, and Slavery* (Oxford: Oxfam).

Mather, J., 2010, 'Ma Jian's *Red Dust*: Global China and the travelling-self', in J. Wilson, C. Sandru and S. Lawson Welsh (eds), *Rerouting the Postcolonial: New Directions for the New Millennium* (London and New York: Routledge), pp. 139–50.

Matthews, S., and Groes, S. (eds), 2009, *Kazuo Ishiguro* (London and New York: Continuum).

Mbembe, J.-A., 2003, 'Necropolitics', trans. L. Meintjes, *Public Culture*, 15:1 (Winter), 11–40.

McGhee, D., 2005, *Intolerant Britain? Hate, Citizenship and Difference* (Maidenhead: The Open University Press).

McVeigh, K., 2011, 'Yarl's Wood detainees "paid 50p an hour"', *The Guardian* (2 January), www.guardian.co.uk/uk/2011/jan/02/yarls-wood-detainees-paid-50p-hour (accessed 15 October 2012).

Meoni, A., 2011, '"Everyone else comes to terms with it, why can't you?": Umanità animale e bestialità umana in *The Lives of Animals* e *Disgrace* di J. M. Coetzee', in L. Giovannelli (ed.), *Interlacing Perspectives: Dialoghi sulla tradizione artistico-letteraria in lingua inglese* (Rome: Aracne), pp. 199–224.

Mezzadra, S., and Neilson, B., 2011, 'Oltre il muro: Topologia dello spazio globale sul confine tra inclusione ed esclusione', in R. Vecchi and R. Monticelli (eds), *Topografia delle culture* (Bologna: I libri di Emil), pp. 29–55.

Milchman, A., and Rosenberg, A., 1992, 'Hannah Arendt and the etiology of the desk killer: The Holocaust as portent', *History of European Ideas*, 14:2, 213–26.

Modiano, R., 1999, 'Sameness or difference? Historicist readings of *The Rime of the Ancient Mariner*', in S. T. Coleridge, *The Rime of the*

Ancient Mariner: Complete, Authoritative Texts of the 1798 and 1817 Versions with Biographical and Historical Contexts, Critical History, and Essays from Contemporary Critical Perspectives, ed. P. H. Fry (Boston: Bedford/St. Martin's), pp. 187–219.

Mohammadi, R., 2012, *Poems*, trans. N. Laird and H. Kabir (London: Poetry Translation Centre).

Moorehead, C., 2006 (2005), *Human Cargo: A Journey among Refugees* (London: Vintage).

Morgan, A. (writer), 2006, *Sex Traffic*, dir. D. Yates (Granada Television / Big Motion Pictures production for Channel Four and the Canadian Broadcasting Corporation).

Morgan, A., 2008, *Fugee*, in T. Wertenbaker, J. Thorne, A. Morgan, N. Wright, B. Lavery, S. Hoggett, S. Graham, N. Williams, A. Furse, M. Ravenhill and M. Buffini, *New Connections 2008: Plays for Young People* (London: Faber and Faber), pp. 139–207.

Mullan, J., 2009, 'Afterword: On first reading *Never Let Me Go*', in S. Matthews and S. Groes (eds), *Kazuo Ishiguro* (London and New York: Continuum), pp. 104–13.

Mynott, E., 2002, 'From a shambles to a new apartheid: Local authorities, dispersal, and the struggle to defend asylum seekers', in S. Cohen, B. Humphreys and E. Mynott (eds), *From Immigration Controls to Welfare Controls* (London and New York: Routledge), pp. 106–25.

Nazer, M. (with D. Lewis), 2003 (2002), *Slave: My True Story* (New York: PublicAffairs).

Nelson, V., 2009, 'Cathedral head: The Gothick cosmos of Guillermo del Toro', *The Believer*, 7:3 (March–April), 17–24.

Oboe, A., and Bassi, S. (eds), 2011, *Experiences of Freedom in Postcolonial Literatures and Cultures* (London and New York: Routledge).

Okpewho, I., 1992, *African Oral Literature: Backgrounds, Characters and Continuity* (Bloomington and Indianapolis: Indiana University Press).

Oldfield, J. R., 2007, *Chords of Freedom: Commemoration, Ritual and British Transatlantic Slavery* (Manchester: Manchester University Press).

O'Reilly, A. M., and Clark, W., 2011, 'All work and no pay: The rise of workfare', *Red Pepper* (16 November), www.redpepper.org.uk/all-work-and-no-pay (accessed 27 May 2013).

Orwell, G., 1968 (1946), 'Why I write', in *The Collected Essays, Journalism and Letters of George Orwell. Volume I: An Age Like This, 1920–1940*, ed. S. Orwell and I. Angus (London: Secker and Warburg), pp. 1–7.

Orwell, G., 1986 (1946), 'Politics and the English language', in *Inside the Whale and Other Essays* (Harmondsworth: Penguin), pp. 143–57.

Orwell, G., 1990 (1949), *Nineteen Eighty-Four* (London: Penguin).

Osborne, D., 2008, 'Introduction' to the collection of Black British plays *Hidden Gems* (London: Oberon), pp. 7–16.

Pai, H.-H., 2008, *Chinese Whispers: The True Story behind Britain's Hidden Army of Labour* (London: Penguin).

Paik, P. P., 2012, 'Apocalypse by subtraction: Late capitalism and the trauma of scarcity', in A. Aneesh, L. Hall and P. Petro (eds), *Beyond Globalization: Making New Worlds in Media, Art, and Social Practices* (New Brunswick: Rutgers University Press), pp. 49–71.

Palidda, S., 2011, 'Introduction', in Palidda (ed.), *Racial Criminalization of Migrants in the 21st Century* (Farnham and Burlington: Ashgate), pp. 1–19.

Pandey, G., 1988, '"Encounters and calamities": The history of a North Indian *Qasha* in the nineteenth century', in R. Guha and G. C. Spivak (eds), *Selected Subaltern Studies* (New York and Oxford: Oxford University Press), pp. 89–128.

Paravisini-Gebert, L., 2002. 'Colonial and postcolonial Gothic: The Caribbean', in J. E. Hogle (ed.), *The Cambridge Companion to Gothic Fiction* (Cambridge: Cambridge University Press), pp. 229–57.

Pawlikowski, P., 2000, *Last Resort*, co-written with R. Joffe (UK: BBC).

Penuel, S., 2005, 'Relocating the heart of darkness in Ruth Rendell', in J. H. Kim (ed.), *Race and Religion in the Postcolonial British Detective Story* (Jefferson, NC, and London: McFarland), pp. 51–70.

Phillips, C., 1999 (1987), *The European Tribe* (London: Faber and Faber).

Phillips, C., 2001a (2000), *The Atlantic Sound* (London: Vintage).

Phillips, C., 2001b, *A New World Order* (London: Secker and Warburg).

Phillips, C., 2004 (2003), *A Distant Shore* (London: Vintage).

Phillips, C., 2010 (2009), *In The Falling Snow* (London: Vintage).

Phillips, C., 2011a, *Colour Me English: Selected Essays* (London: Harvill Secker).

Phillips, C., 2011b, 'Rude am I in my speech', in A. Oboe and S. Bassi (eds), *Experiences of Freedom in Postcolonial Literatures and Cultures* (London and New York: Routledge), pp. 187–91.

Piccino, C., 2010, 'Il ragazzo braccato che canta a Calais', *Il manifesto – Alias* (28 August), p. 20.

Popa, D., 2009, *Not Natasha* (London: Autograph BP).

Punter, D., 1998, *Gothic Pathologies: The Text, the Body and the Law* (New York: St. Martin's Press).

Punter, D., 2000a, *Postcolonial Imaginings: Fictions of a New World Order* (Edinburgh: Edinburgh University Press).

Punter, D. (ed.), 2000b *A Companion to the Gothic* (Malden: Blackwell).

Rankin, I., 2004, *Fleshmarket Close* (London: Orion).

Razac, O., 2003 (2000), *Barbed Wire: A Political History*, trans. J. Kneight (New York: Norton).

Reah, D., 2011, *Not Safe* (Nottingham: Crime Express).

Rendell, R., 1995 (1994), *Simisola* (London: Arrow).

Reporter (The magazine of Anti-Slavery International), 14:3, unspecified author, 'UK trafficking crack down as more than 500 arrested' (Summer 2008), 4.

Reporter, 15:1, unspecified author, 'UK adopts European Trafficking

Convention' (Winter 2009), 5.
Reporter, 16:3, unspecified author, 'Crackdown on Vietnamese trafficking gangs ignores victims' (Summer 2010), 4.
Reporter, 17:2, unspecified author, 'Campaigning works! UK signs up to new EU trafficking law' (Spring 2011), 6.
Reporter, 17:3, unspecified author, 'New UK trafficking strategy will not help victim, say NGOs' (Summer 2011), 4.
Reporter, 17:3, unspecified author, 'Launch of new Slavery-Free London campaign' (Summer 2011), 6.
Reporter, 17:3, unspecified author, 'Domestic workers protest proposed changes to visa' (Autumn 2011), 4.
Reporter, 18:1, unspecified author, 'Child trafficking victims sent back to France' (Winter 2012), 5.
Reporter, 18:2, unspecified author, 'Couple convicted for slavery in first British case' (Summer 2012), 5.
Reporter, 19:1, unspecified author, 'UK fails to fully implement EU Trafficking Directive' (Spring 2013), 4.
Reporter, 19:1, unspecified author, 'Global community takes steps to protect domestic workers' (Spring 2013), 5.
Rice, A., 2003, *Radical Narratives of the Black Atlantic* (London and New York: Continuum).
Rice, A., 2007, 'Naming the money and unveiling the crime: Contemporary British artists and the memorialization of slavery and abolition', *Patterns of Prejudice (special issue 'Imagining transatlantic slavery and abolition')*, ed. J. Oldfield, 41:3–4 (July–September), pp. 321–43.
Roberts, L., 2002a, '"Welcome to Dreamland": From place to non-place and back again in Pawel Pawlikowski's *Last Resort*', *New Cinemas: Journal of Contemporary Film*, 1:2, 78–90.
Roberts, L., 2002b, 'From Sarajevo to Didcot: An interview with Pawel Pawlikowski', *New Cinemas: Journal of Contemporary Film*, 1:2, 91–7.
Robinson, M., 2000, 'The haunted beach' [from *Lyrical Tales*, 1800], in M. H. Abrahams and S. Greenblatt (eds), *The Norton Anthology of English Literature, Seventh Edition*, vol. II (New York and London: Norton), pp. 96–7.
Robinson, V., Andersson, R. and Musterd, S., 2003, *Spreading the 'Burden'? A Review of Policies to Disperse Asylum Seekers and Refugees* (Bristol: The Polity Press).
Rocker, R., 2006, *Sindrome da filo spinato: Rapporto di un tedesco internato a Londra*, trans. P. Di Paola (Santa Maria Capua a Vetere: Spartaco).
Romanek, M. (director), and Garland, A. (script), 2010, *Never Let Me Go*, produced by A. Macdonald and A. Reich for Fox Searchlight and DNA Films and Film4 (executive producers: A. Garland, K. Ishiguro and T. Ross).
Rotas, A., 2004, 'Is "Refugee Art" possible?', *Third Text*, 18:1, 51–60.

Rothberg, M., 2008, 'Decolonizing trauma studies: A response', *Studies in the Novel*, 40:1 and 2 (Spring and Summer), 224–34.

Rothberg, M., 2009, *Multidirectional Memory: Remembering the Holocaust in the Age of Decolonization* (Stanford, CA: Stanford University Press).

Rousset, D., 1951 (1946), *A World Apart* ..., trans. Y. Moise and R. Senhouse (London: Secker and Warburg).

Rowland, S., 2001, *From Agatha Christie to Ruth Rendell: British Women Writers in Detective and Crime Fiction* (Houndmills and New York: Palgrave).

Rushdie, S., 1991, 'Imaginary homelands', in *Imaginary Homelands: Essays and Criticism 1981–1991* (London: Granta/Penguin), pp. 11–20.

Rushdie, S., 1992 (1988), *The Satanic Verses* (Dover, DE: The Consortium).

Said, E. W., 1988, 'Foreword', in R. Guha and G. C. Spivak, *Selected Subaltern Studies* (New York and Oxford: Oxford University Press), pp. v–x.

Said, E. W., 1991 (1983), 'Traveling Theory', in *The World, the Text and the Critic* (London: Vintage), pp. 226–47.

Said, E. W., 1993, *Culture and Imperialism* (London: Chatto and Windus).

Said, E. W., 2004, *Humanism and Democratic Criticism* (Houndmills and New York: Palgrave Macmillan).

Schuster, L., 2003, 'Common sense or racism? The treatment of asylum-seekers in Europe', *Patterns of Prejudice*, 37:3, 233–56.

Sciurba, A., 2009, *Campi di forza: Percorsi confinati di migranti in Europa* (Verona: Ombre corte).

Sealy, M., 2008, 'Mark Sealy: Disposable People 2008 – Hayward Gallery touring exhibition', http://marksealy.com/page14.htm (accessed 7 September 2010).

Sealy, M., 2009, 'Beyond the lens' [portfolio text for Dana Popa's *Not Natasha*], *Foam Magazine*, 18 (March), consulted during my visit to the exhibition, Photofusion Gallery, Brixton, London, on 28 July 2009.

Shaffer, B. W., 1998, *Understanding Kazuo Ishiguro* (Columbia: University of South Carolina Press).

Shaffer, B. W., and Wong, C. F. (eds), 2008, *Conversations with Kazuo Ishiguro* (Jackson: University of Mississippi Press).

Shah, S., 2007, 'Medicine per il Nord, provate sui corpi del Sud', *Le Monde Diplomatique – Il Manifesto* (May), pp. 14–15.

Shelley, P. B., 1888 (1821), 'A defence of poetry', in *The Prose Works of Percy Bysshe Shelley from the Original Editions*, ed., pref. and annotated by R. Herne Shepherd, vol. II (London: Chatto and Windus), pp. 1–38.

Shire, W., 2011, *Teaching My Mother How to Give Birth* (London: the mouthmark series / flipped eye publishing).

Sillitoe, A., 1995 (1959), 'The loneliness of the long distance runner', in *Collected Stories* (London: Flamingo), pp. 1–35.

Sim, W.-C., 2010, *Kazuo Ishiguro* (London and New York: Routledge).
Sinclair, I., 2012 (2011), *Ghost Milk* (London: Penguin).
Skinner, B. E., 2008, *A Crime So Monstrous: Face-to-face with Modern-day Slavery* (New York: Free Press).
Smith, D., 2011, 'Pfizer pays out to Nigerian families of meningitis drug trial victims', *The Guardian* (12 August), www.guardian.co.uk/world/2011/august/11/pfizer-nigeria-meningitis-drug-compensation (accessed 23 April 2013).
Solzhenitsyn, A., 1974 (1973), *The Gulag Archipelago 1918–1956: An Experiment in Literary Investigation*, vol. I, trans. T. P. Whitney (New York, Evanston, San Francisco and London: Harper and Row).
Spencer, R., 2010, 'Cosmopolitan criticism', in J. Wilson, C. Sandru and S. Lawson Welsh (eds), *Rerouting the Postcolonial: New Directions for the New Millennium* (London and New York: Routledge), pp. 36–47.
Spivak, G. C., 1988 (1987), *In Other Worlds: Essays in Cultural Politics* (New York and London: Routledge).
Spivak, G. C., 1995 (1988), 'Can the subaltern speak?', in B. Ashcroft, G. Griffiths and H. Tiffin (eds), *The Post-Colonial Studies Reader* (London: Routledge), pp. 24–8.
Spivak, G. C., 2005, 'Scattered speculations on the subaltern and the popular', *Postcolonial Studies*, 8:4, 475–86.
Spivak, G. C., 2007 (2000), 'The new subaltern: A silent interview', in S. During (ed.), *The Cultural Studies Reader* (London and New York: Routledge), pp. 229–40.
Splendore, P., 2011, 'Un'altra Londra: la città Black British tra utopia e eterotopia', *Lo straniero*, xv:137 (November), 74–81.
Stella, A., 2000, *Histoires d'esclaves dans la Péninsule Ibérique* (Paris: Éditions de l'École des Hautes Études en Sciences Sociales).
Suvin, D., 2004, 'Narciso e Anteo: il collettivismo deve per forza essere contro la gente?', in G. Maniscalco Basile and D. Suvin (eds), *Nuovissime mappe dell'inferno: Distopia oggi* (Rome: Monolite), pp. 149–64.
Syla, S., 2005, 'I hate Wednesdays', in J. Langer (ed.), *The Silver Throat of the Moon: Writing in Exile* (Nottingham: Five Leaves), pp. 22–3.
Tan, K.-A., 2008, '"If you're not on paper, you don't exist": Depictions of illegal immigration and asylum in film: on Michael Winterbottom's *In This World* (2002) and *Code 46* (2003)', in L. Eckstein, B. Korte, E. U. Pirker and C. Reinfandt (eds), *Multi-Ethnic Britain 2000+: New Perspectives in Literature, Film and the Arts* (Amsterdam and New York: Rodopi), pp. 301–14.
Teverson, A., 2007, *Salman Rushdie* (Manchester and New York: Manchester University Press).
Thieme, J., 2003, *Post-Colonial Studies: The Essential Glossary* (London: Arnold).
Tibbles, A., 2008, 'Facing slavery's past: The bicentenary of the abolition of the British slave trade', *Slavery and Abolition: A Journal of Slave and*

Post-Slave Studies (special issue on Public Art, Artefacts and Atlantic Slavery), 29:2 (June), 293–303.

Toscano, A., 2009, 'Dirty deportation tactics at SOAS', *The Guardian* (17 June), www.guardian.co.uk/commentisfeee/libertycentral/2009/jun/17/soas-cleaners (accessed 20 May 2013).

Totten, S., and Bartrop, P. R., 2008, *Dictionary of Genocide*, with contributions by S. L. Jacobs (Westport, CT: Greenwood Press).

Townsend, M., 2011, 'They rescue victims of sex trafficking: Now their funding is to be stopped', *The Observer* (17 April), p. 11.

Travis, A., 2013, 'Conservatives promise to scrap Human Rights Act after next election', *The Guardian* (30 September), www.theguardian.com/law/2013/sep/30/conservatives-scrap-human-rights-act (accessed 2 October 2013).

Turcotte, G., 2009, *Peripheral Fear: Transformations of the Gothic in Canadian and Australian Fiction* (Brussels: P.I.E. Peter Lang).

Van den Anker, C., 'Contemporary slavery, global justice and globalization', in Van den Anker (ed.), *The Political Economy of New Slavery* (Houndmills: Palgrave/Macmillan), pp. 15–36.

Van der Kolk, B. A., and Van der Hart, O., 1995, 'The intrusive past: The flexibility of memory and the engraving of trauma', in C. Caruth (ed.), *Trauma: Explorations in Memory* (Baltimore: Johns Hopkins University Press), pp. 158–82.

Visser, I., 2011, 'Trauma theory and postcolonial literary studies', *Journal of Postcolonial Writing*, 47:3 (July), 270–82.

Volpato, C., 2011, *Deumanizzazione: Come si legittima la violenza* (Bari: Laterza).

Ward, A., 2011 (2009), *Never-Never Land* (London: Ward Wood).

Wasson, S., 2011, '"A butcher's shop where the meat still moved": Gothic doubles, organ harvesting and human cloning', in S. Wasson and E. Alder (eds), *Gothic Science Fiction 1980–2010* (Liverpool: Liverpool University Press), pp. 73–86.

Waugh, L., 2007 (2006), *Selling Olga: Stories of Human Trafficking and Resistance* (London: Phoenix).

White, M., and Epston, D., 1990, *Narrative Means to Therapeutic Ends* (New York and London: Norton).

Whittaker Khan, Y., 2005, *Bells* (and *Chaos* by A. Dar) (London: Oberon).

Williams, P., 2010, '"Outlines of a better world": Rerouting postcolonialism', in J. Wilson, C. Sandru and S. Lawson Welsh (eds), *Rerouting the Postcolonial: New Directions for the New Millennium* (London and New York: Routledge), pp. 86–91.

Williams, P., 2013, 'Overlapping intellectuals, intertwined theories', paper delivered at the 6th AISCLI (Associazione Italiana di Studi sulle Culture e Letterature di lingua Inglese) conference, Rome, 17–18 January.

Wilson, J., Sandru, C. and Lawson Welsh, S., 2010, 'General introduction', in Wilson, Sandru and Lawson Welsh (eds), *Rerouting the Postcolonial:*

New Directions for the New Millennium (London and New York: Routledge), pp. 1–13.

Winterbottom, M. (director), 2002, *In This World* (UK: Film Consortium and BBC and Film Council and Revolution Films production).

Wong, C. F., and Crummett, G., 2008 (2006), 'A conversation about life and art with Kazuo Ishiguro', in B. W. Shaffer and C. F. Wong (eds), *Conversations with Kazuo Ishiguro* (Jackson: University of Mississippi Press), pp. 204–20.

Wormald, M., 2003, 'Kazuo Ishiguro and the work of art: Reading distances', in R. Lane, R. Mengham and P. Tew (eds), *Contemporary British Fiction* (Cambridge: Polity), pp. 226–38.

Yarnall, J., 2011, *Barbed Wire Disease: British and German Prisoners of War 1914–19* (Stroud: Spellmount).

Young, J. E., 2001, 'Daniel Libeskind's Jewish Museum in Berlin: The uncanny arts of memorial architecture', in B. Zelizer (ed.), *Visual Culture and the Holocaust* (London: Athlone), pp. 179–97.

Zephaniah, B., 1996, *Propa Propaganda* (Newcastle-upon-Tyne: Bloodaxe).

Zephaniah, B., 2001, *Refugee Boy* (London: Bloomsbury).

Žižek, S., 2006, 'Comments by Slavoj Žižek', included in the DVD special edition of A. Cuarón's *Children of Men* (Universal).

Index

Note: literary and visual works can be found under authors' names. 'n.' after a page reference indicates the note number(s) on that page

Abani, Chris
   Becoming Abigail 23, 60–9, 84, 119, 124, 141
   Kalakuta Republic 64
Abraham, Nicolas 137n.25
Achebe, Chinua 177
Adorno, Theodor W. 26, 93n.48, 166, 168
Adshead, Kay
   Bogus Woman, The 23, 49, 88n.1, 90n.23–4, 91n.33
Afolabi, Segun
   'Monday morning' 29n.16
Agamben, Giorgio 9–10, 16, 27, 181–3, 187, 205n.40
   concentration camps 23–4, 26, 32n.46, 63, 143, 149–50, 152, 191, 196, 206n.50
   refugees 193–4, 196–7, 200–1, 207n.55, 207n.61
Agbaje, Bola
   Detaining Justice 95n.70
agricultural labourers 77–82, 94n.59, 136n.15
Ahmad, Aijaz 22, 36, 47n.2
AISCLI (Associazione Italiana di Studi sulle Culture e Letterature di lingua Inglese) 30n.25
Albrecht, Hans-Joerg 21
Aldridge, Alexandra 141, 167
Ali, Monica
   In the Kitchen 5, 28, 29n.10, 89n.12, 90n.23–5, 110, 199
alternative history (ucronia) 152, 172n.21
Alvi, Moniza
   'Candle' 93n.43, 139n.52
Amenábar, Alejandro 105
Amnesty International 155, 173n.27, 203n.19
Anderson, Bridget 4, 5, 22, 23, 33–8, 40, 42–3, 47n.3, 48n.10, 48n.13, 49, 51–2, 58, 61–2, 65–6, 77, 190, 206n.44
Andrews, Hazel 89n.4–5, 104–5
animals 78, 80–1, 94n.62, 102, 128–9, 174n.39, 201
Anti-Slavery Day 5
Anti-Slavery International 3
   Reporter 29n.9, 47n.3, 57, 68, 92n.36, 206n.48
Arendt, Hannah 203n.13
   desk killer 24, 73–6, 93n.47, 93n.49–50, 94n.56, 198, 208n.67
   refugees 94n.60, 182–3, 193
   totalitarianism 16, 192
Armitt, Lucy 108, 135n.3
Arrighi, Giovanni 12
Ascari, Maurizio 135n.2
Ashcroft, Bill 64
Atwood, Margaret 174n.45, 175n.52
Augé, Marc 27, 185–7, 189, 204n.25

Bacon, Christine
   Illegals, The 135n.8, 137n.32
Baldick, Chris 108–9, 137n.26
Bales, Kevin 6, 7, 29n.17

Balibar, Étienne 5, 7, 12, 33, 191, 198, 205n.38, 206n.46
European apartheid 6, 28, 29
Bartrop, Paul R. *see* Totten
Bassi, Shaul 143
Baucom, Ian 12, 30n.27
Bauman, Zygmunt
Holocaust 15, 73, 75, 164, 192, 205n.36
human waste 6–7, 19, 30n.23, 61, 91n.26, 160, 199
Bayley, Clare
Container, The 25, 115–20, 134, 188, 192
Beedham, Matthew 172n.21, 174n.45, 175n.52
Behdad, Ali 204n.28
Belbin, David
Secret Gardens 197, 200, 207n.56
Benjamin, Walter 12, 177, 182, 194
Bensoussan, Georges 7, 15, 18, 31n.33, 31n.35, 35, 38, 73, 75, 94n.61, 152, 162, 166, 194, 203n.12
Bissett, Cora 25
Roadkill 119–21, 127–8, 133–4, 137n.35, 141
Black, Shameem 167, 172n.21, 175n.50, 175n.53
Black Britain 38–9, 41–2, 47n.6, 47n.8, 56, 146, 148
Black British studies 20, 27–8, 40–2, 47n.9, 77–80, 83, 90n.22, 95n.70, 187–90, 197, 207n.58
dream-England 77–80
Blanchot, Maurice 139n.53
Boal, Augusto 25, 120, 122, 138n.44
Bohmer, Carol 59–60, 96n.79, 121, 124, 138n.37, 138n.45, 138n.49, 183, 187
Bonini, Tiziano 104
Bosworth, Mary 29n.11, 32n.47, 84, 94n.57, 95n.72–3, 96n.78
Botting, Fred 98–9, 105–6, 108, 137n.24
Boulter, Jonathan 132, 139n.53, 139n.58
Bradman, Tony 92n.35
Brecht, Bertolt 25, 108, 119, 121–2
Brennan, Timothy 1, 93n.44, 142, 171n.7, 172n.11, 173n.22, 205n.33, 205n.43

British institutions 137n.28, 144
asylum proceedings 6, 29n.15–16, 50, 59–60, 76, 90n.21, 90n.23, 138n.45
British National Party 42
Children's Commissioner for England 92n.36
and colonialism 78, 135n.9, 163, 170
Home Office 29n.12, 42, 49, 57, 92n.36, 95n.70, 95n.72, 184, 207n.54, 208n.65
Immigration and Nationality Directorate 184
immigration policies 5–6, 23–4, 26, 29n.9, 29n.11, 29n.15–16, 32n.48, 35–6, 42–3, 47n.3, 50, 57–60, 65–6, 68, 70, 72–6, 83–5, 88n.1, 89n.14, 91n.30, 92n.36, 95n.73, 104, 110, 124–6, 130, 142–5, 171n.7–8, 172n.19, 180–1, 183–4, 195, 202n.10, 206n.45
Immigration Service 87, 96n.82
labour market 5, 29n.10, 77, 110, 143, 194–5, 206n.44, 206n.47
London Metropolitan Police Human Trafficking Team 57
see also detention centres
Brock, Jeremy
I Am Slave 48n.14, 70–1, 89n.11, 92n.41
Broomfield, Nick 188
Ghosts 25, 72, 82, 88, 94n.64, 96n.83, 97–110, 118, 119, 141, 171n.6, 195, 198
Buelens, Gert 31n.40, 133, 141
Bunzl, Matti 189–91, 204n.30
Burton, Antoinette 189–91, 204n.30

Camus, Albert 28, 201, 208n.67
Caruth, Cathy 120, 123–4, 132, 139n.57, 200
Cherniavsky, Eva 208n.66
Chikwava, Brian
Harare North 51, 89n.17, 90n.22, 95n.67
children 49, 57, 62, 68–9, 91n.34–6, 119, 124, 143–4, 151–2, 154, 156, 186
see also detention centres
Chinese migrants 16–17, 77, 81–2, 88,

94n.64, 95n.68, 98–102, 105, 107, 109–10, 135n.4–6, 135n.9, 188, 204n.27
  'Dover 58' 100, 110
  Morecambe Bay tragedy 3, 25, 82, 88, 94n.64, 97–100, 103–5, 110, 206n.44
  see also Broomfield; Pai
Christian, Ed 87
Churchill, Caryl
  Far Away 93n.46
Cimitile, Anna Maria 30n.28
Clarkson, Thomas 2–3
Clean Break theatre company 127
Cleave, Chris 188
  Other Hand, The 24, 66–77, 83, 97, 104, 115, 124, 141, 184, 200–2, 203n.16, 204n.24, 205n.37, 208n.62–6
Coetzee, J. M. 12, 90n.18
Cohen, Steve 1, 6, 7, 29n.14, 85, 140, 142, 149, 183–5, 203n.15, 203n.17
Coleridge, Samuel Taylor 9
  Rime of the Ancient Mariner, The 106, 135n.13
Comaroff, Jean and John L. 30n.29, 206n.46
Commission for Filipino Migrant Workers 32
'concentrationary archipelago' 16–17, 24–5, 50, 82, 102, 109, 149, 162, 181, 185, 191, 199
concentration camps 94n.61, 103, 148–9, 157, 159, 162, 203n.17
  Auschwitz 15, 43, 166, 168, 184, 205n.39
  bodies 24, 48n.11, 63–4, 152, 204n.23
  and British colonialism 16
  and hooded head 179–82, 203n.11
  new forms of 14–18, 31n.34–7, 44, 48n.12–14, 81, 145–6, 150, 157–8, 162, 169, 171, 175n.53, 178, 182–7, 192, 196, 203n.17, 206n.50
  trains to 43–4, 100, 117
  Treblinka 44, 81
  see also Agamben; Holocaust
Conrad, Joseph 140
  Heart of Darkness 41

Cowper, William
  Task, The 33
Craig, Gary 4, 55, 78, 91n.30, 99, 188
Craps, Stef 31n.40–1, 133, 141
Crawley, Heaven 68, 70, 95n.75, 103, 117, 124, 139n.51
Cresswell, Tim 70
crime fiction 23, 24, 38–9, 43, 45–6, 83, 86–7, 96n.83, 97, 135n.2, 141, 188, 191
  see also Rankin; Rendell
Crownshaw, Richard 132
Crummett, Grace 176n.56
Cuarón, Alfonso
  Children of Men 26, 141–50, 158, 188, 198
Currie, Mark 173n.34

D'Aguiar, Fred 137n.25
  Feeding the Ghosts 36, 41
Dalton-Johnson, Kevin
  Captured Africans 2, 3
Dawson, Ashley 78, 171n.8
De Genova, Nicholas P. 7, 28n.7, 29n.19, 135n.7, 195, 205n.32
dehumanisation 30n.21, 38, 43–4, 117–19, 139n.56, 164–5, 192
  animalisation 23, 26, 43–4, 57, 60, 62–3, 81–4, 95n.68, 102, 129, 142–3, 146, 151, 160–1, 168
Del Toro, Guillermo 136n.20
Del Villano, Bianca 13, 36–7, 41, 137n.27
De Michelis, Lidia 76–7, 92n.35, 93n.45, 94n.65
Derrida, Jacques 11, 187
  naming 41
  spectrality 13, 18–22, 36, 40, 107, 191, 195
desaparecidos 154–5, 173n.26–7, 173n.29
detention centres 5–6, 24, 32n.47, 50, 67–71, 85–7, 92n.39, 95n.70, 95n.75, 96n.78, 117, 138n.38, 146, 148–50, 202n.10, 208n.65
  barbed-wire disease 85, 95n.76–7
  children in 24, 68, 70, 86, 92n.35–8, 116–17, 121–6, 138n.38, 139n.50–1
  in coastal towns 50, 89n.4–5, 104, 148, 172n.18

Index

deportations 36, 72–6, 135n.7–8
deterritorialisation 178, 202n.4
exploitation of immigrant labour 6
  private companies 6, 29n.14, 75–6,
    85, 94n.57
  and spectralisation 178, 183–7,
    203n.15–18
  suicides 85, 95n.76
  transfers 102
Dick, Philip K.
  *Do Androids Dream of Electric
    Sheep?* 150, 158, 173n.35,
    174n.39, 175n.49, 175n.51
Dickens, Charles 175n.52
Diemert, Brian 96n.83, 135n.2
Di Nicola, Andrea 29n.8
Di Paola, Pietro 95n.77
documentary 107–9, 119, 136n.22,
    171n.6
domestic workers 22–3, 33–8, 42–5,
    47n.3, 190
Dottridge, Mike 62
Durrant, Sam 12, 13, 19
Dürrenmatt, Friedrich 45
dystopia 26–7, 141–3, 152–3, 167,
    170, 183
  see also Cuarón; Ishiguro; James

Eaglestone, Robert 30n.32, 32n.49
Eckstein, Lars 171n.1, 172n.9, 188
ECPAT (End Child Prostitution,
    Pornography and Trafficking)
    68, 92n.36
Elías, Juan 144
Eliot, Thomas Stearns
  Waste Land, The 67
Engels, Friedrich 36
Epston, David, 54, 60
Equiano, Olaudah 91n.34
Esty, Jed 189–91, 204n.30
European Union 36, 96n.79
  European Convention on Action
    against Trafficking in Human
    Beings 57
  European Convention on Human
    Rights 28, 29n.12, 92n.36
  legislation on immigration 5

Fanon, Frantz 26, 136n.19, 160,
    167–8, 174n.38, 198
  on humanism 10, 30n.26

Farhi, Moris
  Children of the Rainbow 194,
    205n.39
Farrier, David 6, 27, 29n.16, 30n.22,
    31n.41, 31n.44, 32n.46, 32n.50,
    60, 88n.2, 89n.4, 90n.18,
    90n.21, 92n.36, 96n.78, 114,
    118, 120, 122, 136n.23,
    137n.33, 138n.44, 172n.16,
    178, 186, 197, 202n.4, 203n.16,
    203n.18, 204n.21, 204n.29,
    204n.31, 205n.41, 207n.55,
    207n.61
Fekete, Liz 6
Felman, Shoshana 51
Fiedler, Leslie 152
Finley, Moses I. 91n.34, 205n.42
Forti, Simona 153, 157, 164
Foucault, Michel 11, 93n.44, 126, 143,
    147, 152–3, 156, 163, 170, 180
  heterotopia 17, 90n.22, 206n.49
France 92n.36, 106, 115, 150
  Calais 27, 178–83, 185–8,
    202n.1–7, 203n.14, 203n.17,
    204n.23,
  immigration policies 7, 198
  Sangatte 115, 202n.1, 202n.7
Frassinelli, Pier Paolo 30n.26
Frears, Stephen
  Dirty Pretty Things 6, 9, 11, 14,
    29n.16, 47n.9, 89n.3, 98,
    135n.11, 157, 199, 206n.45
Freeman, John 176n.56
Freud, Sigmund 123
Friend, Melanie 203n.18

Galli, Giorgio 45
Garland, Alex see Romanek
Gastarbeiter 20–1
Gatwick 'No border camp' 207n.55
George, Sylvain
  Éclats, Les 202n.5, 204n.23
  Qu'ils reposent en révolte 27,
    178–82, 185–8
Gibney, Matthew J. 95n.74
Gikandi, Simon 189, 204n.22
Gilroy, Paul 191–3
  on Holocaust 31n.38, 192, 205n.36
  on migrations 17, 207n.55
  on slavery 192, 205n.35
Giommi, Francesca 91n.28

Giustini, Alexia 48n.11, 63–4, 91n.27, 91n.34, 103, 149, 159, 174n.37, 204n.23
globalisation 6, 8, 18, 23, 25, 27, 51, 61, 69, 76, 113–14, 141–2, 177, 182, 187, 189–92, 195, 204n.22, 204n.28, 204n.31
Godwin, William
Caleb Williams 109
Goheen Glanville, Erin 204n.31
Gordon, Avery 10, 14, 22, 46, 58, 77, 107, 110, 118, 154–5, 173n.26–7, 184, 196, 199, 203n.19, 207n.59
Gothic 25, 87–8, 96n.83, 97–100, 104–9, 117–18, 129, 135n.2–3, 136n.17–19, 137n.24–7, 141, 154, 191
Greppi, Carlo 117
Gretton, Dan 94n.55
Grigsby Bates, Karen 176n.6
Grisoni, Tony 115
Guantánamo 203n.11
Guild, Mhairi 84, 95n.72–3
Gulf States 33–6, 42–3
Gunning, Dave 7, 31n.44, 58, 77, 89n.15, 95n.74, 118–19
Gupta, Rahila 23, 51–62, 65, 99, 101, 105, 110, 112, 117, 121, 135n.5, 135n.9, 207n.54
Gurnah, Abdulrazak
By the Sea 89n.15–16, 90n.18
Gutman, Israel 182

Haidari, Karim
'The journey' 89n.15
Hall, Stuart 41–2, 188
Hammar, Thomas 207n.55
Hardt, Michael 90n.18, 191
Harris, Nigel 58, 85, 96n.79
Harris, Wilson 12
Hegel, Georg Wilhelm Friedrich 106, 136n.18
Helen Bamber Foundation 127
Helff, Sissy 108
Himid, Lubaina 3
Hoeferlin, Marc 103, 136n.22
Holocaust 32n.46, 72–3, 91n.34, 155, 164, 202n.8
desk killer 24, 73–6, 93n.46–56
Holocaust theory 14–18, 30n.32, 31n.33, 106, 140, 153, 191
suppression of 182–3, 203n.12–13
see also Bauman; Bensoussan; concentration camps; Levi
Horowitz, Mardi J. 60
Horwitz, Gordon 94n.61
Howarth, Anita 21, 178–9, 202n.2, 203n.14
Huggan, Graham 91n.29
Hulme, Peter 187
humour fiction 24, 69–71, 76–82, 94n.65, 133, 141, 191
see also Lewycka
Huxley, Aldous 84

Ibrahim, Yasmin *see* Howarth
ILO (International Labour Organisation)
Domestic Workers Convention 47n.3
intertextuality 140–1, 171n.1, 171n.3
Ishiguro, Kazuo 140
Never Let Me Go 10, 26–7, 150–71, 171n.5, 177–8, 182–4, 195
Isin, Engin F. 31n.37, 202n.1, 202n.4
Islam, Manzu
Burrow 89n.15, 207n.57
Italy 13, 51, 114, 115, 150, 173n.22

James, P. D. 188
Children of Men, The 26, 143–9, 172n.13, 198
Janet, Pierre 126
Jordan, Anna
Chicken Shop 139n.54
Joseph Rowntree Foundation 4

Kalayaan 47n.3, 197
Kaul, Suvir 189–91, 204n.30
Kavka, Misha 98
Kaye, Heidi 108
Kaye, Mike 28n.6
Kelman, Herbert C. 75, 93n.54
Kim, Julie H. 38, 43, 47n.6
Kirkwood, Lucy
It Felt Empty When... 25, 127–34, 141
Kirmayer, Laurence J. 90n.19
Kitson, Peter J. 164
Knox-Shaw, Peter H. 91n.34, 106, 136n.18
Kolodziejczyk, Dorota 204n.26

Korte, Barbara 171n.6, 172n.14–15, 172n.19, 188–9
Koshy, Susan 47n.9
Kosofsky Sedgwick, Eve 100
Kunzru, Hari 203n.17
Kurds 86, 96n.79, 115–16, 179–80, 197, 203n.16

La Capra, Dominick 136n.19
Lachs, John 75, 93n.52
La Guma, Alex
  A Walk in the Night 11
Lal, Vinay 16
Langer, Lawrence L. 91n.24
Lawson Welsh, Sarah *see* Wilson
Lazarus, Neil 204n.29
Left, Sarah 62
Lester, Trine *see* Crawley
Levi, Primo
  Drowned and the Saved, The 14–15, 31n.42, 43–4, 60, 63, 74, 105–7, 152, 164, 192, 198
  If This Is a Man 15–16, 31n.34, 106, 155
Levinas, Emmanuel 192
Lewycka, Marina 188
  Short History of Tractors in Ukrainian, A 81, 94n.63
  Two Caravans 24, 76–82, 102, 116, 141, 206n.53
Linden, Sonja
  Asylum Dialogues (with C. Bacon) 137n.32, 138n.38, 197, 204n.20
  Asylum Monologues 137n.32–3, 184, 197
Lioret, Philippe 202n.8
  Welcome 27, 178–88, 198
literature and art, role of 8–11, 22, 46, 52, 138n.42, 160–1, 165–8, 175n.48–9, 199–200, 207n.60
Loach, Ken
  It's a Free World… 98
Loomba, Ania 8, 11, 56, 59, 61, 189–91, 204n.30
Loshitzky, Yosefa 9, 29n.16, 47n.9, 102, 116, 135n.11, 157
Luckhurst, Roger 171n.3

Makenga, Dieudonnée-Marcelle
  'Tale, A' 29n.15
Mandel, Ernest 38–9, 45

Marx, Karl 13, 36, 109
Mather, Jeffrey 204n.27
Mbembe, Achille 93n.44
McCrum, Robert 96n.85
McGhee, Derek 84, 89n.14, 95n.73
McVeigh, Karen 6
Melville, Herman
  Bartleby, the Scrivener 90n.18
Meoni, Alessandra 94n.62
Mezzadra, Sandro 202n.4, 202n.6
Mighall, Robert *see* Baldick
Migrant and Refugee Manifesto 36, 47n.1
Milchman, Alan 75, 93n.48, 198
Modiano, Raimonda 106, 136n.17
Mohammadi, Reza
  'Illegal immigrant' 132–3
Moldova 51, 54, 71, 77
Montesquieu, Charles-Louis de Secondat 106, 136n.18
Moorehead, Caroline 60, 84, 89n.8, 89n.14, 90n.23, 92n.38–9, 95n.71, 95n.76, 138n.46, 202n.3, 203n.16, 207n.55
Morgan, Abi
  Fugee 25, 121–6, 128, 130, 132–4, 141
  Sex Traffic 71, 137n.31, 139n.56
Morrison, Toni 12, 37, 192
Mullan, John 167, 174n.44
Mynott, Ed 57, 84

naming 41, 45, 52, 61, 70, 134, 139n.59
  see also Derrida
narrative therapy 54, 60, 134
Nazer, Mende
  Slave: My True Story 47n.3, 89n.8
Negri, Toni *see* Hardt
Neilson, Brett *see* Mezzadra
New Labour 32n.48, 50, 88n.1, 95n.73
Nigeria 23–4, 35, 38, 43, 45, 48n.15, 61, 67, 72, 93n.44, 94n.55, 119, 173n.22, 200, 208n.62
Night Shyamalan, M. 105

Okpewho, Isidore 89n.6
Oldfield, J. R. 1–4, 8, 19, 28n.3, 118, 188
old people's homes workers 82, 95n.67

organ trafficking 9, 50, 89n.3, 141, 152–3, 157
  see also Ishiguro
Orwell, George
  Nineteen Eighty-Four 7, 140, 142, 149, 183–5, 203n.15
  'Politics and the English language' 156
  'Why I write' 8, 11

Pai, Hsiao-Hung 12, 17, 29n.18, 56, 94n.59, 99–100, 102, 107, 110, 135n.4, 135n.6, 136n.16, 136n.21, 188, 194
Paik, Peter P. 172n.19
Palidda, Salvatore 195
Pandey, Gyanendra 89n.10
Paravisini-Gebert, Lizabeth 137n.25
Parry, Benita 204n.29
Pawlikowski, Pawel
  Last Resort 23, 50, 137n.23
Penuel, Suzanne 47n.10
Phillips, Caryl
  Atlantic Sound, The 21
  Colour Me English 9, 202n.1
  Distant Shore, A 21, 30n.22, 31n.44, 89n.15, 171n.1
  European Tribe, The 20–1
  Higher Ground, 31n.41
  In the Falling Snow 31n.45
  Nature of Blood, The 31n.41, 47n.9
  New World Order, A 49, 140, 177
  'Rude Am I in My Speech' 31n.43
  see also Rothberg
Piccino, Cristina 179
Poe, Edgar Allan 135n.2
Popa, Dana 188
  Not Natasha 25, 110–14, 141
POPPY Project 127, 197, 206n.54
postcolonial studies 18, 37, 133, 140–1, 153
  and the body 61, 64, 152–3
  magic realism 108, 142–3, 172n.9
  maps 64, 91n.29
  new frontiers of 1, 8, 27–8, 187–202, 204n.26–36, 205n.43
  orality 56, 89n.6
  see also naming
postmodernism 141, 172n.2–3
Post Traumatic Stress Disorder (PTSD) 26, 59–60, 90n.22, 120–1, 127, 131, 203n.16
Punter, David 135n.3, 137n.25–6

racism 39–41, 45, 47n.7, 47n.10, 84, 103, 106, 109, 141–3, 145, 152–3, 178, 183, 192–3, 202n.3, 203n.14, 203n.17
Rankin, Ian 38, 188
  Fleshmarket Close 24–5, 29n.13, 57, 68, 83–8, 94n.64, 97, 135n.1, 141, 194, 198
Razac, Olivier 31n.36
reader-response criticism 45, 171, 176n.57
Reah, Danuta
  Not Safe 139n.53
Refugee Council 49
Rendell, Ruth 47n.5, 49, 188
  Simisola 22–4, 38–47, 52, 55, 58, 61, 62, 65–6, 68, 83, 86–8, 95n.68, 141–2, 145, 188, 198
restaurant workers 82, 94n.66
Rice, Alan 2, 3, 4
Ricoeur, Paul 3, 28n.4
Roberts, Les 89n.4–5, 104–5, 107n.23
Robinson, Mary 136n.13
Robinson, Vaughan 84, 89n.14
Rocker, Rudolph 95n.77, 203n.17
Rogaly, Ben 4, 5, 77, 206n.44
Romanek, Mark
  Never Let Me Go 162, 170, 173n.29, 173n.33, 174n.40–1, 175n.55
Romani culture 205n.39
Romantic poetry 104, 135n.13
Rosenberg, Alan see Milchman
Rotas, Alex 89n.9, 207n.58
Rothberg, Michael 32n.46, 47n.9, 136n.19, 140, 171n.2
  on Caryl Phillips 20, 139n.55, 140
  multidirectional memory 17–20, 177, 179, 192
Rousseau Jean-Jacques 106, 136n.18
Rousset, David 17
Rowland, Susan 39, 45, 46, 47n.5
Roy, Arundhati 137n.25
Rushdie, Salman 140
  on dream-England 78–9
  Satanic Verses, The 26, 142–4, 168, 171n.7–12
Rygiel, Kim see Isin

Index

Said, Edward W. 1, 48n.10, 56, 163, 205n.34
  on humanism 10–11, 30n.25–6
  Traveling Theory 18–19, 48n.10, 191
Salverson, Julie 120, 138n.44
Sandru, Cristina *see* Wilson
Scerbanenco, Giorgio 45
Schlingensief, Christoph 204n.21
Sciurba, Alessandra 178, 202n.1, 202n.7–8
Scotland 24, 83–4, 87–8, 95n.71, 96n.5, 119, 134, 135n.1, 137n.34–51, 138n.38
  Glasgow Campaign to Welcome Refugees and Asylum Seekers 204n.20
  Glasgow's Kingsway estate 197, 207n.55
Scott, Ridley
  Blade Runner 142, 158
Sealy, Mark 110, 114
sexual slavery 6, 23–4, 25, 34, 50, 51–4, 62–4, 67–9, 82, 88n.2, 90n.24, 91n.32–3, 102, 110–14, 116, 119–20, 125–34, 139n.54, 139n.56, 141
Shaffer, Brian W. 173n.24
Shah, Sonia 153
Shakespeare, William 11, 12, 31n.43, 84
Shelley, Percy Bysshe
  Defence of Poetry, A 8–10
Shire, Warsan 91n.32, 114, 120
Shuman, Amy *see* Bohmer
Sillitoe, Alan 136n.19
Sim, Wai-Chew 156, 158, 165, 170, 172n.20, 173n.24, 173n.32, 174n.46–7, 175n.54
Sinclair, Iain 97
Skinner, Benjamin E. 11, 14
Slavery-Free London Campaign 29n.9
slavery, modern definitions and terminology 4–5, 7, 28n.6–7, 29n.18–19
Smith, Steph *see* Bissett
SOAS cleaners 195
Solzhenitsyn, Aleksandr
  Gulag Archipelago, The 17
Southey, Robert 136n.13
spectrality 11–14, 57, 101

abject bodies 153, 157
agency 132–4, 114–15, 162, 163, 197
body writing 64–6, 91n.28, 113, 186–7
and citizens 46, 84, 106–7, 109, 137n.27, 157–9, 170–1, 177, 194–202, 206n.48, 207n.54–5, 208n.61–7
identity 71–2, 80, 94n.60, 105, 115–16, 186–7
invisibility 12, 43–4, 58, 83, 101, 126, 129–30, 143, 164, 178
isolation 20, 43, 55–6, 70–2, 89n.8–9, 92n.40–2, 101–4, 111–13, 115, 123–5, 127, 136n.16, 137n.31, 137n.35, 139n.55, 161–2, 174n.40, 181, 185, 188, 197, 205n.32, 206n.53
liminality 87, 194, 205n.41
literacy 23, 53, 55–6, 158, 165–9
means of transport 74–76, 99–102, 114–19, 132, 138n.38, 178–81, 202n.6, 202n.9
narration 37, 54–5, 60, 90n.25, 124
(post)colonialism 12–13, 30n.31
'right to complex personhood' 10, 58, 65, 76–7, 89n.17, 166, 168–9, 175n.51, 197
silence 36, 45–6, 55–8, 89n.11, 113, 121, 138n.45, 154–5
South Africa 11–12, 30n.29, 173n.22
spectacularisation 84–5
and the underground 12, 51, 57, 89n.12
voices 22–3, 37–8, 46–7, 51–4
witches 88
see also Gothic; concentration camps, new forms of; detention centres; transatlantic slavery
Spencer, Robert 199, 204n.31, 206n.52
Spivak, Gayatri Chakravorty 17, 46–7, 48n.17, 56, 59, 187–8, 208n.66
Splendore, Paola 90n.22
STAMP (Slave Trade Arts Memorial Project) 2, 3
Stella, Alessandro 205n.42
Stop the Traffick 19
subaltern 23, 56, 89n.10
  see also Spivak
Suvin, Darko 170

Syla, Sokol
    'I hate Wednesdays' 202n.10

Tan, Kathy-Ann 98, 115, 137n.36
Teverson, Andrew 171n.8, 172n.12
Tibbles, Anthony 28n.2
Todorov, Tzvetan 145
Torok, Maria *see* Abraham
Totten, Samuel 93n.53, 94n.55
transatlantic slavery 41, 91n.34,
    100, 104, 106, 148, 159, 164,
    174n.45, 179, 192
  2007 abolition bicentenary 1, 2, 5,
    12, 28n.3, 49, 110
  Liverpool International Slavery
    Museum 19, 31n.39
  public memory of 1–3, 18, 118
  and spectrality 2, 12
trauma 54, 61, 71, 93n.43, 99, 113,
    139n.52, 141, 171n.2, 171n.4,
  trauma studies 26, 31n.40, 32n.49,
    90n.20, 90n.24, 120–8, 131–4,
    136n.19, 141, 191, 200,
    207n.60
Truth, Sojourner 41
Tunstall, Kate E. 95n.74
Turcotte, Gerry 12–13, 107

United Nations 4, 28n.5, 82
  Convention against Transnational
    Organised Crime 4
  Universal Declaration of Human
    Rights 144
USA
  asylum proceedings 59–60
  slavery 41, 154
utopia 46, 153, 165, 172n.19, 196,
    206n.51–2

Van den Anker, Christien 7
Van der Hart, Onno 91n.24, 123–4,
    126, 134
Van der Kolk, Bessen A. *see* Van der
    Hart
verbatim theatre 114, 135n.8,
    137n.32–3, 138n.38

Vischer, Adolf Lukas 95n.77
Visser, Irene 90n.20, 207n.60
Volpato, Chiara 30n.21, 161, 165, 178

Ward, Adele
  'Next door' 48n.12, 93n.42
Wasson, Sara 165
Waugh, Louisa 23, 51–62, 65–6,
    98–100, 110, 113, 117, 121,
    206n.44, 207n.54
Wesley, John 91n.34
Westminster Abbey 2–3
Whitaker, Benjamin 28n.5
White, Michael *see* Epston
Whittaker Khan, Yasmin
  Bells 48n.14, 138n.47
Wiene, Robert 130
Wilberforce, William 3
Wilberforce Institute for the Study
    of Slavery and Emancipation
    (WISE) 28n.3
Williams, Patrick 30n.25, 189
Wilson, Janet 189, 191, 205n.33,
    206n.52
Winterbottom, Michael
  In This World 108, 115, 119,
    135n.10, 136n.23, 137n.36,
    202n.1, 202n.9
Wong, Cynthia F. 176n.56
World Health Organization 95n.71
Wormald, Mark 154
Wright, Tom 117

Yarnall, John 96n.77
Young, James E. 2, 28n.1
Young, Robert 13, 30n.30
Young Vic theatre 117, 138n.40
Yugoslavian war 15, 20

Zephaniah, Benjamin
  Refugee Boy 23, 49–50, 91n.34,
    92n.37, 92n.40, 203n.16,
    208n.63
  'The death of Joy Gardner' 206n.48
Žižek, Slavoj 144, 146–7
Zong 12

EU authorised representative for GPSR:
Easy Access System Europe, Mustamäe tee 50,
10621 Tallinn, Estonia
gpsr.requests@easproject.com

www.ingramcontent.com/pod-product-compliance
Ingram Content Group UK Ltd.
Pitfield, Milton Keynes, MK11 3LW, UK
UKHW021840140426
5217IPUK00022B/1531